STUDIES IN ANTIQUITY AND CHRISTIANITY

STUDIES IN ANTIQUITY AND CHRISTIANITY

The Institute for Antiquity and Christianity
Claremont Graduate University
Claremont, California

STUDIES IN ANTIQUITY & CHRISTIANITY

WHOLLY WOMAN HOLY BLOOD

A Feminist Critique of Purity and Impurity

Edited by Kristin De Troyer,
Judith A. Herbert,
Judith Ann Johnson,
Anne-Marie Korte

TRINITY PRESS INTERNATIONAL
A Continuum imprint
HARRISBURG • LONDON • NEW YORK

BL
458
.W52
2003

Trinity Press International
P.O. Box 1321
Harrisburg, PA 17105
Trinity Press International is a member of the Continuum International Publishing Group.

Cover design/illustration: Wesley Hoke

Library of Congress Cataloging-in-Publication Data

Wholly woman, holy blood : a feminist critique of purity and impurity / edited by Kristin De Troyer ... [et al.].
    p. cm.
Includes bibliographical references and index.
ISBN 1-56338-400-0 (pbk.)
1. Women—Religious aspects—Congresses. 2. Menstruation
—Religious aspects—Congresses. 3. Blood—Religious aspects
—Congresses. 4. Purity, Ritual—Congresses. 5. Feminism—
Religious aspects—Congresses.   I. De Troyer, Kristin.
BL458.W48 2003
291.3—dc2
                                                    2002010527

Printed in the United States of America

03 04 05 06 07 08   10 9 8 7 6 5 4 3 2 1

CONTENTS

CONTRIBUTORS

Kathleen O'Grady is a research assistant at the Simone de Beauvoir Institute, Concordia University, Montreal, and the Director of Communications at the Canadian Women's Health Network.

Deborah Ellens is an independent scholar residing in Claremont, California.

Kristin De Troyer is Professor of Hebrew Bible at the Claremont School of Theology and Professor of Religion at the Claremont Graduate University.

Mayer I. Gruber is Associate Professor in the Department of Bible and Ancient Near East at Ben-Gurion University of the Negev, Beer Sheva, Israel.

Kathleen P. Rushton is a Sister of Mercy at Otautahi Christchurch, Aotearoa, New Zealand, where she works as an interpreter of biblical texts.

Jennifer Schultz is a Ph.D. candidate in Early Church History at the University of St. Michael's College, University of Toronto.

Susan K. Roll is Associate Professor of Liturgy and Systematic Theology at Christ the King Seminary in East Aurora, New York.

Grietje Dresen is Lecturer in Moral Theology and Women's Studies at the Catholic University of Nijmegen, the Netherlands.

Anne-Marie Korte is Associate Professor in Theological Women's Studies at the Catholic Theological University in Utrecht, the Netherlands, and Honorary Professor of Theological Women's Studies at Utrecht University.

Judith Ann Johnson is an independent research scholar working with Claremont Graduate University's Women's Studies in Religion and University of Global Ministries.

One of the most recent books on purity and impurity is entitled *Purity and Holiness: The Heritage of Leviticus.*[1] In their introduction, the editors, Marcel Poorthuis and Joshua Schwartz, write that "impurity" appears as a topic of study in biochemistry, cultic religion, and morality. "These three areas," they write, "may be roughly equated with three dimensions of impurity, ranging from physical pollution to internalized guilt."[2] They continue, "This cultic meaning of impurity . . . is connected to the human body and its relation to the holy."[3] The issue of purity and impurity is, indeed, intertwined with both the body and the holy. In this volume, my coauthors and I have focused on one of the most important elements of the body: blood. An ambiguous "thing," blood flows at the edge of purity and impurity.

Purity and Holiness revisits the book of Leviticus. The editors suggest that "purity and impurity appear as the possible states of man's [*sic*] bodily existence oriented toward God and creation, toward holiness and everyday life."[4] When I first read this sentence, I liked it—except for the exclusive language. There was a poetical dimension to it. Then, I noticed the oppositions: God and creation, holiness and everyday life. And I wondered: Are these truly oppositions? Or do these words function as a hendiadys, expressing one idea by using two words connected with "and," hence meaning "divine creation and holy daily life"?

The oppositions reminded me of a text written by Hildegard von Bingen. In her song "Voice of the Blood," she writes:

1. Marcel J. H. M. Poorthuis and Joshua Schwartz, *Purity and Holiness: The Heritage of Leviticus* (Jewish and Christian Perspectives 2; Leiden: Brill, 2000).
2. Ibid., 5.
3. Ibid.
4. Ibid., 7.

O redness of blood,	O rubor sanguinis,
who have flowed down from that height	qui de excelso illo fluxisti.
which divinely touched:	quod Divinitas tetigit,
you are the flower	tu flos es,
that the winter of the serpent's breath	quem hiems de flatu serpentis
never withered.	numquam laesit.[5]

In this text, heaven and earth seem connected through the blood. The text can be read as transcendence touching upon immanence. I, however, also read the text as referring purely to female blood that gives life. Female blood flows down and is the flower out of which life comes forth. When blood is giving life, death cannot touch. Blood is "divinely touched." It is intimately connected with holiness.

In *Purity and Holiness,* the editors write, "Purity rules also seem to reflect man's [*sic*] grappling with the numinous and ambiguous elements of life and death."[6] They explained, for instance, that a corpse is "holy but at the same time a source of impurity."[7] They continue their research on bodily emissions and state that "both semen and menstrual blood convey the loss of potential fertility." Here, I disagree with them. Female blood—whether menstrual or of the parturient—conveys life and death, and not only the loss of potential fertility. When dealing with blood, Poorthuis and Schwartz later write: "Blood is considered holy, but at the same time strictly forbidden within one and the same Biblical culture,"[8] and "blood is the seat of life."[9] I fully agree with the latter statements. For me, an exploration of blood in a most interdisciplinary way became a desired topic.

That female blood has also been an argument in theological politics regarding the ordination of women makes this study even more needed. On January 14, 2000, Sr. Beth Rindler, SFP, sent in a letter to the *National Catholic Reporter* that read:

> In his Dec. 10, 1999, article in NCR, Jesuit Fr. George Wilson raises a point about women's genitalia as being associated with dirt. This reinforces what I learned in a course of canon law when I was studying the social structure of our [= Roman Catholic] church. In my studies I

---

5. Hildegard von Bingen, "Voice of the Blood" (Sequentia; Deutsche harmonia mundi; BMG Classics, 1995).
6. Poorthuis and Schwartz, *Purity and Holiness,* 9.
7. Ibid.
8. Ibid., 11–12.
9. Ibid., 24–25.

learned that it became very difficult for a man to remove himself from
the priesthood after he was ordained. However, if he married a woman,
it was an automatic expulsion. I wondered why this was. When I said
to the professor that it appeared that women were a source of impurity
for the church, the professor accepted my statement. Of course, this
was difficult for me to believe and to accept.

Although I consider the answer given to Sr. Beth erroneous, I hope that
this book will shed a different light on the issue of female blood, purity,
and impurity and its consequences for a sound theology of priesthood.

We have opted for an interdisciplinary approach. All our contributors, however, are also well versed in gender studies and focus their
articles on the relationship between gender and blood purity/impurity.
The contributors to this volume work with different texts ranging from
biblical, classical, patristic, medieval, to modern sources. Their approaches vary from historical critical to postmodern. What weaves the
book together is the issue of "blood."

In the opening article, Kathleen O'Grady (Toronto, Canada) sets the
tone. She offers a semantic analysis of "taboo," connecting the woman
who has a discharge of blood with the vows taken by the *nazirite*. Deborah Ellens (Claremont, California) offers a challenging reading of the
structure and contents of Lev 15—the text dealing with the woman who
has a discharge of blood. Kristin De Troyer (Claremont, California)
focuses on the blood of the parturient and traces the origins of the concept of "impure blood." Mayer Gruber (Beer Sheva, Israel) looks at
Qumran law and halakic sources dealing with women and sources of
pollution. Kathleen P. Rushton (Brisbane, Australia, and Aotearoa,
New Zealand) analyzes John 16:21, a New Testament text, and crosses
boundaries of interpretation. Jennifer Schultz (Toronto, Canada) ex-
plores the classical medical texts dealing with female blood. She ties the
Christian fathers to their Greek background. Susan K. Roll (Buffalo,
New York) offers an impressive survey of the early patristic and medieval
texts that deal with the rite of "the churching of women." Grietje Dresen
(Nijmegen, the Netherlands) continues the theme of the churching of
women and looks at its cultic expressions in the nineteenth and twentieth centuries. Anne-Marie Korte (Utrecht, the Netherlands) offers a
cultural anthropological reflection and stipulates feminist theological
conclusions. Judith Ann Johnson (Virginia Beach, Virginia) opens a
final window unto the broader societal aspects. She takes the reader into
the future by analyzing the shedding of blood—especially male blood—
in a military context.

A word about the genesis of this book. In 1999, the Linguistic Agency of the University of Duisburg (LAUD) in cooperation with the Religion and Discourse team (RAD) had its biannual symposium in *Schloss Krickenbeck*, near Duisburg, Germany. The topic of the meeting was "Women and Religious Discourses: An Interdisciplinary and Cross-cultural Approach." Anne-Marie Korte chaired the session entitled "Female Corporeality and Theology." Three people presented a paper: Jennifer Schultz, Kathleen O'Grady, and Kristin De Troyer. A long and fine discussion followed the presentations. In a subsequent board meeting of LAUD and RAD, members decided to devote a book to this topic. The title became *Wholly Woman, Holy Blood: A Feminist Critique of Purity and Impurity*. May it definitively connect female blood with holiness!

Kristin De Troyer,
On behalf of the editors: Kristin De Troyer, Judith A. Herbert, Judith Ann Johnson, and Anne-Marie Korte.

ABBREVIATIONS

ABRL	Anchor Bible Reference Library
ASOR	American Schools of Oriental Research
BAR	*Biblical Archaeology Review*
BASOR	*Bulletin of the American Schools of Oriental Research*
CCSL	Corpus Christianorum: Series latina
CSCO	Corpus scriptorum christianorum orientalium
DSD	*Dead Sea Discoveries*
EncJud	*Encyclopaedia Judaica*
FOTL	Forms of the Old Testament Literature
HAR	*Hebrew Annual Review*
HTR	*Harvard Theological Review*
JANES	*Journal of the Ancient Near Eastern Society*
JBL	*Journal of Biblical Literature*
JECS	*Journal of Early Christian Studies*
JPS	*Jewish Publication Society*
JQR	*Jewish Quarterly Review*
JSOT	*Journal for the Study of the Old Testament*
JSOTSup	Journal for the Study of the Old Testament: Supplements Series
NRSV	New Revised Standard Version

PG	Patrologia graeca
PL	Patrologia latina
RevQ	*Revue de Qumran*
SBL	Society of Biblical Literature
SBLDS	Society of Biblical Literature Dissertation Series
SBLMS	Society of Biblical Literature Monograph Series
SC	Sources chrétiennes
TAPA	*Transactions of the American Philological Association*
TSAJ	Texte und Studien zum antiken Judentum
TynBul	*Tyndale Bulletin*
VC	*Vigilae christianae*
VT	*Vetus Testamentum*
WCC	World Council of Churches
ZAW	*Zeitschrift für die alttestamentliche Wissenschaft*

The Semantics of Taboo
Menstrual Prohibitions in the Hebrew Bible
Kathleen O'Grady

Introduction: Holy Dread

In its contemporary usage the word "taboo" signifies the prohibitions attached to a particular inviolable substance or action. Often the word is assimilated for its capacity to convey a negative (impure, immoral, or unholy) activity or object. But as Sigmund Freud observes in *Totem and Taboo*, and later Mary Douglas in *Purity and Danger*, there is an implicit polysemic capacity in the term itself. The semantics of the word "taboo" are dominated, not by a single polarity of negativity, but by a double, seemingly contradictory, valence. The term "taboo" is able to represent something "sacred," "consecrated," and at the same time, something "uncanny," "dangerous," "forbidden," and "unclean."[1]

The first European record of the term comes from the journals of Captain James Cook from his eighteenth-century sea voyage to Polynesia. In his records he notes that the Polynesian word *tapu* (and its variants) denotes those things or actions that are "forbidden," including all "religious interdictions," as well as "anything sacred, or eminent, or devoted" or "consecrated."[2] As later analyzed by Edward Shortland, and echoed in Franz Steiner and James Frazer, the verbal roots of *tapu* consist of the word *ta*, that which is "marked," combined with *pu*, an adverbial form connoting "intensity." Together, "ta-pu literally signifies 'marked thoroughly' or 'marked off.'"[3] *Tapu* is not assessed through a polarity of negative or positive denotation, since the same term can be used to

---

1. Sigmund Freud, *Totem and Taboo* (trans. and ed. J. Strachey; Origins of Religion 13; London: Penguin, 1990), 71.
2. Franz Steiner, *Taboo* (London: Penguin, 1956), 27, 25.
3. Ibid., 32, 31; James Frazer, "Taboo," *Encyclopedia Britannica* 23:15.

denote something "holy" as well as something "impure," something "sacred" as well as something "unclean," something "consecrated" as well as something "forbidden."

Perhaps the positive or negative valence of the signifier is incidental, contingent upon its application and constituting only a secondary characteristic of the term. But a more radical interpretation is in order. As Steiner argues, in its original usage *tapu* did not separate holy from forbidden; in fact, it made no such distinction at all.[4] *Tapu* collapses any semantic bifurcation by denoting both polarities. Frazer too observes that "sacredness and uncleanness [are] indistinguishable [in 'taboo']," for the word conveys, not holiness *or* defilement, but both at the same time.[5] This does not amount to a conflation of separate and distinct concepts; rather, as Steiner explains, "Taboo is a single, not an 'undifferentiated' concept."[6] *Tapu* is a complex linguistic configuration that fuses together particular concepts—sanctity and uncleanness—in the same verbal structure.

The contrary denotations contained in the single sign (*tapu*) imply, not a collapse of contrary positions, but the logic by which the disparate terms function. What remains focal in *tapu* is the concept of something separated or differed from the norm, something, as the etymology would have it, "marked" or set apart from the ordinary order of life. As Frazer states, "It [taboo] does not . . . imply any moral quality but only a connexion with the gods or a separation from ordinary purposes."[7] Thus, the only appropriate antonym for *tapu* would be neither "sacred" nor "polluted," since the term can convey both simultaneously, but as Northcote Thomas and Frazer both observe, the Polynesian *noa*, a term denoting something "common," "general," or "accessible."[8]

Freud further states that the Polynesian tapu is structured in the same way as the Roman *sacer*, both meaning "set apart."[9] Douglas translates the Hebrew *k-d-sh*—traditionally defined as "holy"—as "set apart," with the Latin *sacer* conveying both "desecration" and "consecration."[10] And Frazer indicates that the Greek ἅγιος conflates both the polarity of "sacredness" and "pollution" and translates the Latin *sacer* as both

---

4. Steiner, *Taboo*, 33.
5. Frazer, "Taboo," 18.
6. Steiner, *Taboo*, 34.
7. Frazer, "Taboo," 15.
8. Northcote Thomas, cited by Freud, *Totem and Taboo*, 72.
9. Freud, *Totem and Taboo*, 71.
10. Mary Douglas, *Purity and Danger: An Analysis of the Concepts of Pollution and Taboo* (London: Routledge, 1966, 1992), 8.

"sacred" and "accursed."[11] In each expression the same sign is capable of conveying opposing meanings since it is structured not on a bipolar oppositional framework, but on the logic of separation itself.

The contemporary English term "taboo" thus has its semantic origins in the Polynesian word *tapu*. Etymologies do not necessarily constitute reliable definitions. However, in the case of "taboo," the English word (and its counterparts in other modern European languages, e.g., the French *tabou*) maintains the underlying logic of its verbal root and remains for many (Douglas, Freud, and Steiner included) a continuing "linguistic problem."[12] Modern dictionaries attempt to circumvent the ambiguity of meaning by defining "taboo" in two distinct manners as: (1) "sacred" or "holy" and (2) "unclean." They do not reckon with the contradictory nature of their definitions but summarize the two aspects of "taboo" as equally "prohibited" or "inviolable."[13] So while contemporary definitions appear to wish upon the word "taboo" a clear demarcation of purity *or* impurity, in each particular usage of the word—a moral distinction—the semantic ambiguity nevertheless remains intact. Perhaps the most succinct definition of the dissonant meanings that characterize "taboo" remains Freud's expression: "holy dread."[14]

In this chapter I wish to unravel further the dynamics of "taboo." I will demonstrate, through a detailed reading of Lev 15, that the semantic confusion of "taboo," with menstrual prohibitions as a defined type, may function to elucidate the very foundations of our conceptual categories and grant us knowledge concerning our configuration of the divine order. Further, a parallel reading between Lev 15 (the *niddah*) and Num 6 (the *nazir*) will demonstrate that while that which is marked impure is occluded from the sacred order, the same order is also inscribed by (and thus founded on) that which it jettisoned from its system. This engenders a new understanding of the dynamic between "the impure" and "the sacred" as encapsulated in the single semantic container "taboo." I will suggest that the parallel logic of exclusion existing between the *niddah* and the *nazir* in the Hebrew Bible has often been obscured by centuries of biblical commentary and translation—particularly Christian renderings—that have interpreted menstruation as both an "unnatural" (defective) and "immoral" (sinful) process.

---

11. Frazer, "Taboo," 18.
12. Steiner, *Taboo*, 31.
13. Cf. *Collins New English Dictionary, American Heritage Dictionary, Webster's II New Riverside University Dictionary.*
14. Freud, *Totem and Taboo*, 71.

Menstrual Prohibitions in the Hebrew Bible
Lev 15:19–23

Leviticus 15 contains a lengthy discussion of the ceremonial impurity occasioned by male and female sexual discharges. The passage progresses from a discussion of irregular male emissions (gonorrhea or blennorrhea) and normal seminal discharge to regulations for menstruation and instructions for irregular menstrual bleeding. Thus the statements regarding regular physiological processes (seminal emissions and menstruation) for men and women follow one another, framed by the discussion of irregular discharges (a symmetric organizational pattern of 1-2-2-1).

Leviticus 15 delineates menstruation, as well as male discharges, in terms of ritual uncleanness and detailed interdictions. A menstruating woman is designated unclean for a period of seven days, during which time she cannot take part in sexual relations. Any persons in direct contact (physical) or indirect contact (by means of an object) with a menstruant are also deemed unclean until the evening of their infraction and after ritual ablution:

> When a woman has a discharge of blood that is her regular discharge from her body, she shall be in her impurity for seven days, and whoever touches her shall be unclean until the evening. Everything upon which she lies during her impurity shall be unclean; everything also upon which she sits shall be unclean. Whoever touches her bed shall wash his clothes, and bathe in water, and be unclean until the evening. (Lev 15:19–23 NRSV)

The passage indicates that the menstruant is to remain in a state of ritual impurity for seven days, a time period that constitutes the approximate duration of a woman's natural menstruation. The menstruant is capable of transmitting her polluted state to others, specifically from her touch and from those items on which she sits or reclines. Further, the passage implies the potential communication of impurity from any object that has been handled by the menstruating woman (since her very touch defiles).

The passage continues in its specificity to include the occasion of menstrual irregularities. If a woman menstruates outside of her regular cycle or for a prolonged period of time, the same code of conduct applies: "If a woman has a discharge of blood for many days, not at the time of her impurity, or if she has a discharge beyond the time of her impurity, all of the days of the discharge she shall continue in her uncleanness; as in the days of her impurity, she shall be unclean" (Lev 15:25–26 NRSV). A woman with irregular bleeding, like the menstruant, can communicate her polluted state to others through immediate or indirect contact, with the defilement absolved through ritual cleansing. In addition to the standard menstrual regulations, however, a woman with irregular bleeding must count seven full days after the cessation of her menses: "If she is cleansed of her discharge, she shall count seven days, and after that she shall be clean" (Lev 15:28 NRSV). On the eighth day she is required to make a small sacrifice—two turtledoves or two young pigeons—to the priest for a sin offering and a burnt offering as expiation for her impurity, to "make atonement on her behalf before the LORD for her unclean discharge" (Lev 15:30 NRSV). After seven "clean" days and a ritual sacrifice, her state of impurity comes to an end.

Leviticus 15 thus marks a distinction between regular and irregular menstrual bleeding. The passage describes the ritual segregation required during a normal menstruation, not as a punitive measure for a sinful nature or behavior, but rather as a code of conduct to ensure "cleanliness." A menstruant is deemed at danger of communicating her unclean state to other members of the community, and the restrictions on her behavior are to inhibit this possible contagion. The Levitical passage defines menstrual blood in terms not of deviance or immorality, but of hygiene. Only abnormal menstrual bleeding requires "atonement," and the reparation necessary (sacrifice of two turtledoves) is equal to that required for male gonorrhea (see Lev 15:14); both irregular bleeding and gonorrhea are thus considered transgressions from the desired norm and, therefore, necessitate ritual sacrifice and purification. A regular menstrual cycle requires neither sin nor burnt offering to mark a renewed period of purity. The cessation of the menses itself is enough to complete the period of ritual uncleanness.

Nevertheless, many biblical commentators throughout history have viewed the Levitical menstrual prohibitions as divine punishment for the sinful nature of woman, which, through the actions of Eve, effected the fall of humankind. Menstruation becomes the divine "curse" of women. Presented here and elsewhere throughout this chapter is a random and eclectic sampling of the many available examples that demonstrate how pervasive this general view has been in various sources (different traditions) and throughout different historical time periods:

Because woman spilled the first man's blood, therefore to her was handed over the religious duty involving menstruation. (*Midr. Gen. Rab.* 1, 17:7r [Neusner, p. 188])

Why is *the woman's* case dealt with so severely [in Lev 15]? Perhaps, to keep up the memory of "*The Fall.*" The woman was in the transgression. "Remember whence thou art fallen."[15]

Eve's sin means that all women must "suffer torment and misfortune." And therefore she must have her period every month, and must fast once or twice [a month], so that she will always remember her sin and remain in a constant state of repentance. Just as a murderer constantly does.[16]

Paul Gauguin captures the link between Eve's consumption of the forbidden fruit with menstruation in his *Parua na te Varua Ino* ("Words of the Evil Spirit"), where Eve is shown in the garden pressing a white cloth to her newly menstrous vagina.[17] A variation on this link between menstruation and "the fall" appears in Kabbalistic literature where Eve is said to have seduced Adam to have sexual relations during her menstruation, thus transgressing a sacred law and initiating their expulsion from the garden.[18] The "forbidden fruit" in this reading is none other than the menstruous woman herself.

Many biblical commentaries, even up to the present day, continue to view menstruation as "symbolical of sin"[19] or as a "type of sinfulness" that must be contained, since, as one source states, "evil persons [i.e., menstruants] tend to contaminate anything or anybody they touch."[20] Levitical menstrual "uncleanness" thus becomes transformed through disparate interpretations to signify the "natural" immorality and sinfulness of woman.

While Christian commentators have generally presented a consonant understanding of the menstruant of Lev 15 (as immoral and sinful—

15. Andrew Bonar, *A Commentary on Leviticus* (London: Banner of Truth Trust, 1846), 295, Bonar's emphasis.

16. *Sefer mitsvas ha-noshim*, Solnik, as cited by Chava Weissler, "Mizvot Built into the Body: Tkhines for Niddah, Pregnancy, and Childbirth," in *People of the Body: Jews and Judaism from an Embodied Perspective* (ed. Howard Eilberg-Schwartz; New York: State University of New York Press, 1992), 104.

17. 1892; National Gallery of Art, Washington, D.C.

18. Naftali Herz Bacharach, *Emeq haMelekh* (Amsterdam: 1648), 23c–d, as cited by Raphael Patai, *Gates to the Old City* (New York: Avon, 1980), 456.

19. John Peter Lange, *Commentary on the Holy Scriptures: Leviticus* (Grand Rapids: Zondervan, 1876), 121; John Calvin, *Commentaries on the Four Last Books of Moses* (trans. C. W. Bingham; Grand Rapids: Eerdmans, 1950), 32; Bonar, *Commentary on Leviticus*, 287.

20. Armor D. Peisker, ed., *The Wesleyan Bible Commentary* (Grand Rapids: Eerdmans, 1967), 333.

which I will develop further), the Jewish interpretations of the same text vary significantly. The rabbinical tradition permits and often encourages conflicting readings, while Christian, particularly early Christian understandings of biblical texts, have a more doctrinal foundation. It could even be argued that early rabbinic scholars have already intimated the semantic ambiguity of the menstruant in Lev 15, clearing the way for contemporary Jewish feminist scholars to declare the Levitical proscriptions "celebratory" of women's specificity and in no manner punitive.[21]

This chapter will not concern itself with a historical account of the Judaic renderings of Lev 15, already detailed in many excellent studies. Nor does the chapter provide a detailed historic overview of the Christian treatment of this biblical passage (also widely treated). Rather, I hope to elucidate clearly the configuration of "holy dread" (taboo) on which the menstruant of Lev 15 rests, and to establish that this complex valence has been lost in many renderings of Lev 15 that function through a bipolar (pure-impure) understanding of "taboo." I will provide a close reading of the text itself to demonstrate that a more dynamic semantics is at work, one that will draw together and make parallel biblical passages on the menstruant and the holy person.

Historical Assessments

The misconceptions and negative views of menstruation put forth by Aristotle and Pliny highly influenced early views of menstruation. In his first-century C.E. account of menstruation or, as he labels it, "pernicious mischief," Pliny includes the following description:

> But nothing could easily be found that is more remarkable than the monthly flux of women. Contact with it turns new wine sour, crops touched by it become barren, grafts die, seeds in gardens are dried up, the fruit of trees falls off, the bright surface of mirrors in which it is merely reflected is dimmed, the edge of steel and the gleam of ivory are dulled, hives of bees die, even bronze and iron are at once seized by rust, and a horrible smell fills the air; to taste it drives dogs mad and infects their bites with an incurable poison. (Pliny, *Nat.* 7.15.64–66 [Rackham, LCL])

While these particular views were not maintained by religious writers, the views perpetuated the notion of menstruation as a powerful, unnatural force.

---

21. See Ellens, this volume.

Further, the process of menstruation became conflated with an aborted or miscarried fetus. Aristotle mistakenly understood menstrual blood to be the constitutive matter for the growth of a fetus after conception and semen to be the formative activity that shapes the physical and spiritual elements of a child:

> The contribution which the female makes to generation [of a fetus] is the *matter* used therein, this is to be found in the substance constituting the menstrual fluid. . . . The male provides the "form" and the "principle of the movement," the female provides the body, in other words, the material. . . . [Menstrual blood is] "an impure condition"; i.e., it lacks one constituent, and one only, the principle of Soul. . . . This principle has to be supplied by the semen of the male. (Aristotle, *Gen. an.* 727b, 19; 729a, 15; 737a, 25–35 [Peck])[22]

The view that the male sperm is the active component in procreation was accepted for centuries in Europe and was reiterated as late as Freud.[23]

Pliny's first-century account of menstruation echoes Aristotle: "The substance in question [menstrual blood] is the material for human generation" (Pliny, *Nat.* 7.15.66–67 [Rackham, LCL]). Moses Maimonides adopts this position in his influential twelfth-century rabbinic commentary: "All the [menstrual] liquid that is found there [in the uterus] becomes solidified, and thus the embryo is formed, as has been elucidated in natural science."[24] The resulting effect of this view of menstrual blood as the formative matter of conception is that the menstrual process itself becomes defined as failed conception, with the unformed matter (blood) constituting an undeveloped "corpse." Menstruation is thus not equated with a cleansing or regenerative process but is commensurate with death (the failure of life-creation). Western views of menstruation today continue to be informed by Aristotle's definition of menstruation as unsuccessful conception.[25]

Thomas Aquinas cited Aristotle's negative account of menstruation in his *Summa Theologica*, where he also added that "the menstrual blood, the flow of which is subject to monthly periods, has a certain natural

---

22. See also Aristotle, *Gen. an.* 726b–731b; 775b–778a.
23. Sigmund Freud, *New Introductory Lectures on Psychoanalysis* (New York: W.W. Norton, 1965), 114.
24. Moses Maimonides, *Commentary on the Mishnah: Introduction to Seder Zeraim and Commentary on Tractate Berachoth* (trans. F. Rosner; New York: Feldheim, 1975), 184.
25. Emily Martin, *The Woman in the Body* (Boston: Beacon, 1987), 47–48.

impurity . . . [it is] infected with corruption and repudiated by nature" (*Summa Theologica* 2:2189 [pt. 2, q. 31, art. 5]). Aquinas's writings on menstruation generally combine the view of menstrual blood as a representation of women's natural impurity (as descendants of Eve) and as a perversion of nature (i.e., aborted life). His view of menstruation informed various sources on the topic well into the nineteenth century and continues to inform current readings of Lev 15.

Menstruation and Sexual Relations: Lev 15:24

The prohibition against sexual relations during menstruation is repeated several times throughout the Hebrew Bible (Lev 15:24; 18:19–20; 20:18; Ezek 18:6). The Lev 15 passage declares that if a man has sexual relations with a menstruating woman he will, like the menstruant herself, remain in a state of ceremonial impurity for a period of seven days and is capable, like the menstruant, of communicating his pollution to others: "If any man lies with her, and her impurity falls on him, he shall be unclean seven days; and every bed on which he lies shall be unclean" (Lev 15:24 NRSV). In this passage a violation of the ban against sexual relations during menstruation involves only a period of ritual impurity for the man, who is believed to have contracted the menstruant's uncleanness. A later passage, however, increases the punitive measures to be taken: "If a man lies with a woman having her sickness and uncovers her nakedness, he has laid bare her flow and she has laid bare her flow of blood; both of them shall be cut off from their people" (Lev 20:18 NRSV). The more severe punishment for sexual relations during menses prescribed in this later Levitical passage—"both of them shall be cut off (*karet*) from their people"—has been understood as either a sentence of excommunication from the community or penalty by death.[26]

At first glance it appears as if the two Levitical passages—one admonishing a temporary ceremonial impurity, the other exile or death—detail extreme contradictory measures for the same transgression. But a number of different possible interpretations exist for the inconsistency between the two injunctions: (1) The first section describes sexual relations between a man and wife, while the latter

---

26. Francis Brown, ed., *The New Jerome Biblical Commentary*, 4:33; Carl Friedrich Keil and Franz Delitzsch, *Biblical Commentary on the Old Testament* (Grand Rapids: Eerdmans, 1949), 393; Joshua Porter, *Leviticus* (Cambridge: Cambridge University Press, 1976), 122; Gordon J. Wenham, *The Book of Leviticus* (Grand Rapids: Eerdmans, 1979), 221.

describes intercourse between unmarried or adulterous partners; thus, the extreme punitive measures in the second passage are a reflection of the doubly transgressive character of the act (unlawful sexual relations and violation of the menstrual prohibitions).[27] This reading relies on the context of the second Levitical passage, which discusses a number of sexual prohibitions (incest, adultery, homosexuality) that do not take place between a husband and wife. (2) The former legislates laws for cleanliness, while the subsequent passage focuses on moral conduct and discipline.[28] This conclusion is based on a contextual reading of Lev 15, which does not ascribe any punitive measures to an infringement of the code, while Lev 20 details punishments for a number of different (primarily sexual) violations. (3) The early passage refers to the accidental transgression of the ban (the onset of the menses occurring during intercourse), while the later passage details the punishment for a deliberate violation of the law.[29] This view recognizes the willful nature of the offenses listed in Lev 20, while Lev 15 outlines regulations for unintentional contact with the menstruant. (4) The latter passage is the product of a different historical time period with a more stringent legal code.[30] The evolution of judiciary laws is a legitimate option for reconciling the opposing passages, since most biblical commentators agree that the two passages originated in different historical periods: that is, Lev 20 falls within the sphere of the "holiness period," while Lev 15 is part of the "Priestly Code."[31] (Debates continue on which of the codes precedes the other, with the traditional documentary hypothesis ascribing the earlier age to the holiness period.)

An examination of each of these possibilities for reconciling the two passages demonstrates that a definitive interpretation is impossible. Yet all interpretations but the last (historical) reading of the texts actually circumvent the problem since they discern no contradiction between the two passages. The latter penalty simply complements the former (with

---

27. See, e.g., Reginald C. Fuller et al., eds., *A New Catholic Commentary on Holy Scripture* (Don Mills, Ontario: Nelson, 1969), 236.
28. See Raymond Brown et al., eds., *Jerome Bible Commentary* (Englewood Cliffs, N.J.: Prentice-Hall, 1968), 4:34; Wenham, *Book of Leviticus*, 220.
29. See Keil and Delitzsch, *Biblical Commentary*, 394; Lange, *Leviticus*, 120; Erhard S. Gerstenberger, *Leviticus: A Commentary* (Old Testament Library; Louisville: Westminster John Knox, 1996), 204.
30. See George Arthur Buttrick et al., eds., *The Interpreter's Bible* (New York: Abingdon, 1953), 2:76; and Joshua Porter, *Leviticus*, 122. Noth asserts a similar position, stating that v. 18 was likely a later addition to the Lev 15 passage; see Martin Noth, *Leviticus: A Commentary* (trans. J. E. Andersen; London: SCM Press, 1962), 113.
31. Lester L. Grabbe, *Leviticus* (Sheffield: Sheffield Academic Press, 1993), 12–20.

qualifying factors). And each of the diverse readings accept that at some time or in some conditions sexual relations during menstruation were punishable by exile or death. No reading questions the restriction against sexual relations during menstruation.

Historical Assessments

A historic text reflects the emphasis placed on the sexual ban in the Jewish tradition. The *Midrash Rabbah* tells the story of Jehoiakim, who was imprisoned for a variety of crimes. During his confinement he was permitted to have sexual relations with his wife but refused her during her menses. The text concludes by revealing the true reason for Jehoiakim's incarceration and provides an explanation for his subsequent release: "In Jerusalem you did not observe the precept relating to issues [menstruation], but now you are fulfilling it . . . for this do *I send forth the prisoners*" (*Midr. Rab.* [Lev.; Metzora] 4.19:6 [Freedman and Simon, 245–49], original emphasis). The story of Jehoiakim demonstrates the severity of the menstrual ban in historical Judaism. Today the contemporary Jewish position (for Orthodox, Conservative, and many Reform traditions) remains firm in its prohibition of sexual relations during menstruation.

Many major Christian thinkers have advocated maintaining the Levitical prohibitions for menstruation, particularly the ban on sexual relations during menstruation. Again we can turn to Aristotle as a source of influence on these early commentators. Aristotle postulated that conception during menstruation would be certain to produce physical abominations and abnormalities in the child since the prime matter for the fetus is polluted (i.e., menstruous). Jerome adopted this view, and it is further cited in Aquinas: "Men ought to keep away from their [menstruous] wives, because thus is a deformed, blind, lame, leprous offspring conceived" (*Summa Theologica* 2802 [q. 64, art. 3, suppl.]). Augustine states that the Levitical prohibitions concerning contact with a menstruous woman should be maintained literally and not figuratively, and his views are echoed in Aquinas.[32] Aquinas described the Levitical menstrual regulations as a "ceremonial precept," because of the menstruant's "uncleanness," but also added that it was a "*moral precept*," because of the "harm that frequently resulted to the offspring from such intercourse" (*Summa Theologica* 2802 [q. 64, art. 3, suppl.], emphasis added).

---

32. Augustine, "Forgiveness 21, XII"; and Thomas Aquinas, *Summa Theologica*, 2802 (q. 64, art. 3, suppl.).

John Calvin affirmed the Levitical views on the menstruant and referred to menstruation as a "shameful thing."[33] Bible commentaries reinforce the notion of moral pollution associated with menstruation, particularly of sexual relations during the flow. A late nineteenth-century Levitical discussion of menstruation entitled "The Secret Flow of Sin from the Natural Heart" refers to menstruation as a "miserable state," an "illness" (i.e., as "unnatural"), and a "sin."[34] A late twentieth-century commentary refers to the "sense of *natural* disgust or shame [that] has developed into an *ethical* and religious feeling of uncleanness" in the Levitical menstrual ban on sexual intercourse.[35]

During the history of Christianity this interpretation of the Levitical menstrual regulations has supported the view that menstruation is an abomination of the natural order (i.e., it is "abnormal"). This reading of Lev 15 has been used to prohibit women, always potential menstruants, from approaching the altar and from entering the church.[36] Dionysius, the archbishop of Alexandria in the third century, declared that menstruants should not take Communion: "Menstruous women ought not to come to the Holy Table, or touch the Holy of Holies, nor to churches, but pray elsewhere."[37] The Greek Orthodox Church to this day restricts menstruants from participation in Communion. The Roman Catholic Church and the Eastern Orthodox Church continue to list the moral impurity of menstruation as one of their reasons for resisting the ordination of women priests.[38] Until Vatican II, the Catholic tradition prohibited women in general from reading Scripture within the sanctuary because of their polluted state.[39] Menstrual taboos in Judaism and Christianity have functioned to keep women from attaining high-ranking positions and excluded them from ceremonial participation. While I have already demonstrated that this understanding of menstruation as a

---

33. Calvin, *Four Last Books of Moses*, 2:33.
34. Bonar, *Commentary on Leviticus*, 287–98.
35. Paul Haupt, *The Sacred Books of the Old and New Testament* (New York: Dodd, Mead, 1898), 78; also cited as a reliable argument in Buttrick et al., *Interpreter's Bible*, 2:74, emphasis added.
36. Theodore Balsamon, *Interrogatio* 35, as cited by William Phipps, "The Menstrual Taboo in Judeo-Christian Tradition," *Journal of Religion and Health* 19 (1980): 300; Theodore Balsamon, seventh century, bishop of Canterbury, *Penitential of Theodore* 14, 17.
37. Dionysius of Alexandria, *Canon II*. Response to letter from Basilidea the Bishop.
38. Rosemary Radford Ruether, "Women's Body and Blood: The Sacred and the Impure," in *Through the Devil's Gateway: Women, Religion, and Taboo* (ed. A. Joseph; London: SPCK and Channel Four Television, 1990), 7.
39. Ibid., 9.

punitive measure for a moral infraction is unfounded (not established as such in Lev 15), and that neither is menstruation defined in the Levitical passage as unnatural, it is still necessary to explore further the biblical sanctions concerning menstruation to understand more fully the underlying logic of the menstrual prohibitions.[40]

Menstrual Segregation: Lev 15:31

A further emphasis on punishment for violations of the purity regulations appears in the summary statement of Lev 15, which immediately follows the discussion of regular and irregular menstrual bleeding: "Thus you shall keep the people of Israel separate from their uncleanness, so that they do not die in their uncleanness by defiling my tabernacle that is in their midst" (Lev 15:31 NRSV).

This passage appears to confirm the penalty by "death" (either literal, communal, or spiritual) mentioned in Lev 20 ("so that they do not die").

While this passage supports the reading of severe disciplinary measures for transgressions of the Levitical code, it also opens up other possibilities for understanding the menstrual prohibitions themselves. One possible reading of the above passage is that the "tabernacle . . . in their midst" refers to the constant presence of the Lord within the community of his chosen people, and thus, the segregation practiced for uncleanness ("You shall keep the people of Israel *separate* from their uncleanness" [emphasis added]) is a "code of conduct" to be followed, with defiance of these regulations resulting in "spiritual death" or "divine punishment."[41] The passage simply reflects the proscriptions already detailed in the specific passages on uncleanness and directs submission to this legislation. It functions as a concluding statement to the section on discharges generally and does not contain further proscriptions.

A second reading, however, views this passage as a clear injunction against religious worship for those with impurities. There are no religious restrictions delineated in the sections specific to menstruation. However, if one reads "my tabernacle" in this passage as constituting a physical place of worship, rather than the presence of the Lord within the community, an added regulation falls on the menstruant, prohibiting her from formal religious practice, with an infraction being punished by

---

40. See De Troyer and Roll, this volume.
41. See Fuller et al., *New Catholic Commentary*, 236; Keil and Delitzsch, *Biblical Commentary*, 394; Baruch A. Levine, *Leviticus* (JPS Torah Commentary; Philadelphia: Jewish Publication Society, 1989), 98; Wenham, *Book of Leviticus*, 220; George A. F. Knight, *Leviticus* (Daily Study Bible Series; Edinburgh: Saint Andrews Press, 1981), 83.

death.[42] This reading can be augmented from historical texts that indicate that menstruants were banned from the temple during the time of Herod.[43] In addition to the sexual prohibitions and the possible transmission of pollution, menstruants are further restricted in this passage from religious worship.

The Levitical proscriptions for menstruation discussed above prevent direct contact between a menstruant and her community, already suggesting an implicit practice of menstrual seclusion (an individual cannot touch the menstruant or the objects associated with her). The third and most convincing reading of the concluding passage to Lev 15 builds on the notion of menstrual isolation and understands the passage to be a call for the practice of *total* menstrual segregation. The statement "You shall keep the people of Israel separate from their uncleanness" can be understood as a *physical* segregation of those with impurities, such as menstruation, from their community. Some historic evidence for this practice exists, though it comes from a period significantly later than the one in which Lev 15 was written. Josephus, in the first century C.E., supports this reading when he states, "He removed the women, when they had their natural purgations, till the seventh day; after which he looked on them as pure and permitted them to come in again [to the city/camp]" (*Ant.* 3.11.3 [p. 220]). *The Temple Scroll* also affirms this reading: "And in every city you shall allot places . . . for women during their menstrual uncleanness and after giving birth, so that they may not defile in their midst / with their menstrual uncleanness."[44] The Mishnah also indicates that menstrual separation was common practice in the Tannaitic period, with special houses available for menstruants (m. *Nid.* 7:4A). In this third reading the concluding Levitical passage refers to a temporary exile from the city or community itself, with violations punished by death.[45]

This third reading of the concluding Levitical passage is not in contradiction with the first two readings insofar as it admits to the presence of the Lord within the camp itself ("my tabernacle," first reading) and

---

42. See Peisker, *Wesleyan Bible Commentary,* 334; Raymond Brown et al., *Jerome Biblical Commentary,* 4:33; Keil and Delitzsch, *Biblical Commentary,* 394; Wenham, *Book of Leviticus,* 221; Gerstenberger, *Leviticus,* 205; Bonar, *Commentary on Leviticus,* 298.

43. Josephus, *Ag. Ap.* 2.8 (p. 210). Cf. Yigael Yadin, ed., *The Temple Scroll* (Jerusalem: Israel Exploration Society, Institute of Archaeology of the Hebrew University of Jerusalem, and Shrine of the Book, 1983), 2:192 (XLV, 10).

44. Yadin, *Temple Scroll,* 1:306 (XLVIII, 14–17). See Gruber, this volume.

45. See Calvin, *Four Last Books of Moses,* 2:33 (where he also implies the first reading); Lange, *Leviticus,* 120. See Gruber, this volume.

the prohibition of menstruants from endangering this presence (through entering the temple, second reading); rather, it draws the most extreme consequences from the logic of both the first and second readings and advances the practice of full menstrual seclusion. The understanding of "separation" as central to the prohibitions on menstruation is underlined in each case.

Niddah: Etymology

There is a large variation in interpretation for the Hebrew term for menstruation, *niddah*, which lies at the heart of the Lev 15 passage. The traditional definitions and translations for *niddah* are as follows: "impurity," "immorality," "abomination," "abhorrent thing," "filth," "excretion," "something to be shunned," "especially of menstruation."[46] Each of the terms employed suggests an extreme negative view of the physiological process of menstruation, connoting pollution (a normative interpretation) as well as sinfulness (a moral interpretation). As we have seen, historical discourses on menstruation confirm this general outlook.

The origins for the Hebrew *niddah* are not evident, but a look at its etymology may afford an entry into its biblical semantics. Baruch Levine locates the verbal root for *niddah* in *n-d-h*, which signifies "to cast, hurl, throw" [away]."[47] Jacob Milgrom also comments on this verbal root but defines it in a mildly different fashion as "to chase away or put aside."[48] Another possible root, *n-d-d*, similarly signifies "depart, go, flee, wander." Milgrom, like Levine, associates the possible root words with the "discharge" of the menstrual blood from the uterus of the menstruating woman, thus the blood is "cast out" of the menstruant. With such a definition, Levine concludes that the term *niddah* "does not connote impurity in and of itself but, rather, describes the physiological process of the

---

46. Francis Brown defines *niddah* as (1) "ceremonial impurity, especially of menstruation" and (2) "impure thing" (*New Brown-Driver-Briggs-Gesenius Hebrew and English Lexicon*, 622c); Koehler and Baumgartner define it as (1) "excretion, abhorrent thing" and (2) "impurity, menstruation" (*Lexicon*, 596d); Tregelles defines it as "abomination," "filth, menstrual uncleanness," "something unclean, or filthy" (*Hebrew and Chaldee Lexicon*, 535). Jacob Milgrom defines it as "impurity," "abomination," and "lustration"; see *Leviticus 1–16* (Anchor Bible; New York: Doubleday, 1991), 744. Gerstenberger defines *niddah* as "something abhorrent" and "menstruation" (*Leviticus*, 203). W. Gunther Plaut defines *niddah* as "something to be shunned"; see *The Torah: A Modern Commentary* (New York: Union of American Hebrew Congregations, 1981), 850.
47. Levine, *Leviticus*, JPS Torah Commentary, 97.
48. Milgrom, *Leviticus 1–16*, 744–45.

flow of blood."[49] Hence a definition and translation of *niddah* would be rendered appropriately as "menstruation," a more neutral term than the traditionally supplied, and frequently employed (still, in contemporary commentaries and Bibles), "impurity" or "abomination," which contain both normative and moral judgments. Quite to the contrary, in some biblical passages (Num 8:7; 19:9; Zech 13:1) the word *niddah* conveys "lustration" or "water used to cleanse" (parallel in pattern to the Egyptian word for menstruation, *ir hsnn*, which also means both menstruation and ritual purification).[50]

There is, however, another possible conclusion that can be formed from the same etymology. The concept of "separation" that is evident in both verbal roots for *niddah* (put aside, depart) could just as easily (or simultaneously) refer to the Levitical regulations of separation for menstruation. Talmudic and midrashic literature defines *niddah* literally as "separation,"[51] referring to the time period of the menstrual seclusion, but niddah is equally used to indicate the menstruant herself, understood in these early rabbinic commentaries as the "one who is excluded," or the "one set aside."[52] Milgrom also accounts for this possibility in his analysis, "In addition, niddâ came to refer not just to the menstrual discharge but to the menstruant herself, for she too was 'discharged' and 'excluded' from her society."[53] Evidence for a system of menstrual seclusion and for the withdrawal of the menstruant from ordinary society is thus available in the etymology of the Hebrew term itself.

The traditional definitions for *niddah* as "immorality" or "abomination" are not evident in its etymological roots. As we have already demonstrated above, neither are these connotations present in the Lev 15 passage itself, which simply describes the menstruant as "unclean," and not with the more weighted classifications of "abomination" or "immorality." The verbal shift is dramatic when this new translation of *niddah* as "She shall be in her (period of) separation for seven days" replaces "She shall be in her impurity for seven days." The focus of the Lev 15 passage then rests, not as traditional rendering would imply on notions of "pollution," but on menstruation as a time of *separation*.

---

49. Levine, *Leviticus*, JPS Torah Commentary, 97.
50. As noted by Milgrom, *Leviticus 1–16*, 744.
51. Geoffrey Wigoder, ed., *The Encyclopedia of Judaism* (New York: Macmillan, 1989), 524.
52. Adrienne Baker, ed., *The Jewish Woman in Contemporary Society* (New York: New York University Press, 1993), 155; and Louis Jacobs, ed., *The Jewish Religion: A Companion* (Oxford: Oxford University Press, 1995), 342.
53. Milgrom, *Leviticus 1–16*, 745.

A further emphasis on *separation* is evident in the concluding section of the Lev 15 passage already discussed: "Thus you shall keep the people of Israel *separate* from their uncleanness" (emphasis added). As previously noted, this passage functions as a concluding statement to the Lev 15 passage and immediately follows the discussion of menstrual regulations. *Niddah*, literally as "separation," is further augmented here with the injunction to isolate the menstruant from her community. Thus the logic of separation for menstruation is doubly invoked in the Levitical laws.[54]

But this concluding statement of Lev 15 employs an unusual form of the verb *hizzîr (ve-hizartem; ve-yinnazru)*.[55] This verb form (verbal root *h-z-r*) denotes "set aside, dedicate, or separate, *in a religious and ceremonial sense*."[56] The specific "religious" valence of division is lost in the English translation, which simply offers the word "separate." Further, and importantly, the verb form is linked to *n-z-r*, from which the word *nazir* or *nazirite*, that is, "holy person," derives.[57] Here, *h-z-r* is applied directly to the menstruant; yet this verb form is used in only one other place in the entirety of the Hebrew Scriptures, where it is traditionally understood and translated as "*sacred* separation," since it is applied directly to the *nazir*, that is, the holy person of Numbers (Num 6:2–3, 5–6, 12).[58]

The *Nazir*: Num 6:1-21

The *nazir* (or *nazirite*) first appears in Num 6: "The LORD spoke to Moses, saying: 'Speak to the Israelites and say to them: When either men or women make a special vow, the vow of a nazirite, to separate themselves to the LORD, they shall separate themselves from wine and strong drink" (vv. 1–3 NRSV).[59] The "separation" of the *nazir* to the Lord

---

54. See De Troyer, this volume.
55. Norman Henry Snaith, who first commented on this verb form, does not import this significant linguistic observation to his very standard reading of the *niddah*; see *The Century Bible: Leviticus and Numbers* (London: Nelson, 1967), 109.
56. Julius H. Greenstone, *The Holy Scriptures: Numbers, with Commentary* (Philadelphia: Jewish Publication Society, 1939), 59, emphasis added. See also Green et al., *Concise Lexicon*, 154 (5144).
57. This observation was made by Levine, though he does not develop why these two passages might share linguistic similarities (*JPS Torah Commentary*, 98).
58. This was first observed by Wenham, who said that "*hizzîr*," as used in Lev 15:31, is used only in Num 6:2, 3, 4, 6, 12, and in a related form in Lev 22:2 (*Book of Leviticus*, 221). Wenham does not draw any conclusions from this observation, however. Subsequent arguments on this verbal "coincidence" are my own.
59. Related literature on the biblical *nazir* can be found in the Mishnah tractatem *Naz.* and the tractate *Nazir* in the *Talmud of the Land of Israel*, vol. 24 (*y. Naz.*), as well as in the midrashic Num. *Rab.*

is the linguistic equivalent of menstrual "separation" in the concluding passage of Lev 15, with both employing the exclusive usage of the anomalous verb form based on the root *h-z-r.*

A list of regulations then follows: *nazirs* are prohibited from cutting their hair (Num 6:5), eating or drinking products made from grapes (vv. 3–4), and having contact with the dead, including deceased family members (vv. 6–12). The rules for the *nazir* are more strict than those outlined for the priest, and equal in austerity only to those required of the high priest. Yet, though the regulations are similar, the vows of the *nazir* do not confer priestly status but rather declare participation in a kind of holy order, where one separates oneself for God: "All their days as nazirites they are holy to the LORD" (v. 8 NRSV). Significantly, women are permitted equal participation in the vow of the *nazir,* while they are prohibited from the priesthood.

Though the passage ascribes no time limit to the vow of the *nazir,* it appears to be a temporary status that could be concluded with the shaving of the head, along with the ritual burning of the hair in the tent of meeting (Num 6:18), a ceremonial gesture to be rid of—as one commentator suggests (making manifest Freud's "holy dread")—"something holy, *hence dangerous.*"[60] Those concluding the state of separation conferred upon them in the vow of the *nazir* (vv. 13–20) did so ceremonially by presenting lavish amounts of animal and food offerings at the tent of meeting.[61]

Just as the etymology for niddah rests on notions of "separation," so too is the *nazir* defined. As Levine argues, the verbs *nadar* and *nazar,* from which the term *nazir* arises and the terms in which the Num 6 passage is defined, "are sufficiently close in meaning and sound to suggest

---

60. Timothy R. Ashley, *The Book of Numbers* (Grand Rapids: Eerdmans, 1993), 148, emphasis added.
61. Few other references to the *nazir* appear in the Bible. Samson (Judg. 13:3–7) is clearly called a *nazir,* though he did not follow the prohibitions laid out in Num 6 (such as abstaining from wine). Levites similarly consecrated themselves to the Lord but were not *nazirs.* Samuel, often considered a nazir, is not named as such in the Bible, but in the manner of a *nazir* he did not shave or cut his hair. As Ashley observes, however, it is more likely from the genealogy of 1 Chr 6:25–28, 33, that Samuel was a Levite rather than a *nazir* (Ashley, *Book of Numbers,* 139). Several commentators also infer from textual evidence that John the Baptist was a *nazir,* but again this is not openly stated (see Greenstone, *Holy Scriptures,* 58). Dennis T. Olson argues that Joseph of Gen 49:26 was a *nazir,* since he is defined as "set apart," but the text does not explicitly name him as such. Olson also indicates that Jesus is named as a "Nazarene" not only because of his birth in Nazareth but also to connote his position as a *nazir.* See his *Numbers: Interpretation* (Bible Commentary for Teaching and Preaching; Louisville: John Knox, 1996), 39–40.

that they are related etymologically." The roots *n-d-r* and *n-z-r* are, Levine states, "phonetic variants of the same verbal root" and are analogous in pattern to *n-d-h* and *n-z-h*.[62] As we have already seen, *n-d-h* and *n-z-h* are the verbal roots that constitute the word *niddah* and imply "separation." In the case of the *nazir,* the verbal roots convey the similar meanings of one "set apart," "set aside," "separated," but also of one "dedicated," "devoted," or "consecrated," especially in a "religious sense."[63]

Many commentators have mistakenly used this etymology to associate the *nazir* with concepts of "holiness," "piety" or "purity." Philip Budd, for example, states that the verbal roots for the *nazir* "convey the idea of purity . . . but the ideas are not obviously present."[64] But the positive valence given to the *nazir* is not implicit in its construction, but contingent upon its usage. While *n-z-r* is able to convey the notion of one set apart as in a "dedication" (of "holiness"), it also carries the opposite meaning of one set apart as "cursed."[65] The notion of purity is not the focus of the term, but incidental, conditional upon application. Instead, the *nazir* rests on the concept of separation—one set apart—which is implicit in states both of being "blessed" or "cursed." As with *niddah,* where "impurity" does not constitute its central semantics, so *nazir* is defined not by its relation to "purity," but by the notion of separation. The midrashic literature similarly disassociates the *nazir* from necessary connotations of "holiness" or "purity," stating, "*Neziruth* (n-z-r) [*nazir*] in every instance denotes nought but separation" (*Midr. Rab.* [Num.] 10.8 [Freedman and Simon, 378]). In a move that anticipates Freudian psychoanalytic theory, the *Midrash Rabbah* adopts the story of none other than Narcissus to convey the proper behavior of the *nazir* as one set apart (*Midr. Rab.* [Num.] 10.7 [Freedman and Simon, 371–72]). And from what is the *nazir* separated? As one commentator has stated, the *nazir* is "set apart" from "wine, grape products and dead bodies," but

---

62. Levine, *Numbers 1–20,* 218.
63. See Ashley, *Book of Numbers,* 135, 141; Martin Noth, *Numbers: A Commentary* (trans. J. E. Andersen; Old Testament Library; Philadelphia: Westminster, 1968), 54; Olson, *Numbers,* 39; Walter Riggans, *Numbers* (Philadelphia: Westminster, 1983), 53; Wenham, *Book of Leviticus,* 86; John Sturdy, *Numbers* (Cambridge Bible Commentary; Cambridge: Cambridge University Press, 1976), 48; Alan Hugh McNeile, *The Book of Numbers* (Cambridge: Cambridge University Press, 1931), 31; Leonard Elliot Binns, *Numbers* (Westminster Commentaries; London: Methuen, 1927), 37; Francis Brown, *New Brown-Driver-Briggs-Gesenius Hebrew and English Lexicon,* 634 (5144).
64. Philip J. Budd, *Numbers* (Word Biblical Commentary; Waco, Tex.: Word, 1984), 71.
65. Plaut, *Torah,* 1058; also as "dedication to shame," Green et al., *Concise Lexicon,* 154 (5144).

more significantly the *nazir* is "separated *to the LORD*."[66] Division characterizes the semantics of the *nazir*.

While most contemporary analysis would locate the *nazir* as the
polar opposite of the *niddah*, the highest of the holy and the lowest of
the impure, a linguistic analysis demonstrates that the two actually function on the same paradigm of separation. Both figures are set apart from
the normal order of society, marked out by a "sacred separation" (as the
anomalous usage of the *h-z-r* verb form, shared only by Lev 15 and
Num 6, indicates). This shared verbal patterning, which highlights division at the heart of the sacred, is not incidental but intrinsic to the oper-
ation of the two passages. Leviticus 15 admonishes a "sacred separation"
of the menstruant from her community in order to maintain the sanctity
of the "tabernacle that is in their midst" (v. 31 NRSV). *Nazirs* are required
to "separate themselves to the LORD" in order to make themselves "holy
to the LORD" (Num 6:2, 8). Sanctification in both passages functions
through division.

The historical proximity of the two passages makes such semantic
parallels significant. Numbers 6 is traditionally dated as part of the
Priestly Code (as is Lev 15) or as a supplement to it, with the passage on
the *nazir* specifically concluding the segment of legal codes that begins
in Lev 1.[67] Thus Lev 15 and Num 6 share historic textual origins in
addition to their shared linguistic elements. The midrashic literature too
recognizes a common structural pattern in Lev 15 and Num 6, placing a
discourse on the prohibitions of the *niddah* at the center of its discussion
of the *nazir* (*Midr. Rab.* [Num.] 10.8 [Freedman and Simon, 375–76]).

An explicit parallel in the two passages concerns the sacrificial proscriptions for a deviation in status. When a woman experiences an irregularity in her menstrual cycle, the Levitical passage calls for a ritual
sacrifice of two turtledoves or small pigeons on the eighth day, after a
seven-day period of separation (15:29). The same ritual requirement
applies to an aberration of the status of *nazir*. When those who have
taken the vow of *nazir* come into contact with a corpse, thereby compro-
mising their vow, they are told to begin their "cleansing" for seven days,
and "on the eighth day they shall bring two turtledoves or two young
pigeons to the priest at the entrance of the tent of meeting, and the
priest shall offer one as a sin offering and the other as a burnt offering,
and make atonement for them" (Num 6:9–10 NRSV). The menstruant
with an irregular discharge has the identical requirement of waiting

---

66. Wenham, *Book of Leviticus*, 86.
67. Ashley, *Book of Numbers*, 137, 149.

seven "clean" days and then, "on the eigth day she shall take two turtledoves or two pigeons and bring them to the priest at the entrance of the
tent of meeting. The priest shall offer one for a sin offering and the other
for a burnt offering; and the priest shall make atonement on her behalf
(Lev 15:30 NRSV).

The consequences for an irregularity in the status of the *niddah* and
the *nazir* are thus analogous. Most sources, including the midrashic
texts, overlook this obvious parallel, preferring to attribute the remarkably small offering required of the *nazir* to economic fairness, which
would allow the poor to partake in the *nazirite* office (*Midr. Rab.* [Num.]
10.25 [Freedman and Simon, 406]).[68] And while other situations require
the same animals for sacrifice,[69] such as the leper or the parturient, only
the menstruant with an irregular flow requires the same seven-day
period of cleansing with the exact ritual prescription as the contaminated
nazir. The leper, for example, provides a similar animal sacrifice but is
also to include an offering of oil and grain, with the order of sacrifice
described in different terms (Lev 14:21–22). To my knowledge, only one
biblical commentator has commented upon the exceptional similarity
between the ritual requirements of the corrupted *nazir* and the menstruant with irregular flow and simply amended his observation with a confused, "It is not clear why."[70]

Revealingly, a *nazir* who comes in contact with a menstruant or a
nazir who menstruates (since women, too, may take the vow) does not
invalidate the status of the *nazirite*-ship. No ceremonial cleansing or ritual offering is required, and the *nazir* may count the days of *niddah* as
part of the *nazirite* consecration. Explicitly stated in the talmudic literature (*y. Naz.* 7:3 G, p. 194), this is implicit in the biblical passage, which
does not indicate any impurity from contact with menstruants. Since
Num 6 clearly states that women are able to take part in the *nazirite* vow,
we can infer that such prohibitions would be provided if menstruation
were to obstruct the vow of the *nazir.* As one separated, the *niddah* does
not negate the vow of the *nazir* since they occupy a similar structural
space.

---

68. Binns, *Numbers,* 39; Budd, *Numbers,* 72.
69. See Lev 5:7; 12:8; 14:21–30; 15:14–15, 29–30.
70. Sturdy, *Numbers,* 51.

The Logic of "Taboo"
Explaining Lev 15

Those modern and contemporary biblical commentaries that reject the notion of menstruation as a moral infraction (still too few) have attempted to understand Lev 15 in a new light. An explanation that has been gaining currency in feminist circles is the view that the menstrual regulations are not "prohibitive" but "celebratory" of women and their physiology. Wishing to free menstruation from negative connotations, these well-meaning critics regard the regulations of Lev 15 as a period of rest and relaxation for the menstruant, who is now free of her household and sexual "duties."[71] Thus the establishment of the menstrual regulations in this account is attributed to women, not to a patriarchal society nor to God.[72] While noble in its attempt, this explanation remains a simplistic inversion of the standard biblical reading of menstruation as state of defilement. Although the notions of "uncleanness" and "contamination" are evident and incontrovertible in the biblical passage, these critics do not engage them or dismiss them as misrepresentations of the "original" meaning. In one sense, the current feminist analyses of menstrual prohibitions are flawed in exactly the same manner as those of early biblical commentators whom they claim to refute. Both demonstrate the incapacity of contemporary analytical structures to align conceptual polar opposites (holy-impure) in the same framework. Menstrual taboos, as are the proscriptions surrounding the nazir, are defined not by moral distinctions (negative-positive; pure-impure), but by the logic of separation inherent in both. Laws of morality and the logic of separation are not commensurate but competing systemic patterns of organization.

By far the most common modern explanation for the Levitical passage is a "primitive" association of menstrual blood with "demonic powers," which thus equates the menstrual prohibitions with a kind of "superstition." Milgrom summarizes this position when he states that "it was the worldwide fear of menstrual blood as the repository of demonic forces that is most likely the cause of the isolation of the menstruant."[73] Julia Kristeva observes Levine's assertion that menstrual blood functions

---

71. Roland Kenneth Harrison, *Leviticus: An Introduction and Commentary* (Downers Grove, Ill.: InterVarsity Press, 1980), 164; Gerstenberger, *Leviticus*, 204. This view is also common in a number of feminist analyses.

72. See Judith S. Antonelli, *In the Image of God: A Feminist Commentary on the Torah* (London: Jason Aronson, 19950, 276–87.

73. Milgrom, *Leviticus 1–16*, 766.

as a diabolical force that potentially threatens the divine order.[74] Menstruation, as a negative agency, can thus be posited against the positive forces of God.

The "universal demonic" nature of menstrual blood in Milgrom's argument can be easily refuted by the most recent research on the treatment of menstruation in numerous traditions and throughout history, which demonstrates that attitudes and conceptions vary as widely as the number of traditions studied (save for the ambiguous semantics of menstrual blood and the menstruant that appears to be consonant in widely varying traditions).[75] These accounts further indicate that the notion of a "universal menstrual taboo" is more likely attributable to the cultural biases and shortcomings of nineteenth- and early twentieth-century anthropology and sociology than to a unified portrayal of the menstruant as "demonic." To notice this shortcoming in Milgrom's argument does not refute the argument itself. What Milgrom and Levine suggest is that two distinct orders operate within the Levitical passage: that of a divine agent and that which threatens it. This system of analysis has systematically divided the pentateuchal passages into two ("moral" or even "religious") categories: the holy and the unholy.

We can attribute this dichotomous reading of biblical regulations to W. Robertson Smith's *Lectures on the Religion of the Semites*. Smith neatly separates into positive and negative categories the rules and regulations laid out in the Pentateuch. On one side, he collects together all rules of "holiness" that relate to the worship of the Lord. On the other, he places rules of "uncleanness," which seem to him "irrational" and "illogical."[76] To the former he attributes the "true" essence of the Semitic religion (i.e., sacrality), while to the latter he ascribes earlier, primitive notions of diabolic forces that had not yet been outgrown by the Semites. Smith further encapsulates all religious traditions along these lines:

> The irrationality of the laws of uncleanness, from the standpoint of spiritual religion or even of the higher heathenism, is so manifest, that they must necessarily be looked on as having survived from an earlier form of faith and of society. . . . As regards holy things in the proper sense of the word, i.e., such as are directly connected with the worship and service of the gods . . . [they] have a good and reasonable sense

---

74. Julia Kristeva, *Pouvoirs de l'horreur: Essai sur l'abjection* (Paris: Du Seuil, 1980), 109.
75. See Buckley and Gottlieb, *Blood Magic*.
76. W. Robertson Smith, *Lectures on the Religion of the Semites: The Fundamental Institutions* (New York: Ktav, 1969), 449.

even in the higher forms of religion, and find their sufficient explanation in the habits and institutions of advanced societies.[77]

According to Smith, the laws of uncleanness in the Hebrew Bible,
which includes "menstrual blood *in particular*," "can only be [the]
remains of a primitive superstition" and have "nothing to do with respect
for the gods," while the laws of "holiness" constitute the evolved sacred
code of the Semites.[78] Smith thus offers the first modern analysis of the
Hebrew Bible that would definitively (one could say "necessarily") separate the nazir (holy "man") from the realm of the *niddah* (unholy woman)
in all subsequent interpretations.

However, Smith himself remained troubled that the "boundary
between the two [superstition and holiness] is often vague, and that the
former as well as the latter present the most startling agreement in point
of detail." Further he states that "holiness is contagious, just as uncleanness is, and that things [that] are to be retained for ordinary use must be
kept out of the way of the sacred infection."[79] Still he insists on the distinction between the two, without providing evidence further than that
one category (the holy) makes "sense" while the other does not. Smith's
model implicitly places the *nazir* in polar opposition to the *niddah*; his
system indicates that they could not exist within the same order (or
logic).

It is precisely this binary classification that Steiner finds problematic
with Smith's account. He indicates that there is no evidence for a bipolar
arrangement of regulations in the Hebrew Bible and that Smith provides
none other than his contemporary nineteenth-century projections of
"logicality." Steiner further argues that Smith (and others) incorrectly
"claim that interdiction is older and more primitive than . . . sacredness,
and conclude . . . that the latter derived from the former through the
alchemy of evolution" while not substantiating this claim with historical
facts.[80] No evidence supports Smith's assertion that the practice of the
niddah is more primitive or historically precedes the practice of the *nazir*.
Also nothing makes one more "logical" than the other.

Like Steiner, Frazer understood that the relegation of the sacred and
impure to binary distinctions was not wholly accurate. Frazer comes
closest to my understanding of the *niddah-nazir* relation by noting the

---

77. Ibid., 449.
78. Ibid., 448, emphasis added.
79. Ibid., 450.
80. Steiner, *Taboo,* 130.

correspondence between the *nazir* and the concept of taboo: "Amongst the Jews—(1) the vow of the Nazarite (Num. VI. 1–21) presents the closest resemblance to the Polynesian taboo. The meaning of the word Nazarite is 'one separated or consecrated,' and this, as we saw (p. 15) is precisely the meaning of taboo."[81] Frazer also went so far as to remark upon the similarity between regulations applied to holy "men" in general and to menstruating women in various "primitive" societies (though he did not comment upon this same parallel in the Hebrew Bible between the *niddah* and the *nazir*):

> The same explanation applies to the observance of the same rules by divine kings and priests; for the uncleanness, as it is called, of girls at puberty [menstruation] and the sanctity of holy men do not . . . differ materially from each other, being only different manifestations of the same mysterious energy which, like energy in general, is in itself neither good nor bad, but becomes beneficent or maleficent according to its application.[82]

The uniting feature is not their holiness or pollution, Frazer contends, but their level of "danger" (to themselves and those around them) and the need to keep this danger "separate" from the community. Thus Freud can say, "This power is attached to all special individuals, such as kings, priests . . . and to all *exceptional states*, such as the physical states of menstruation."[83] Again, as Frazer indicates:

> We are tempted to divide them [taboos] into two general classes, taboos of privilege and taboos of disability. Thus the taboo of chiefs, priests, and temples might be described as a privilege, while the taboo imposed on the sick and on persons who had come in contact with the dead might be regarded as a disability . . . the former rendered persons and things sacred or holy, while the latter rendered them unclean or accursed. But that no such distinction ought to be drawn is clear from the fact that the rules to be observed in the one case and in the other were identical.[84]

---

81. Frazer, "Taboo," 17. He does not go on to make a comparison between *niddah* and the *nazir*. These observations are my own.
82. James Frazer, *The Golden Bough* (ed. Th. H. Gaster; Criterion Books 490; New York: Criterion Books, 1959), 587; see also no. 489, 584–87, and nos. 165–71, 166–75.
83. Freud, *Totem and Taboo*, 75.
84. Frazer, "Taboo," 17.

While both Steiner and Frazer acknowledge and provide evidence that "the sacred" and "the unclean" do not belong to separate orders but partake of the same logic (as also discussed in detail in the introduction), they refrain from unraveling the implications of this observation.

Concluding Remarks

Douglas takes us beyond Steiner and Frazer by establishing that the shared logic underlying both sacredness and pollution (as expressed in the semantic container "taboo") elucidates our very conceptual systems. In *Purity and Danger* she argues that there can be no clear understanding of that which is expelled from a cultural system through interdictions and restrictions (impure) unless one first examines the organizational patterns of a given society. Conversely, one cannot comprehend a cultural order without acknowledging that this order is first configured through that which is jettisoned from organization itself. In other words, nothing is naturally or "innately" to be negated from the social order; rather, this classification is culturally relative and dependent upon the way in which a society perceives and organizes the world. That which is negated is constituted as such since it defies the classificatory system of a society; the "unclean" or "impure" is that which exceeds the categories inscribed in the social order. The impure is that which is "out of place," that which denies the boundaries and borders established by the cultural realm. The impure is the result of a conceptual construction; thus, *we* "create" that which is impure.

Similarly, the cultural order itself cannot be instituted without first establishing that which is "impure" (unclean, dirty). The establishment of order itself is contingent upon our creation of the impure. That which is expelled from the system constitutes the system itself. For Douglas, this is the great paradox of human conceptual categories and is also what infuses the "impure" with great power. On the one hand, the "impure" has destructive potential. That which is marginalized from the social order has the power to destroy the arbitrary nature of the classificatory structures themselves, hence the feelings of foreboding and anxiety that accompany the transgression of prohibitions that protect these boundaries; the unclean substance both threatens and demonstrates the tenuous foundations of order. It endangers the boundaries that could only be constituted through its expulsion. On the other hand, the impure also has a tremendous creative capacity. "Dirt" has the power to create since it is the very stuff from which order was created in the first place. A normative order is not possible without marking something outside of that order, yet all order is first made from that which is unordered (hence "other"). Douglas uncovers the complex contingent relationship between that which is of the cultural order and that which is expelled from it, with the latter founding, grounding, yet perpetually threatening the former.

What underlies Douglas's reading of the relation between purity and impurity is that the cultural order of sanctity is established through the rejection of the "impure," and yet this same "impurity" underwrites the sacred, not as polar opposites but as part of the same order. This is not to say the obvious—that the impure and the holy are *the same thing*—but rather that they are constructed from the same (and not oppositional) logic and thereby are inscribed within one another. This functions to disclose the semantic ambiguity at work in the word "taboo." How can something be both "sanctified/consecrated," and "uncanny/forbidden/unclean," as the term, throughout its history and to the present day, affirms? Quite simply, as Douglas demonstrates, a substance that defies the classifications of normative order necessarily is "consecrated" in its ambiguity ("uncleanness"), since at its heart it is dedicated to the very principle of order/classification—that is, by exceeding it.

Hence the parallels between the *niddah* and the *nazir* are not incidental but arise out of the same reasoning that undergirds our very conceptual systems. It is more than a simple misreading (based on current cultural biases) to understand Lev 15 as a system of prohibitions that establish punitive measures on an immoral (sinful) or defective (unnormative) process. A careful reading of Lev 15, rather, makes clear that the underlying motive for the prohibitions, as are the prohibitions for Num 6, is to emphasize the need for separation between the sanctified order and these phenomena in order to establish and perpetuate the sanctified order itself.

In this chapter, I have tried to refute those readings of Lev 15 that consign the menstrual prohibitions listed therein to punitive measures against women for the transgressions of Eve. As my examination has demonstrated, several centuries of Christian and Jewish biblical commentary have implicitly framed their reading of the Levitical passage with an understanding of menstruation as a sinful, unethical, or immoral infraction of the "natural" order; that is, the menstrual prohibitions are viewed as a divine ordinance against the abnormal and deviant nature of women themselves. A careful reexamination of Lev 15, however, demonstrates that the passage in question does not situate menstruation within the realm of immorality or abnormality, and neither are the regulations detailed as punishments. Rather, the ritual observations of Lev 15 focus, as do the ritual observances for the *nazir* or holy person, on the practice of separation as a means for maintaining the sanctified order. Thus, the menstrual prohibitions are not concerned with punishment, as most commentaries surmise, but with the maintenance of the divine order itself. The *niddah*, while excluded from this order, is also the means through which this order is founded and thus is inscribed at the very heart of the sacred. That which is marginalized from the sacred constitutes the heart of the divine order—its shadowy lining; this dynamic accounts for the semantic ambivalence that characterizes all things "taboo" (i.e., as consecrated, uncanny, and polluted).

This study raises more questions than it answers. It is not likely incidental that the body of a woman "engenders" the sacred since in a patriarchal-defined society her body necessarily exceeds the boundaries and borders established by the (male) normative order. Too, it is not likely incidental that menstrual blood becomes a primary focus of so many sacred texts (in every major religious tradition) since menstrual blood, more clearly than any other taboo substance or state, is situated at an ambiguous semantic crossroads, expressing both the blood of life itself, the most sacred of substances, with the shedding of blood, in a "sacrificial" gesture. Not surprisingly, this shifting valence between life and death requires ritual attention. Menstruation, in all of its ambiguity, becomes the epitome of the ambivalent resonance (purity-impurity; sacred-unclean) imprinted in the linguistic container "taboo."

2

Menstrual Impurity and Innovation in Leviticus 15

Deborah Ellens

Leviticus 15, organized according to a taxonomy of genital flows, instructs the reader in the science of the mediation of impurities resulting from those flows. Setting standards and prescribing remedies, it "maps" the way from impurity to purity for the menstruant, the man discharging semen, the lover, and the individual who suffers from genital disease. The author's treatment of the woman in this "instructional guide" is intriguing, for it consists of two sets of contrasting, if not opposing, conceptual associations. One set of associations is implicitly assumed by the author. It is part of his worldview and the culture from which he comes. The second set of associations, on the other hand, is the result of a conscious decision made in the course of his taxonomic analysis. In the context of the first set of associations, the second set of associations amounts to nothing short of a deliberate innovation.[1]

The First Set of Conceptual Associations

A single word occurring in Lév 15:33 is the strongest representation in the chapter of the first set of conceptual associations. That word is *dawah* and signifies the woman from whom blood issues, during either an anomalous or a nonanomalous flow. This is its only occurrence in the chapter. Nevertheless, it is an especially powerful indicator of a gender

---

This essay is a revision of a portion of my dissertation, "A Comparison of the Conceptualization of Women in the Sex Laws of Leviticus and in the Sex Laws of Deuteronomy" (Ph.D. diss., Claremont Graduate University, 1998).

1. This second set of associations might be considered, to use the terminology set out by Rolf P. Knierim, a "transformation" from the first set of associations. It is most certainly a reconceptualization of the problem of the impurity of genital flows. See his *Text and Concept in Leviticus 1:1–9: A Case in Exegetical Method* (Tübingen: Mohr, 1992), n. 1.

polarization of the genital-discharge problem since it appears in the summary of the chapter.

The meaning of *dawah* is charged. It connects menstruation with illness. While the illness connection with menstruation is inconclusive in Lev 15 by itself,[2] both the cognate associations of *dawah* and its metaphorical and literal applications in other parts of the Hebrew corpus strongly suggest that connection.[3] Lamentations 5:17 states that, on account of our sins, "our heart has become *dawah*; our eyes have grown dim," a parallelism aligning *dawah* with a bodily weakness, loss of eyesight (RSV). Psalm 41:4 establishes a parallel between *dawa* and illness (*holi*), as does Isa 1:5. *Madawe* is used twice in Deuteronomy to refer to the diseases of Egypt (7:15; 28:60). Other occurrences of the root, lacking such clear-cut signification of illness, nevertheless refer to something negative in association with things like desolation (Lam 1:13), defilement and scattering (Isa 30:22), tasteless food (Job 6:7), a desperate future on account of past sins (Jer 8:18), and despair on account of past rebellion (Lam 1:22). At most, the illness associations and, at least, the negative associations of *dawah* are difficult to avoid.

Furthermore, whereas *dawah*, with its charged meaning, signifies the woman, a neutral word (*hazzabh*) meaning "the one flowing" signifies the man. Thus, *dawah* polarizes the problem of genital discharge. It brands the woman's normal genital discharge as necessarily unhealthy and perhaps, therefore, dangerous, as compared to the man's genital discharge.[4] At least two other features of the text support this polarization. The first is the point of view of the chapter.[5] The second is the language depicting the sex act.

---

2. The illness connection is inconclusive in both Lev 12 and Lev 15. Milgrom suggests that the expression using *dawah* in Lev 15:33 is an "idiom" "borrowed" from Lev 12:2 where the impurity of birth is mediated (*Leviticus 1–16*, 947).
3. Deut 7:15; 28:60; Isa 1:5; 30:22; Jer. 8:18; Ps 41:4; Job 6:7; Lam 1:13, 22; 5:17. See Milgrom, *Leviticus 1–16*, 745–46.
4. My reading of Lev 15:32–33 is as follows:
    This is the law of the one flowing: (32a)
      that is—
        the one from whom an emission of semen goes out so that he becomes
          unclean by it, (32b)
        and the dawah during her menstrual impurity, (v. 33aα)
        and the one flowing with his [or her] flow: (33aβ)
          for a male, (33aγ1)
          and for a female, (33aγ2)
        and for a man who lies with an unclean woman. (33b)
5. I use "point of view" to refer to the author's relationship to the audience that he addresses in the text. For a more thorough explanation of my use of this term, see Ellens, "Conceptualization of Women," 2–3.

The point of view of Lev 15 is apparent in the first verse of the chapter. *Yhwh* instructs Moses and Aaron to address the "sons of Israel," a male collective. Thus, the first two groups of laws begin respectively with "If any man . . ." (v. 2b) and "If a man . . ." (v. 16). However, the next two groups of laws begin with "If a woman . . ." (vv. 19 and 25). These latter two groups of laws pertain to the uncleanness derived from the bodily emissions of women. Explicit reference to the man in these two groups of laws occurs only in v. 24.

The content of these latter two groups of laws in vv. 19–30 and the absence in the chapter as a whole of a male character who relays the information of vv. 19–30 to the woman suggest that "sons of Israel" addresses a male collective in the midst of which stand women who are also listening to Moses and Aaron. Nevertheless, the men are the ones named, the ones to whom the narrator/author speaks explicitly. Women are implicit addressees only, marginalized to the background.[6]

The language depicting the sex act in Lev 15 offers an even more pronounced circumscription than point of view. It consistently places the man in the dominant position as subject. The woman is always object. In vv. 18 and 24 she is the direct object. In v. 33b she is the object of a preposition. In the sex act she is never initiator, never actor. She is only the receptor of the man's actions.[7] Furthermore, the description of the sex act is designated by a function that occurs with respect to the male body, "emission of semen," and not with respect to anything specific to the female body.[8]

Thus, the use of *dawah*, the point of view, and the language depicting the sex act support a set of conceptual associations that picture woman as marginalized, objectified, and necessarily periodically unhealthy or

---

6. Another feature in the text, perhaps related to point of view, supports this marginalization. Although the author inserts no explicit male character between Moses and the woman in order to mediate her instruction, mediation is apparent in the ritual for presentation of offerings. Men bring their offering to *Yhwh* at the door of the tent of meeting. Women bring it to the priest at the door of the tent of meeting. Men and women bring the same offering, both go to the door of the tent of meeting, and the priest propitiates "before *Yhwh*" on behalf of both of them. Nevertheless, the man approaches *Yhwh*, and the woman does not.

7. In fact, the woman's grammatical placement in the chapter as a whole is consonant with her placement in the verses in which the sex act is depicted (vv. 18, 24, and 33b). In the chapter as a whole, she is subject only with respect to inanimate objects and with respect to remediation of her own impurity.

8. In v. 18 this subject/object polarity is mitigated somewhat in the Hebrew text by the emphasis of the proleptic referent "a woman." The proleptic referent cannot, however, counterbalance the effects of the language depicting the sex act.

dangerous. Her agency is curtailed, and her normal menstrual flow is associated with illness. The same features in Lev 15 suggest a concept of man as central, subject, and never unhealthy on account of his normal seminal emissions. This might be all that need be said about the conceptualization of woman in Lev 15 except for one other feature of the text that is so powerful in its support of a contrasting set of conceptual associations that it must be regarded as an innovation in the context of the first set of associations. That feature is the structure of the text, the larger organizing principles operative in the text.

The structure pictures the woman equal to the man. She is as responsible as he is for maintaining the laws of purity with respect to genital discharge. Her status as agent in this respect is equivalent to his. Mediation of impurity caused by her genital discharge is equivalent in its significance to mediation of impurity caused by his genital discharge. Her jeopardy in the presence of impurity by genital discharge is equivalent to his. Seminal emission is a normal condition lacking association with illness. So also, according to the structure, is menstruation. In this way, her flow is typologically equivalent to his.[9] A look at the structure of Lev 15 confirms these assertions: [10]

---

9. Several scholars have recently posited that the menstrual taboo exemplified in the Bible is ultimately responsible for the subsequent isolation of women and their exclusion from religious practice in Judaism. Cf. Leonie J. Archer, "Bound by Blood: Circumcision and Menstrual Taboo in Post-Exilic Judaism," in *After Eve: Women, Theology, and the Christian Traditions* (ed. J. M. Soskice; London: Marshall Pickering, 1990), 45; "The Role of Jewish Women in the Religion, Ritual, and Cult of Graeco-Roman Palestine," in *Images of Women in Antiquity* (ed. A. Cameron and A. Kuhrt; Detroit: Wayne State University Press, 1983), 275; Shaye J. D. Cohen, "Menstruants and the Sacred in Judaism and Christianity," in *Women's History and Ancient History* (ed. S. B. Pomeroy; Chapel Hill: University of North Carolina Press, 1991), 273–99; Howard Eilberg-Schwartz, *The Savage in Judaism* (Bloomington: Indiana University Press, 1990), 171, 177–94; Lawrence A. Hoffman, *Covenant of Blood: Circumcision and Gender in Rabbinic Judaism* (Studies in the History of Judaism; Chicago: University of Chicago Press, 1996), 146–54, 171–72, 190–91; Judith Romney Wegner, *Chattel or Person: The Status of Women in the Mishnah* (New York: Oxford University Press, 1988), 162–66. This development, as well as the broader implications of fluid symbolism as described by people like Eilberg-Schwartz (*Savage in Judaism*, 147) and Hoffman (*Covenant of Blood*, 181–82), does not define the conceptuality of Lev 15. Leviticus 15, in fact, does not exhibit this isolation and exclusion. Rather it demonstrates considerable equity in the treatment of men and women with respect to the purity issues, as even scholars like Eilberg-Schwartz and Hoffman recognize.

10. The organizing signals used for this structure follow the precedent set by the Forms of the Old Testament Literature commentary series, which is edited by Knierim and Tucker.

a) emission of semen	32b
b) menstruation	33aα
2) *anomalous cases*	33aβ–33b
a) basic statement	33aβ
b) specification: naming the source	33aγ–33b
(1) by gender	33aγ
(a) male	33aγ₁
(b) female	33aγ₂
(2) by special case: intercourse	33b

Conditionals introduce each of the four major sections of the "main body of the speech," which details legal instruction for four basic scenarios.[11] The four conditionals are the following:

1. A man: if his flow is flowing from his flesh (vv. 2b–15)
2. A man: if an emission of semen goes out from him (vv. 16–18)
3. A woman: if she is flowing; blood is her flow from her flesh (vv. 19–24)
4. A woman: if a flow of her blood is flowing (vv. 25–30)

Each conditional identifies the topic of its respective section. Each of the four sections treats the mediation of the impurity of a particular genital flow. The "summary," underscoring the same concern, begins with an adjuration to separate the Israelites from their uncleanness. It then recapitulates the above scenarios and adds a new one.

The four major sections fall into two larger divisions, which constitute the main body of the *Yhwh* speech.[12] These larger divisions divide according to gender. The first division concerns male genital discharge, and the second, female genital discharge. These two divisions each consist of an anomalous and a nonanomalous subunit, the "four major sections." Each anomalous section divides into two units: one concerning purity, the other impurity. The anomalous/nonanomalous subunits of the divisions are reversed from one another, producing a chiasm of the form

---

11. The four sections are referenced in the outline above in section II.B. ("Main Body of Speech") as 1.a.1); 1.a.2); 1.b.1); and 1.b.2).
12. See the italicized type in the above structure analysis.

ABBA. The two larger divisions are, thus, schematic reverse images. These structural correspondences between the male and female sections are the most apparent indication that the concerns and categories addressed for both sections—and therefore for both genders—are the same.[13] Structural symmetry constitutes gender symmetry.

Furthermore, the chapter contains three "sex verses" (vv. 18, 24, 33b).[14] Two of these verses, 18 and 24, conclude the men's and women's nonanomalous sections respectively. They are both conditionals. The third verse, 33b, concludes the summary of the entire chapter. The placement of these verses is significant. It suggests a deliberate attempt to organize with considerable gender equity the problem of genital flow.[15]

The most significant challenge to the above interpretation is the structural solution that Jacob Milgrom and Richard Whitekettle propose for the perceived syntactic and conceptual problems of v. 18.[16] This solution

---

13. The following scholars make similar statements: Eilberg-Schwartz, *Savage in Judaism,* 181; Hoffman, *Covenant of Blood,* 148; Cohen, "Menstruants and the Sacred," 276, 291.

14. Cross-gender contamination is, of course, particularly acute during sexual intercourse. The three sex verses are, therefore, especially revealing for the conceptualization of women in the chapter. Analysis of their content and their placement in the chapter is key to understanding the author's organizing principles, his primary concern, and by extension, therefore, his second set of conceptual associations regarding women. A close reading of the three sex verses is helpful for understanding the structure of the chapter as a whole. In all three verses the content and syntax as well as the microstructure of the verse demonstrate that, with respect to purity issues related to sexual intercourse, the author treats the man and woman equally. For a close reading and detailed discussion supporting these assertions, see Ellens, "Conceptualization of Women," 59–67; "Leviticus 15: Contrasting Conceptual Associations regarding Women," in *Reading the Hebrew Bible for a New Millennium* (ed. W. Kim et al.; Harrisburg: Trinity Press International, 2000), 2:131–36, 138–41

15. For arguments supporting this statement with respect to v. 33b, see Ellens, "Conceptualization of Women," 62–67; "Leviticus 15," 133–36. A failure to understand the nature and placement of v. 33b gives rise to statements like the following from Wegner, *Chattel or Person,* 165:

> Scripture applies the rules of contamination to "*anyone, male or female, who has a discharge,* and also the man who lies with a cultically unclean woman" (Lev 15:33, emphasis added). A woman who has intercourse with a cultically unclean man is not mentioned because the only pollution that matters is contamination of male by female. Mishnah, following Scripture, worries about woman's cultic purity only as it affects their male contacts. The woman is a polluting *object,* the man is a *person.*

In fact, this statement reveals a misunderstanding of the nature of v. 33b, its place in the structure, and the structure as a whole.

16. An additional significant challenge is the suggestion that the blood of menstruation pollutes because of the *gender* of the blood. This conclusion is drawn by Eilberg-Schwartz and other scholars who compare the blood of menstruation with the blood

posits an introverted structure for Lev 15.[17] In this structure v. 18 is the center of a chiasm of the form ABCBA, belonging to neither the male nor female sections. While this structure demonstrates gender symmetry with respect to organization of the general subject of genital flow,[18] gender symmetry with respect to sexual intercourse and, therefore, purity/impurity is at least potentially compromised. If this ABCBA chiasm is accurate, the male, nonanomalous section lacks a verse corresponding to v. 24 in the female section. The nonanomalous sections no longer mirror one another. The man is protected within the woman's nonanomalous section, but she is no longer protected within his section. Her protection is absent from the thematic concern of his normal flow. Intercourse in the context of his nonanomalous flow becomes a special case, with protection of both the man and the woman at the center of the chapter. The result is a slight bias for protection of the man in the context of genital flow and intercourse.

One might assert that v. 18, even as an independent unit, provides the balance. But v. 18 as an independent unit carries a different message than v. 18 as an integral part of vv. 16–18.[19] Verse 18 as an independent unit

---

of circumcision. They see circumcision and menstruation functioning as a polarity that ultimately has deleterious effects for women. Eilberg-Schwartz writes: "The difference between semen and menstrual blood might also be part of the symbolic domination of women. Although the loss of both fluids represents a missed opportunity for procreation, menstrual blood is more contaminating simply because of its gender" (*Savage in Judaism,* 186). Cf. also Hoffman, *Covenant of Blood,* 136–54; Leonie J. Archer, *Her Price Is beyond Rubies* (Sheffield: Sheffield Academic Press, 1990), 37; "Bound by Blood," 38–61. Significantly, both Eilberg-Schwartz and Hoffman themselves observe that the gender polarity, in fact, does not govern the fluid symbolism of Lev 15 (Eilberg-Schwartz, *Savage in Judaism,* 181; Hoffman, *Covenant of Blood,* 147–48). In the interest of simplicity and space constraints, I have left aside the full discussion concerning this subject, concentrating only upon the structural statement in the context of point of view, language depicting the sex act, and the use of *dawah*. For more detailed arguments as to why the gender of the blood is not a factor in Lev 15, see Ellens, "Leviticus 15," 142–50

17. For the use of the term "introverted structure," see Isaac M. Kikawada, "The Shape of Genesis 11:1–9," in *Rhetorical Criticism* (ed. J. J. Jackson and M. Kessler; Pittsburgh: Pickwick, 1974), 23.

18. Hoffman, *Covenant of Blood,* 147–50. Hoffman uses this structure to demonstrate that the taxonomy of genital impurity is based not on gender, but on the normal/abnormal polarity.

19. In fact, Whitekettle argues for the distinctive import of v. 18 as an independent center, which leads him finally to conclude that the primary concern of the chapter is "ideal physiological functioning of the reproductive system." See his "Leviticus 15.18 Reconsidered: Chiasm, Spatial Structure, and the Body," *JSOT* 49 (1991): 31–45. At

biases the chapter protecting the man against the impurity of the woman.

However, a reading that places v. 18 at the center of an ABCBA chiasm is problematic. One of the major syntactic puzzles of v. 18 is the initial placement of the word for "woman" (*iššah*).[20] That placement emphasizes the woman where one would expect emphasis to remain with the man.[21] Milgrom's solution to this puzzle suggests that v. 18 is an inverted hinge, an independent connecting unit between two texts. A preceding word (woman) within the hinge echoes the text following, and a following word (man) echoes the text preceding (see fig. 1).[22] This inverted hinge is the foundation of Milgrom's introverted structure, which is the ABCBA chiasm.[23] Milgrom cites H. Van Dyke Parunak as the source of his "hinge" model.[24] Of the several literary connectors Parunak describes, the inverted hinge is certainly the closest approximation to what we have in the text.[25] However, Parunak does not claim, nor can we assume, that he has described every type of linking structure that is either possible or that ever occurs. If v. 18 functions as a hinge, it follows a pattern that Parunak has not addressed.

---

the very least, the chiastic structure ABCBA fails to account for the deliberate placement of a sex verse at the conclusion of each nonanomalous section. Such placement underscores the fact that no special danger comes from intercourse because of the *gender* of the flow.

20. English translations generally do not reveal this problem.

21. The masoretic division immediately preceding v. 18 indicates that the Masoretes also puzzled over this placement. See Milgrom, *Leviticus 1–16*, 930. Milgrom observes that the woman is the subject of the verse. I have argued elsewhere that the woman is not the subject (Ellens, "Conceptualization of Women," 60). However, the question remains concerning the pronounced emphasis given to her within the man's section.

22. This feature is not apparent in English translation. See Milgrom, *Leviticus 1–16*, 905, 930–31; H. Van Dyke Parunak, "Transitional Techniques in the Bible," *JBL* 102, no. 4 (1983): 541. This pattern is not to be confused with the chiastic pattern of which v. 18 is the center (ABCBA) and which Milgrom and Whitekettle suggest is the structure of the chapter. The pattern A/ba/B is formed by elements *within* v. 18, in relationship to preceding and following sections. By contrast, the presumed pattern ABCBA is formed by v. 18 as *a whole* with what precedes and follows as *a whole*. The first pattern has to do with grammatical elements. The second pattern has to do with content.

23. Milgrom, *Leviticus 1–16*, 905.

24. Ibid., 930–31.

25. Parunak, "Transitional Techniques," 541. He writes, "The inverted hinge, on the other hand, offers the pattern A/ba/B and reverses the order of the joining elements from that of the larger blocks of text."

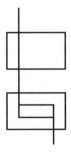

Figure 1 Inverted Hinge

That v. 18 contains reverse echoes of preceding and following text is undeniable. However, as a hinge it is asymmetrically placed, embedded in one side of the structure. One might call it an "inverted hanging hinge": Aba/B (see fig. 2). This understanding reveals two features of the text that Milgrom's structure ignores: (1) the similar subject matter (semen) of v. 18 and vv. 16–17 and (2) the symmetry created by the conclusion of each nonanomalous section with a verse on intercourse. While v. 18 may indeed function as an inverted hinge, such a function does not necessarily designate it as a separate case, as Milgrom suggests. Nor does it entail chiasm of the form ABCBA as the fundamental structure of the chapter. The fact that Milgrom offers two structures even while calling the introverted structure a "more meaningful division" supports this observation.[26]

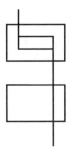

Figure 2 Inverted Hanging Hinge

---

26. Milgrom, *Leviticus 1–16,* 904–5.

These are the syntactic problems of v. 18. The conceptual difficulty of v. 18 has to do with the following question: Why does emission of semen or sexual intercourse, which is necessary to obtain something so highly valued as progeny, cause impurity?[27] Whitekettle's study ultimately attempts to answer this question. As part of his argument, which concludes that the functional ambiguity of the penis is the source of impurity,[28] he posits the structural and thematic independence of v. 18 and, thus, the chapter's "interlocking pivotal structure."[29] A related conclusion is that the primary concern of Lev 15 is the "ideal physiological functioning of the reproductive system" rather than mediation of impurity caused by genital discharge.[30]

Whitekettle posits the structural independence of v. 18 based on two prior suppositions: (1) 'šr in v. 18 necessarily demarcates a distinct legal unit, and (2) the noncontagious impurity of v. 18 indicates that it is not a subcase and is, therefore, independent of vv. 16–17.[31] These suppositions are erroneous. In the first place, Whitekettle has failed to notice the use of the 'šr construction throughout the chapter. It occurs similarly in other clauses (vv. 4a, 4b, 9, 11, 12a, 20a, and 20b), which Whitekettle himself would not identify as distinct legal units. The difference between them and v. 18 is that they can be read more easily as relatives than v. 18, since the subjects and verbs of their protases and apodoses agree in number. Nevertheless, like v. 18, they can also be read as conditionals with *casus pendens.*[32] The similarity is not accidental. In the second place, Whitekettle's conclusion that v. 18 is the independent center of the chapter because it is not a subcase of vv. 16–17 is also misguided. However, the literary phenomenon on which he bases his conclusion is real. The law on sexual intercourse concluding the men's nonanomalous

---

27. Whitekettle, "Leviticus 15.18 Reconsidered," 31. Gordon J. Wenham, "Why Does Sexual Intercourse Defile (Lev. 15:18)?" *ZAW* 95 (1983): 432. Cf. also Eilberg-Schwartz, *Savage in Judaism,* 186; Milgrom, *Leviticus 1–16,* 933–34.

28. Whitekettle, "Leviticus 15.18 Reconsidered," 43–44.

29. Ibid., 37. This is his name for the introverted structure.

30. Whitekettle, "Leviticus 15.18 Reconsidered," 36–37.

31. The word 'šr can be read as a conditional or a relative in the present context. Whitekettle reads it as a conditional. See "Leviticus 15.18 Reconsidered," 35–36.

32. *Casus pendens* might be understood in English as the naming of a topic followed by a colon and a discussion of the topic. For examples of *casus pendens* that do not use 'šr, see the four conditionals above. Verses 4, 5, 10, 11, 18, 20, 22, 26 might all be read as *casus* using 'šr. Bruce K. Waltke and Michael Patrick O'Conner, *Biblical Hebrew Syntax* (Winona Lake, Ind.: Eisenbrauns, 1990), 77, paragraph 5. See Waltke's example of a relative, very similar to the ones used in Lev 15, under his discussion on the nominative absolute (i.e., *casus pendens*).

section is a separate case, whereas in the women's nonanomalous section, that concluding law is a subcase of the case that begins the section.[33] In fact, this construction, two separate but related cases, in the men's section is unique in the chapter.

Whitekettle, however, suggests more than this. Not only is v. 18 not a subcase, it is also an independent unit. He bases this assumption on the conclusion that whereas the impurity of the other sections is contagion, the impurity of v. 18 is not. He bases this conclusion on three factors: (1) the subject of v. 18, unlike all other instruction in Lev 15, is plural;[34] (2) a phrase analogous to the phrase in v. 24 ("and her monthly flow touches him") is absent from v. 18; and (3) the man is explicitly mentioned in v. 18, even though we know already from vv. 16–17 that he is unclean during intercourse. Since these three factors occur, he concludes that the impurity of v. 18 is not contagion.[35] Therefore, v. 18 is independent of vv. 16–17.

However, the plural subject and explicit mention of the man are present for emphasis: *both* man and woman become impure during the desirable act of intercourse. Verse 24 lacks the same emphasis because vv. 19–23 unambiguously had described the woman's impurity already. Verse 24 emphasizes the fact that the man contracts the same level of impurity as the woman. The lack of the "analogous phrase" in v. 18 is a function of the number of discharges involved. In v. 18 only one discharge is involved. Thus, the reader knows without a doubt that the prescription applies to seminal discharge. In v. 24 two discharges of differing severity are involved: semen and blood. The author wants unambiguously to state that in v. 24 *blood* is the cause of the impurity under discussion. Thus, the phrase "and her menstrual impurity is upon him" occurs in v. 24, whereas no such phrase occurs in v. 18.

In fact, contrary to Whitekettle's contention, v. 18b indicates that contagion is at work. It concludes with the phrase "and *they* shall be unclean until evening." Nothing could be plainer. Even Whitekettle's final answer concerning the source of impurity of v. 18, the functional ambiguity of the penis, must admit contagion because of v. 18b.[36] Thus the men's nonanomalous section is unique, not because contagion is lacking, but because the "physiology" of that section in connection with impurity is open to confusion and misunderstanding.

---

33. See structure above. Whitekettle, "Leviticus 15.18 Reconsidered," 35.
34. Ibid., 35.
35. Ibid., 36.
36. Ibid., 44.

The writer foresaw that if he allowed vv. 16–17 to encompass the situation of v. 18 analogously to the woman's nonanomalous section, or if he framed v. 18 exactly as he framed v. 24, confusion might arise. The "desirability" and "normalcy" of intercourse create the potential for misunderstanding and confusion. Who can believe that sexual intercourse, necessary for the production of progeny, defiles? Not even twentieth-century scholars believe that the author of this ancient text believed it. The fact that they have taken the impurity caused by emission of semen during intercourse to be such a puzzle demonstrates that writer's remarkable foresight.

Thus, the writer includes an explicit stipulation to dispel the potential confusion. He wants it understood that, contrary to what we might consider to be common sense, emission of semen causes impurity in both man and woman under *any* circumstance, even the desirable circumstance necessary for the production of progeny, sexual intercourse. The author mentions *šikhbhath-zara`* ("emission of semen"), a seeming repetition in v. 18, because he wants no confusion to arise over the fact that specifically this genital discharge causes the impurity under discussion.

Thus, genital discharge, not the woman, not the man, not intercourse per se,[37] not the functional ambiguity of the penis, is the source of the impurity of v. 18.[38] The construction of v. 18 is a result of the writer's concern to emphasize the fact that during the "desirable" act of intercourse, which every married couple was expected to perform, both individuals are defiled by impurity. The logic of the impurity of genital discharge rules the chapter, without exception—not even the exception of intercourse. The operative question is not, Why does semen or intercourse defile? It is, rather, Why does genital discharge defile? And this is a question that we must put to the entire chapter, not just to v. 18.

The arguments that support the introverted structure from both Milgrom and Whitekettle cannot be sustained. While awkwardness and idiosyncrasies may characterize v. 18, far simpler solutions than that of the introverted structure explain them. The two-part structure, which demonstrates gender symmetry with respect to purity issues related to genital discharge in general as well as sexual intercourse in particular, is a more accurate rendering. This structure presents the woman's flow as typologically equivalent to the man's. Purity issues connected with her

---

37. Ibid., 33, 36.
38. Milgrom, *Leviticus 1–16*, 44: "It is the discharge that contaminates, not the person. Hence, objects that are underneath him—bed, seat, saddle—but no others are considered impure."

flow are also typologically equivalent.[39] Her status as agent in this respect is, therefore, equivalent to his.

Thus, in Lev 15, two sets of contrasting conceptual associations comprise the author's conceptualization of women. One set—suggested by point of view, language depicting the sex act, and vocabulary signifying the menstruant—picture the woman as marginalized, objectified, and periodically unhealthy on account of her *normal* bodily discharge. Her agency is curtailed. Her discharge is "different." Its danger is different.

The second set of conceptual associations, suggested by the structure, pictures the woman as equal to the man. She, like he, is responsible for maintaining the purity of the community. She, like he, is protected. Her agency is equal to his. Furthermore, her discharge is typologically equivalent to his discharge. The structure of the text, which pairs seminal emission with menstrual flow, vis-à-vis the category of anomalous flow, makes a conceptual statement that diverges from the conceptual effects of point of view, language depicting the sex act, and vocabulary signifying the menstruant. Seminal emission is a normal condition decidedly not associated with illness. So also, according to the structure, is menstruation.[40]

Conclusion

The structure of Lev 15 suggests a conceptualization of women that diverges from the conceptualization suggested by point of view, language depicting the sex act, and the use of *dawah*.

If *dawah*, indeed, associates menstruation with illness, then Lev 15 is, in fact, a reconceptualization or transformation of the very problem of genital flow as it was perhaps commonly understood within the worldview of the author. The nature of these four features—viewpoint, grammar, vocabulary, and structure—determines that the reverse is not true. The author has *selected* viewpoint, grammar, and vocabulary, con-

---

39. For a discussion as to why the blood factor does not disturb this equivalence in Lev 15, see Ellens, "Conceptualization of Women," 76–88.
40. Susan Brooks Thistlethwaite, "You May Enjoy the Spoil of Your Enemies: Rape as a Biblical Metaphor for War," *Semeia* 61 (1993): 63. The structure is the reason that statements such as the following by Thistlethwaite cannot describe Lev 15: "Pollution concepts are essential to understanding women's 'otherness' in the biblical worldviews. . . . The reproductive secretions of women are dirty because this particular cultural system has set off the reproductive capacity of women in a particular way." In Lev 15, to the contrary, her reproductive secretions are dirty because, like the man's secretions, they are genital discharges.

sciously or unconsciously. He has, by contrast, *constructed* the structure—and done so with meticulous deliberation. As a reconceptualization or transformation of the genital-flow problem, the structure amounts to nothing less than an astonishing innovation.[41]

This innovation prompts the question concerning identity: Who is this author that dares to innovate? And why? How does the author come by such meticulously structured knowledge of both male and female discharge? What is the author's stance within the community that motivates or enables the unabashed and confident articulation of this knowledge? Undoubtedly, answers to these questions would fruitfully extend the discussion concerning women and impurity as well as the sociohistorical context of Lev 15.

---

41. Milgrom's comments underscore the point:

> Against this backdrop of Israel's immediate and remote contemporaries and what was probably the dominant practice within Israel itself . . . , the Priestly legislation on the menstruant is all the more remarkable. First and foremost, she is neither banished from the community nor even isolated within her home. The implicit assumption of the pericope on the menstruant is that she lives at home, communicating with her family and performing her household chores. (*Leviticus 1–16*, 952–53)

3

Blood
A Threat to Holiness or toward (Another) Holiness?
Kristin De Troyer

Introduction: The *Pollutio* of the Divine Sacraments

Why are women in some churches and religious communities still excluded from ordination?[1] In the debate on the ordination of women, the argument of "impurity" is sometimes used. For example, the *Apostolic Constitutions* records a prayer in which the bishop says, "Now look upon this your servant who is being ordained as a deaconess, and give her the Holy Spirit, and purify her from any defilement of the flesh and spirit" (8.20). The woman is said to be impure, and in order to be ordained she is to be purified. The defilement must be taken away from her. At first sight this text appears to refer to the actual ordaining of women, albeit as deaconess. However, the *Apostolic Constitutions* also has a restriction, for it says that "a deaconess does not bless, nor perform anything belonging to the office of presbyters or deacons" (8.28).

Anne Jensen has done extensive research on these sorts of statements. She remarks that "from the third century onwards there was an intense debate on whether women could perform ministries that presupposed an ordination of higher clergy."[2] Why was there such a debate? In the *Testament of Our Lord* we read, "During their menstrual period women are to

---

1. We think especially about the Roman Catholic Church and about women's exclusion from the office of priest and Levite in the Bible; cf. Manfred Hauke, *Women in the Priesthood? A Systematic Analysis in the Light of Creation and Redemption* (San Francisco: Ignatius Press, 1988), 212; orig. published *Die Problematik um das Frauenpriestertum vor dem Hintergrund der Schöpfungs- und Erlösungsordnung* (Paderborn, Germany: Bonifatius, 1986).

2. Anne Jensen, *God's Self-Confident Daughters: Early Christianity and the Liberation of Women* (Louisville: Westminster John Knox, 1996), 25; orig. published *Gottes selbstbewusste Töchter: Frauenemanzipation im frühen Christentum* (Freiburg i.B., Germany: Herder, 1992).

stay away from the altar" (1.23.23).³ Do women have to stay away from
the altar because of their menstruation? No, for the text continues: "The
same rule applies to men after the involuntary ejaculation of semen. The
individual is not unclean; it is a matter of showing reverence for the holiness of the altar." However, women were banned from the altar because
their menstruation was regarded as cultic impurity.⁴ According to Jensen
the biblical concepts of impurity and uncleanness were reinterpreted in a
Christian way, giving way to banning women from the altar.⁵ Haye Van
der Meer offers some excellent examples:

> Women in general should not approach the altar . . . for the women
> should be conscious of their own weakness and the weakness of their
> sex, and therefore they must scrupulously guard that they do not touch
> anything consecrated to the service of the church. (Theodolf, bishop of
> Orleans)

> It is also clear that the bishops are especially annoyed over the fact that
> the priests live together with these women and in one breath speak
> about the *pollutio* of the divine sacraments because they are distributed
> by women. (Three French bishops: Lucinius of Tours, Melanius of
> Rennes, and Eustochius of Angiers)

Van der Meer concudes that "by the prohibition of the council of
Laodicea women seem to be banished from the area of official cult. . . .
And many synods have repeated that."⁶ The words "the *pollutio* of the
divine sacraments because they are distributed by women" struck me
with its stark clarity. The bishops really considered women as polluting
and therefore unclean. That women too thought that they were unclean
can be gleaned from the *Didascalia Apostolorum*, whose author criticizes
women who believe that they are filled with unclean spirits during their
seven days and can only be purified by bathing. He opposes this view

---

3. I quote from Jensen, *God's Self-Confident Daughters*, 70.
4. Ibid.
5. Jensen refers to the work of Wendebourg on the Christian reinterpretation of the
cultic laws. Ibid.; cf. Dorothea Wendebourg, "Die alttestamentlichen Reinheitsgesetze
in der frühen Kirche," *ZKG* 95 (1984): 149–70.
6. Haye Van der Meer, *Women Priests in the Catholic Church? A Theological-Historical
Investigation* (Philadelphia: Temple University Press, 1973), 96, 98–99; orig. published
Priestertum der Frau (Freiburg: Herder, 1969). Van der Meer offers a very balanced
view on the teaching and the practice of the church. His conclusion is that there was
from the beginning (of the church) a strong opposition against the ordination of
women and that, however, there was far less unanimity than is assumed.

and says that there is no uncleanness involved in menstruation (26, 1.14–15, 24–25, 27–28). This comment, however, reveals that there were indeed women who believed that menstruation rendered them unclean.[7]

The uncleanness of women was associated with their weakness and with their inferiority.[8] Since Augustine, women were regarded as only good enough for procreation.[9] Thomas Aquinas enforced this statement by saying that women were only created for procreation.[10] Only virgins (along with widows and martyrs) have a better place in their theology: "Blessed are the bodies of virgins, for they shall be well-pleasing to God and shall not lose the reward of their purity" (*Acts Paul* 6).[11] According to Manfred Hauke neither the inferiority of women nor the lack of education accounts for the ban on ordination of women throughout the period of the church fathers.[12] Rosemary Radford Ruether, however, points to the uncleanness of women, as the *Apostolic Constitutions* did, and we will continue along that line of thought. Radford Ruether adds, "Until recent times it was believed to be more pious if women did not come to communion when they were menstruating."[13] "Come to communion" implies "come to the altar." Women have to stay away from the altar.

I propose that "female blood" is one of the major reasons why "women are not being ordained."[14] I will analyze a passage from the biblical book of Leviticus that is immediately concerned with blood. I will not only look at the Hebrew text of Leviticus but also trace the translations of this book to see how the concepts have changed when translated into another language. The section on the different translations of the Hebrew text might seem complex. However, only when looking at all

---

7. See Roll, this volume.

8. Cf. Jensen, *God's Self-Confident Daughters,* pt. 1, chs. 3–4. See Ellens, this volume, for a counterproposal.

9. "The natural good of marriage is thus sexual intercourse between male and female for the sake of procreation": Augustine, *Nupt.* 1.4.5.

10. Thomas Aquinas, *Summa Theologica* I, q. 92, art.1.

11. In my opinion, it is no accident that John Paul II refers to virgins (along with holy martyrs and mothers of families—replacing the widows? *my question*) in his apostolic letter "*Ordinatio Sacerdotalis,*" May 26, 1994.

12. See Hauke, *Women in the Priesthood?* 434. Hauke states that the "will of Christ" is the crucial reference point. In his conclusion he writes, "Non-ordination of women is grounded, however, in a high estimation of the specifically female nature" (ibid., 471). Børresen offers another interpretation of the texts of Augustine and Aquinas; cf. Kari Elisabeth Børresen, *Subordination and Equivalence: The Nature and Role of Women in Augustine and Thomas Aquinas* (repr., Kampen, Netherlands: Kok Pharos, 1993).

13. Rosemary Radford Ruether, "Male Clericalism and the Dread of Women," in *Women and Orders* (ed. R. J. Heyer; New York: Paulist, 1974), 6.

14. See Dresen, this volume.

possible translations can one see how a concept changed and how it affected the history of interpretation.

The Hebrew Text
The Difference between Boys and Girls . . .

Leviticus 12 is a strange text. When a woman gives birth to a male child, she is unclean for seven days. When, however, she gives birth to a female child, she is unclean for two weeks. Worse, after the initial period of uncleanness she remains unclean thirty-three days in the case of a little boy and sixty-six days in the case of a girl. How does one explain these differences in time?

> The Lord spoke to Moses, saying: (2) Speak to the Israelite people thus: When a woman at childbirth bears a male, she shall be unclean seven days; she shall be unclean as at the time of her menstrual infirmity.—(3) On the eighth day the flesh of his foreskin shall be circumcised.—(4) She shall remain in a state of blood purification for thirty-three days: she shall not touch any consecrated thing, nor enter the sanctuary until her period of purification is completed. (5) If she bears a female, she shall be unclean two weeks as during her menstruation, and she shall remain in a state of blood purification for sixty-six days. (6) On the completion of her period of purification, for either son or daughter, she shall bring to the priest, at the entrance of the Tent of Meeting, a lamb in its first year for a burnt offering, and a pigeon or a turtledove for a sin offering. (7) He shall offer it before the Lord and make expiation on her behalf; she shall then be clean from her flow of blood.[15]

The text compares the initial periods of uncleanness with a woman's uncleanness at the time of her menstrual infirmity.[16] The author observes, of course, the difference between the "normal" seven days of uncleanness and the doubled amount in the second case. Therefore he wrote in the first comparison between the initial period of uncleanness and a woman's uncleanness because of her menstruation "as at the time of" and in the second comparison "as during the time of"—the translation reflecting the difference in the Hebrew prepositions. The author explains the second period of uncleanness in v. 4: "she shall not touch any

---

15. The translation is from Levine, *Leviticus,* 72–75.
16. Ibid., 73.

consecrated thing, nor enter the sanctuary until her period of purification is completed." After her expanded time of uncleanness, the woman has to bring a lamb and a pigeon or turtledove to the priest for a burnt offering and a sin offering. The reader might wonder about the double offering or be puzzled about the insertion of the circumcision. I will not comment on these issues,[17] but I will focus on the strange concept of blood purification: "She shall remain in a state of blood purification (*bideme tahara*)" (vv. 4–5). This concept might be the key for explaining the differences in the length of periods of uncleanness in case of a boy or a girl.

On Purifying and Cleansing

The central words of Lev 12 follow:

unclean ("she shall be unclean": vv. 2, 5)
purification/cleansing ("blood [of] purification": vv. 4, 5; "period of purification": v. 6; "she shall then be clean": v. 7—verbal form)
days (days of purification: vv. 4, 6; seven days: v. 2; days of menstruation: v. 2; day of circumcision: v. 3; thirty-three days: v. 4; sixty-six days: v. 5)
blood (blood [of] purification: vv. 4, 5; flow of blood: v. 7)

Although the contrast between "unclean" and "clean," and/or "unclean" and "cleansing" is more obvious in English, I prefer to use the expression "blood of purification" over "blood of cleansing." This stylistic choice has its advantages and disadvantages. Although stemming from the same verbal root (*tahar*), the "days of her purification" are lexicographically differentiated from the "blood of her purification," the former derived from *tohar*, the latter from *tahara*. We will distinguish these two categories by using the expression "the days of purification" and "blood of purification." The disadvantage of using "purification" or

---

17. Nobuyoshi Kiuchi, *The Purification Offering in the Priestly Literature: Its Meaning and Function* (JSOTSup 56; Sheffield: Sheffield Academic Press, 1987), 119–30. Kiuchi refers to Bernd Janowski, *Sühne als Heilsgesehen* (Neukirchen-Vluyn: Neukirchener Verlag, 1982), 227. For the circumcision, see Levine, *Leviticus*, 73. Let me also quote Gerstenberger: "The primary focus of this text is the circumcision of the eight-day-old boy—a topic utterly out of place in this passage (v. 3)—and the woman's requisite purificatory offerings (vv. 6–8). Of course, the duration of the impurity is also of significance (vv. 2, 4 f.). All this betrays the male-priestly or male-congregational perspective" (Gerstenberger, *Leviticus*, 148).

"purifying," as in "purifying blood," is that the opposition of unclean versus clean is no longer clear. But as the opposition is also not clear in Hebrew, and as the verbal root *tahar* can be translated by "to be clean" and—in another verbal form—"to cleanse" and "to purify," we will use the concepts "days of purification" and "purifying blood/blood of purification." However, since "purifying" blood could be interpreted as a verbal form (a participle)—which it is not—my preferred rendering is "blood of purification."

Purifying the Blood or the Blood That Purifies?

The expression "blood of purification" only occurs in Lev 12. In Lev 16:19 the blood is cleansed and hallowed from the "uncleannesses" of the people of Israel. This blood is the blood of the bull and the blood of the goat mentioned in Lev 16:18. The ritual is described in vv. 11–19. By slaughtering the bull and the goat, bringing the blood inside the sanctuary inside the curtain, and sprinkling the blood with his finger seven times upon and before the mercy seat, Aaron makes atonement for the sanctuary. He does so because of the uncleannesses of the people of Israel and because of their transgressions, all their sins. Blood is a very important element in the reconciliation process between humankind and God. But if blood is part of reconciliation, why then must the women stay away from the sanctuary in Lev 12? "She shall not touch any consecrated thing, nor enter the sanctuary." What is the relation between the blood that purifies and the purifying blood? Which blood should be carried into the sanctuary, and which blood should be kept out of the sanctuary? And why is that so?

Blood unlike Menstrual Blood

Walter Kornfeld explains the difference in length of days after a woman's giving birth to a male child or a female child as resulting from the fact that female children are seen as women who are more inclined to uncleanness due to their menstruation and their capacity of giving birth.[18] The woman had to be kept separate from God because her health was seriously endangered after giving birth. The woman suffering from lack of blood, due to her losing blood, and therefore suffering from a lack of her life source, had to be kept away from God, the source of life.[19] Kornfeld

---

18. Walter Kornfeld, *Levitikus* (NEchtB; Würzburg, Germany: Echter, 1983), 49.
19. Ibid., 48.

compares the blood emission after giving birth with the emission of menstrual blood and the emission of male semen.[20] According to Jewish law the emission of menstrual blood and the emission of male semen render the person unclean.[21] That person should indeed be kept far away from the sancta. But the text makes a distinction between the initial period of uncleanness that has to be compared with menstrual uncleanness and the extended period of uncleanness. It is not clear whether Kornfeld makes a distinction between these two periods. He simply speaks about the loss of blood. Mary Douglas too holds an inadequate view about this particular issue. She assumes that all bodily emissions were considered polluting.[22] Tikva Frymer-Kensky critically alters this statement: "The only bodily emissions that pollute are those involved with sex."[23] The initial period of uncleanness may be compared with the period of uncleanness of menstrual blood. The extended period of uncleanness, however, should not be compared to the uncleanness of the menstrual blood. Baruch Levine states, "Discharges of blood that occur after the initial period of impurity are unlike menstrual blood and are not regarded as being impure."[24] The list of things that render one unclean does not include human blood as such.[25]

Jacob Milgrom cannot explain the difference in length of days after giving birth to a female or male child. He refers to other religions that also "duplicate the disparity in the purification periods following the

---

20. Ibid.

21. Cf. also Herbert Danby, *The Mishnah* (Oxford: Oxford University Press, 1933).

22. Tikva Frymer-Kensky, "Pollution, Purification, and Purgation in Biblical Israel," in *The Word of the Lord Shall Go Forth: Essays in Honor of David Noel Freedman in Celebration of His Sixtieth Birthday* (ed. C. L. Meyers and M. O'Connor; Winona Lake, Ind.: Eisenbrauns, 1983), 401.

23. Ibid.

24. Levine, *Leviticus*, 73. To my surprise Gerstenberger mixes up the two periods of time as well. The goal of the second period of uncleanness is that the woman remains "out of reach of male sexual desire." But marital intercourse is only forbidden in the first menstruation-like period. Gerstenberger continues:

> Only on the second pass is the uniqueness of birth taken into consideration: The waiting period between the end of "defilement," that is, bleeding, and complete reestablishment of "purity" is longer than after regular monthly bleeding (v. 4; cf. Lev 15:28). This period of reprieve for the parturient derives on the one hand from the male fear [of] "infecting" himself through sexual intercourse with an "impure" woman. . . . On the other hand, this postpartum reprieve also represents protection for the woman. Her organism can recuperate and focus on the infant; she can also concentrate psychologically on her new role as a mother.

25. Frymer-Kensky, "Pollution, Purification, and Purgation," 402. See also Danby, *Mishnah*, esp. app. 4: "The Rules of Uncleanness as Summarized by Eliyahu, the Gaon of Wilna."

birth of a boy and that of a girl, with the period following a girl's birth nearly always being longer."[26] Levine agrees that the status of a new mother during the extended period of time was a complex one. He refers to the rabbinic sages who compared the status of the new mother to that of a person impure for a day: "Until sunset, rites of purification could not be undertaken; and yet such a person was on his way to final purification, and only time separated him from it."[27] This explanation however does not explain the difference in length of the periods after a boy or a girl is born.

Holy Books Render the Hands Unclean

Most of the commentators agree that "by declaring the new mother impure, the community sought to protect and shelter her."[28] Kornfeld explicitly refers to the new mother's health being in danger after giving birth.[29] Commenting on the widespread belief that menstrual blood was seen as the repository of demonic forces, Milgrom, with the consciousness of a Jew, offers a statement about Israel's nonbelief in demons: "The demons disappeared, but not the demonic—it was continued in man. . . . But also in physical impurity too, the demonic continued to reside. . . . The loss of vaginal blood and semen . . . meant the diminution of life and, if unchecked, destruction and death. And it was a process unalterably opposed by Israel's God, the source of life."[30] Levine, in his comment as well as in his excursus, correctly distinguishes between the initial period and the extended period of uncleanness.[31] He too refers to the belief in destructive, demonic, or antilife forces. Levine even accepts that similar anxieties were current among the Israelites as well.[32] He then comments on the extended period of uncleanness: "Going beyond the protection of mother and child, the legislation also aimed at safeguarding the purity of the sanctuary and the surrounding community from defilement. To this end, the new mother was barred from the sanctuary and from contact with sacred things."[33] Levine explains this "out of the

---

26. Milgrom, *Leviticus 1–16*, 750.
27. Levine, *Leviticus*, 74.
28. Ibid., 249; Mayer I. Gruber, "Women in the Cult according to the Priestly Code," in *Judaic Perspectives on Ancient Israel* (ed. J. Neusner, B. A. Levine, and E. S. Frerichs; Philadelphia: Fortress, 1987), 47–48 n. 40.
29. Kornfeld, *Levitikus*, 48; Gerstenberger, *Leviticus*, 149.
30. Milgrom, *Leviticus 1–16*, 766–67.
31. Levine, *Leviticus*, 73–74, 249.
32. Ibid.
33. Ibid.

apprehension that the antilife forces, which prey upon the newborn and the mother in her state of vulnerability, would be carried with her into the sanctuary."[34] Here, Levine uses the explanation for the fear of menstrual blood as explanation for banning the new mother from the sanctuary. I wonder whether this is correct.

It is better to compare the mother's uncleanness with the uncleanness of the holy books, as Mayer Gruber does and as underwritten by Milgrom.[35] The new mother and the holy books are protected. At first sight this explanation recalls the demonic elements, which might attack the new mother or her child. The extended period is seen in the context of demonic forces again. At the same time this explanation offers a positive element: it is not only because of the possible demonic forces that a woman should be banned from the sanctuary but also because there is something holy about new mothers, which they have in common with holy books. Both are to be protected, the books and the new mothers. And both rendered unclean!

Holy Books, Holy Mothers, Holy God

But if the new mother resembles the holy books, then why is she banned from the sanctuary? "She shall not touch any consecrated thing, nor enter the sanctuary until her period of purification is completed." On the one hand, the new mother is protected—as are the holy books—and on the other hand, the sanctuary is protected from the mother. This contradiction can also be read in Frymer-Kensky's article: "The condition of impurity becomes actively dangerous *to the individual* only when it comes into contact with the sacred. Since the impure can defile the sacred, the *sacred* must be protected."[36] Is it the individual or the sacred that must be protected?

Maybe the expression "purifying blood" should be seen in a more positive way. As Milgrom says: "The plural *damim* most often connotes 'blood guilt' . . . or '(illicit) bloodshed.' . . . But it can also refer simply to blood without a pejorative connotation (e.g., Lev 20:18; Ezek 16:6). Blood never defiles, except if spilled illicitly (Num 35:33–34); otherwise it only purifies and sanctifies (e.g., Lev 16:19)."[37] Unlike Erhard Gerstenberger, who defines the purificatory process as "a gradual elimination of even the

---

34. Ibid.
35. Milgrom, *Leviticus 1–16,* 751; Gruber, "Women in the Cult," 43n. 13.
36. Frymer-Kensky, "Pollution, Purification, and Purgation," 403, emphasis added.
37. Milgrom, *Leviticus 1–16,* 749.

last remnants of blood,"[38] I would, like Milgrom, emphasize the positive connotations of blood. I am thinking especially about the blood in Exod 12: "The blood shall be a sign for you on the houses where you live: when I see the blood, I will pass over you, and no plague shall destroy you when I strike the land of Egypt." The blood protects the Israelites from the divine destruction. The blood is also part of the ritual that takes away the sins and uncleanness of the Israelites. Gen 9:4 identifies blood as the source of life.

Frymer-Kensky adds an important element to the discussion.[39] She first discusses the case of the leper (Lev 13–14). The leper remains impure for seven days after the leprosy is pronounced healed (Lev 13:45–46). She clarifies this strange law in this manner: "In Israelite cosmology it was considered vitally important to maintain the structure of the universe by keeping all distinctions (boundaries) firm.[40] The boundaries between life and death are crucial and no individual who has had contact with the world of death can be part of life."[41] She then offers the following explanation for the additional semi-impure period: "It may be that, like the person who has touched death, the person who has experienced birth has been at the boundaries of life/nonlife and therefore cannot directly reenter the community. She therefore must undergo a long period of transition before she can re-approach the sacred."[42] Milgrom quotes Rachel Adler on this point: "Begetting and birth are the nexus points at which life and death are coupled. . . . The nexus points are those in which there appears to be departure or a transfer of vital force"[43] We will return to the last element later on.

Giving birth is indeed associated with an excessive flow of blood. Ezekiel 16:6–9 reflects the common association between giving birth and blood. Moreover the passage tells us something about giving birth, blood, and the relation with God, who happens to pass by: "I passed by you, and saw you flailing about in your blood. As you lay in your blood, I said to you, 'Live! and grow up like a plant of the field'" (NRSV). After some time God passes by another time: "I passed by you again and looked on you; you were at the age for love. . . . I pledged myself to you

---

38. Gerstenberger, *Leviticus,* 149.

39. Frymer-Kensky, "Pollution, Purification, and Purgation," 400.

40. With reference to Douglas, *Purity and Danger,* 53.

41. Frymer-Kensky, "Pollution, Purification, and Purgation," 400.

42. Ibid., 401.

43. Milgrom, *Leviticus 1–16,* 768. Cf. Rachel Adler, "Tumah and Taharah: Ends and Beginnings," in *The Jewish Woman: New Perspectives* (ed. E. Koltun; New York: Schocken, 1976).

and entered into a covenant with you, says the Lord GOD, and you became mine. Then I bathed you with water and washed off the blood from you, and anointed you with oil" (NRSV). I will not comment here on the image of God's washing off the blood. But it is clear to me that God acts twice here: once after the person's birth and once again when blood is present in the young girl's life, that is, when the young girl is ready to make love.

The first part of this passage establishes a link between life, blood, and God. It is God who gives life to the child, for it is God who says to the person in blood, "Live." I propose that the extended time period of uncleanness is the result of the relation between giving birth and the activity of God. In Ezekiel God is said to be the one who gives life. I would say that the woman gives life. And exactly this aspect seems to be crucial. On a theological level, God is seen as the source of life. Putting a woman at the border of life and death is giving a theological qualification to a woman. To give a theological qualification to a woman is in itself, of course, not such a big problem. But, to give the qualification "giver of life" to a human person, and not to God, could be seen as an offense to God.[44] As Adler said, it is the woman who transfers vital force. And that is exactly the problem.

Moreover, I consider the Ezekiel passage as a key text for the second problem: the different lengths of time after giving birth to a boy and a girl. I will now use the second part of the passage (Ezek 16:8–9): "I passed by you again and looked on you; you were at the age for love. . . . I pledged myself to you and entered into a covenant with you, says the Lord GOD, and you became mine." That God makes a covenant with the young girl at the time that she is ready for loving and giving birth strikes me. The male god binds this girl to him: "you became mine." God not only gives life to a newborn but also makes sure that the fertility of the grown-up "newborn" belongs to him, and no one else.[45] Because of the life-giving capacity of a female grown-up "newborn," the mother is to be kept far away from the sanctuary. The mother who just gave birth to a baby girl is more dangerous to God than the one who gave birth to a baby boy. The mother not only gave life: she gave life to a child who one day may give life. As Gerstenberger puts it, "The female newborn represented a double antipower to the (male?) element of the sacred."[46] The

---

44. We admit that Eve, however, is called "the mother of life."
45. Cf. also the meaning of the names in 1 Sam 1:2–2:5; Gen 4:1; 21:6; and Jer 18:13. God is really the "spiritual" father of the children, and Israel is "his" (?) virgin.
46. Gerstenberger, *Leviticus*, 153.

"punishment" for giving life is to be kept away from the *sancta* for an extended time period. The additional "punishment" for giving life to a baby girl is that the long period of transition before the new mother can reapproach the sacred is doubled—I will return to the word "punishment" later.[47] I fully agree with Levine's statement, "It may have reflected apprehension and anticipation regarding the infant daughter's potential fertility, the expectation that she herself would someday become a new mother."[48] I prefer "It reflects."

Towards Another Holiness

Let me now come to my final point. The new mother is to be kept away from the *sancta*. From a Jewish perspective the sacred has to be protected, and maybe even the new mother has to be protected. I wonder however from what the sacred must be protected? Is it from defilement? Or is it from something or somebody? On the one hand, Levine points to the practices of ancient Near Eastern polytheism: "The regulations governing a new mother may also represent a strong response to the emphasis on fertility in ancient Near Eastern polytheism."[49] Levine continues to say that there is, of course, no such thing in Israelite religion. By keeping the young mother out of the temple, the Israelites opposed the pagan association between the worship of God and the event of birth. According to Jewish rules, God is not "subject to the natural processes of procreation."[50] On the other hand, Gerstenberger thinks that "v. 4 alludes to a certain participation of women in the post exilic cult, though such participation is very difficult to describe concretely."[51] Whether this passage refers to ancient Near Eastern practices or to postexilic common practice, it is clear that Lev 12 tries "to ban women out of the zone of holiness."[52]

The honor of coming up with the pivotal point in this discussion however should go to Gruber. In his outstanding article "Women in the

---

47. I am aware that some people will say that the permission to stay away from the sanctuary can be regarded as a positive law for women, for it can be a release for them not to go to the sanctuary and act according to the law.
48. Levine, *Leviticus*, 250.
49. Ibid.
50. Ibid. That the Israelites opposed the pagan association between the worship of God and the event of childbirth might also have been the reason why the sanctuary is said to be "dangerous to people." God might become jealous when pagan gods come into his realm.
51. Gerstenberger, *Leviticus*, 149. Gerstenberger uses adequate language: "the woman *penetrates* all the way to the 'entrance of the tent of meeting'" (emphasis added).
52. Ibid., 150.

Cult according to the Priestly Code," he clearly demonstrates that women were participating in preexilic and postexilic liturgies.[53] He kindly remarks, "It is equally clear, however, that P has many more positive possibilities to suggest to us about the place of women in biblical thought than we could possibly learn from the repetition of the standard cliché that P with its laws of purity led to the virtual exclusion of women from the cult."[54]

I interpret the restrictive rules about the new mother as follows. First, the rules acknowledge the mother's capacity of giving life. Second, the extended period of blood purification proves that the mother is seen as being on the border between life and not-life. The mother—like God— is giving life. Third, in doubling the time periods in case of a baby girl, the author of these restrictive rules seems to be pointing toward rituals from other pagan religions. Fourth, these rituals are to be seen as referring to gods that were competitors to the God of Israel. Fifth, the new-mother regulations recall what went "wrong" in the "other" religions, or what is to be avoided in Jewish religion. Although the regulations can be read as some kind of protective rules for new mothers, I believe them to be "punishments" for the women's inherent capacity to give life. The new mother is a reminder of pagan religions and is "punished" for it. If one reads these rules as protecting the new mother, then again, they should be read as protection against a God who does not tolerate other gods.

Tracing the Ancient Translations
Unclean Blood in LXX Lev 12

The Greek text of Leviticus translates the Hebrew text and, as usual, also interprets the Hebrew text: "After having given birth to a baby boy, the woman is unclean for seven days. She shall be unclean according to the days of the separation of her menstruation. For thirty-three days, she shall sit in her unclean blood. She shall not touch anything Holy and she shall not enter the sanctuary until the days of her purification are fulfilled" (Lev 12:2–4).[55] For a baby girl, the times are doubled. Then follows the description of the offerings and the expiation.

---

53. We acknowledge that women's functioning in liturgy could be compared to the Levites' functioning.

54. Gruber, "Women in the Cult," 40.

55. Paraphrasing Lancelot Charles Lee Brenton's English translation, *The Septuagint Version of the Old Testament and Apocrypha* (London: Bagster, 1851; repr., Grand Rapids: Zondervan, 1978), 141.

I notice two divergences from the Hebrew. First, the text states that the woman has to sit in her unclean blood (v. 4). When I first read the Greek text, I thought I had misread it. However, the text does read "unclean blood," which has replaced the Hebrew "blood of purification." Second, "the time of her menstruation" is described using the Greek word for "separation." John Wevers translates this passage as "the days of isolation for her menstrual period."[56] Wevers then compares the Greek translation with the Hebrew text, saying: "The Hebrew term 'nidah' is usually rendered by a Hellenistic euphemism, meaning a 'sitting apart,' but it is also translated as 'isolation.' The word *dawah*, related to *niddah*, means 'sick, unwell,' hence 'infirmity.'" He, then, states that "the translator disregarded this word (= *dawah*, *kdt*) in favor of a descriptive (or doublet) rendering of nidah." Wevers continues, saying, "Thus for him (*sic*, *kdt!*) the norm for the period of her uncleanness means the period of her being isolated for a menstrual period, which is a sensible interpretation."[57] In simple words, the translator rendered the first word twice and skipped the following word. Next, Wevers comments on the additional period of "sitting apart," namely, the period of thirty-three or sixty-six days of sitting (apart) in her unclean blood. Wevers does not really address the change to unclean blood; however, he remarks that in some textual traditions "unclean" has changed to "clean."[58] According to Wevers, this change "can only be either based on a complete misunderstanding of what is intended or is a thoughtless mistake."[59] Although I usually agree with Wevers—one of the grandfathers of LXX research—this time I do not buy his rationale.

Lev 12 in Some Ancient Witnesses

The Syriac text translates the Hebrew text in a very simple way. The initial period of uncleanness is compared to the (woman's) days of menstruation. The Syriac text has even simplified the Hebrew expression by using only one word for "menstruation." Next, the woman sits in "her blood of purification" for thirty-three or sixty-six days.[60] The Vulgate has "the days of separation of menstruation" and "the blood of purification."

---

56. John W. Wevers, *Notes on the Greek Text of Leviticus* (Septuagint and Cognate Studies 44; Altanta: Scholars Press, 1997), 165.
57. Ibid., 165–66.
58. Ibid., 167.
59. Ibid.
60. D. J. Lane et al., *Leviticus-Numbers-Deuteronomy-Joshua* (Old Testament in Syriac according to the Peshitta Version, 1.2. II/1b; Leiden: Brill, 1991), 24–25.

The Vetus Latina reads in v. 2 that the woman is unclean during the seven days of segregation for her purification. Then, the text continues, stating that the woman has to sit for thirty-three (or sixty-six) days "in sanguine suo mundo" (vv. 4, 5), which can be interpreted as a reference to "clean" blood. During those days she was forbidden to touch anything holy or to enter into the sanctuary (v. 4). Only when the days of purification (*dies purgationis ejus*) were completed, could she fulfill her obligation at the sanctuary (vv. 6 ff.).[61]

Targum Onqelos also has "the blood of purification"; however, it renders v. 2 by "the isolation period for her menstrual defilement."[62] The text speaks about an isolation period. *Targum Neofiti 1*, too, has kept "the blood of purification." However, it renders v. 2 as "the days of the removal of her menstrual flow."[63] *Targum Pseudo-Jonathan* has an interesting reading.[64] It clearly makes a distinction between the first and second periods. In the first seven/fourteen days, the woman "shall be unclean as at the time of the isolation for her (menstrual) uncleanness."[65] The Targum then continues that the woman shall be "released" on the eighth or fifteenth day.[66] Then, "for thirty-three (or sixty-six, *kdt*) consecutive days, her blood shall be clean." The two time periods are distinguished from one another. Verse 4 (concerning the thirty-three days) adds, "but she shall not touch any holy things, nor enter the sanctuary until the days of her purification are completed." This sentence creates a tension. Although it is said that the blood is clean, the woman has to refrain from entering the sanctuary or touching any holy things "until her days of purification are completed." Aquila, one of the early Jewish revisers of the Old Greek text, does not use the word "unclean" in Leviticus.[67] However, he does have "cleansing/purification."

It seems that the Hebrew expression "the days of separation of menstruation" can be translated in two different ways. First, it can be

---

61. Petrus Sabatier, *Bibliorum Sacrorum Latinae versions antiqua seu vetus italica et caeterae quaecunque in Codicibus Mss. & antiquorum libris reperiri potuerunt* (Reims, France: apud Reginaldus Florentain, 1743; repr., Turnhout, Belgium: Brepols, 1987).
62. B. Grossfeld, *The Targum Onkelos to Leviticus and the Targum Onkelos to Numbers* (ArBib 8; Edinburgh: T&T Clark, 1987), 22–23.
63. Martin McNamara and Robert Hayward, *Targum Neofiti 1: Leviticus* (ArBib 3; Edinburgh: T&T Clark, 1994), 48.
64. Michael Maher, *Targum Pseudo-Jonathan: Leviticus* (ArBib 3; Edinburgh: T&T Clark, 1994), 152–53.
65. Verse 5 reads, "fourteen consecutive days, as at her isolation," and thus, *Targum Pseudo-Jonathan* does not mention the menstrual uncleanness.
66. I suppose that this implies that the woman was kept in isolation.
67. Joseph Reider, *An Index to Aquila* (VTSup 12; Leiden: Brill, 1966).

translated as "the days of secretion of menstruation," that is, simply the flowing out of the body of the menstruation, which is how the Hebrew was understood in the Peshitta and in *Targum Neofiti 1*. Secondly, it can be translated as "the days of isolation of menstruation," which is how *Targum Onqelos* and *Targum Pseudo-Jonathan* have interpreted the Hebrew text. I also read the Vetus Latina in this way. In my opinion, there is a difference between the "secretion" and "isolation." In this case, however, both words could be seen as two sides of the same coin. Next, all witnesses have "blood of purification"; *Targum Pseudo-Jonathan* speaks of "clean blood," as does the Vetus Latina in a certain sense.

Rereading the LXX of Lev 12

The LXX translated the Hebrew words for "at the time of her menstruation" by "in the days of isolation for her menstrual period." The word "isolation," however, can be translated in different ways, namely, "separation," "secretion of sap," "abstraction," and "seclusion." Both "secretion" and "seclusion" can function as translations of *niddah*, for it means both menstruation and separation. The Greek expression can indeed be translated in two ways: "the secretion of her menstruation" or "the isolation of her menstruation." In combination with the word "the days," the translations run as follows: "the days of the secretion of her menstruation" or "the days of the isolation of her menstruation." In the former case, only the menstruation act is meant; in the latter, separation from the community.[68] Consequently, we can say that the translator rendered both the first word (*niddah*) and the second word (*dawah*) of the Hebrew expression. The first is translated with "separation" and the second with "of her menstruation."

So far, we have discussed the translation of v. 2. However, we have not yet touched upon the most visible change of the LXX of Lev 12, namely, the switch from "blood of purification" into "unclean blood." I propose that the translation of the above-mentioned Hebrew expression, combining *niddah* and *dawah* into "the isolation for her menstrual period," is also responsible for the translation of "blood of purification" as "unclean blood" and thus for the switch from "blood of purification" into "unclean blood." My reasoning follows:

---

68. Note that we can use the word "separation" in two different ways. We can use "separation" to indicate one's exclusion from a community, thus, being outside of the community. Moreover, we can use the word "separation" for someone who is separated from the community but still "included" within the community. In this case, the person is "secluded."

1. The term *niddah* and its translation "isolation" imply uncleanness. Leviticus 18:19 is very clear on this point. Menstruation is called "menstrual uncleanness." The Greek translation is "the woman in the separation of her uncleanness." The idea of unclean menstruation is also present in Lev 15, which discusses some bodily discharges. Women are unclean during the seven days of their menstruation. Literally, the text says that the woman is in her impurity and that anyone who touches her shall be unclean (v. 19). The rules are repeated at the end of the chapter. "This is the ritual for those who have a discharge: for him who has an emission of semen, becoming unclean thereby, for her who is in the infirmity of her period, for anyone, male or female, who has a discharge, and for the man who lies with a woman who is unclean" (v. 32 NRSV). In v. 33, the woman is referred to as follows: "for her who is in the infirmity of her period." Verse 33 is freely translated in the Septuagint, and the translator uses the synonym "menses." As said earlier, the latter word is also a rendering of the Hebrew *dawah*. In Lev 15, the word *dawah* has many translations: "the one who sits apart" and "the one who loses blood." The menstruating woman is evidently "unclean" in both the Hebrew and the Greek text.[69]

2. Uncleanness implies separation from the community. Leviticus 13:46 says that the leper shall live alone. His dwelling shall be outside the camp. The Greek text characterizes the leper as "unclean." Again, in Lev 15:31 the command is given to keep the people of Israel separated from the unclean people: "You shall keep the people of Israel separate from their uncleanness, so that they do not die in their uncleanness by defiling my tabernacle" (NRSV). The Greek text twice uses the word ἀκαθαρσία (uncleanness). The unclean person shall live outside the camp. Moreover, the Greek word used in the translation of the Hebrew text also means "separation." Next, Lev 12 is one of the chapters of Leviticus dealing with uncleanness and its consequences for the Israelite community. Chapter 11 deals with clean and unclean food. Touching or eating unclean food results in a state of uncleanness for a set period, in this case until evening. Chapter 13 deals with lepers—all sorts of lepers—and its set period of uncleanness and separation, namely, seven days. Chapter 14 continues with the ritual of purification of lepers and their houses. Chapter 15 describes all sorts of bodily discharges and quotes the appropriate periods of uncleanness, be it until the evening or seven days. The context, the choice of the Greek word, and the clear

---

69. See Ellens, this volume.

identification of the menstruating woman set the tone for the interpretation of the verses of ch. 12.

3. The woman who sits in her unclean blood for thirty-three or sixty-
six days is not allowed to touch anything holy nor to go into the sanctuary. These stipulations reinforce the idea that the woman is in a state of
uncleanness, for in different passages the warning is given to the sons of
Israel not to touch anything holy, except when they are clean or holy.
LXX Exod 29:37 says, "Every one that touches the altar shall be hallowed." Similar commands are given in LXX Exod 30:29; LXX Lev
6:27; LXX Lev 22:4, 6; LXX Num 3:38; LXX Hag 2:13; and LXX Ezek
42:14. LXX Num 4:15 is a very good parallel to LXX Lev 12:4: "The
sons of Caath shall not touch the holy things, lest they die." At least for
the Greek reader, it was clear that the woman, who was told not to touch
anything holy, was an unclean woman. The woman had to be separated
from the holy things. The woman had to remain in a state of separation.

4. Although the menstruating woman is considered unclean (1.), and
the immediate context (2.), as well as the wording regarding holy things
(3.), point to separation, the text of Lev 12:4–5 does not say that. The
second period of days, be it thirty-three days or sixty-six days, is not—I
repeat not—compared with the days of menstruation. The extra days of
cleansing are not compared to the days of menstruation. The text only
says that "the woman shall sit in her blood of purification" and that "she
shall not touch anything holy, nor enter into the sanctuary." This reading
is also found in the Syriac text, the Vulgate, and the three Targumim.

After the preceding analysis, I have come to the following conclusion.
The comparison of the initial seven or fourteen days of uncleanness with
the days and the uncleanness of menstruation; the use of the term
χωρισμός; the context of chapter 12; and, finally, the commands given
to the woman not to touch anything holy, nor to enter into the sanctuary,
have led to the idea that the woman was unclean and separated from the
community in the second and extended period of time after childbirth.
The translator, most probably, has interpreted the woman's "state of
separation" as a "state of uncleanness." Hence, "blood of purification"
became "unclean blood."

The Separation of Women after Childbirth in Some Texts of Qumran

Let me, briefly, indicate what happens with women after childbirth
according to some documents of Qumran. Unclean people are separated
from the community. *The Rule of the Congregation* "prohibits anyone who

is stricken with any of the human uncleanness from entering the council of the community in the end of days" (1QSa 2.3–4).[70] According to the *War Scroll*, they are not allowed to go into battle (1QM 7.4–5).[71] This rule also applies to persons who had seminal emissions (1QM 7.5–6).[72] Yigael Yadin remarks that the formulation concerning men who had seminal emissions "is less severe than that regarding women and children who are excluded from the camp."[73] In the *Temple Scroll*, it is obvious that women who have their menstruation should, like lepers and other unclean people, refrain from coming into the city: "And in every city you shall allot places for those afflicted with leprosy or with plague or with scab, who may not enter your cities and defile them, and also for those who have a discharge and for women during their menstrual uncleanness, so that they may not defile in their midst."[74] The author of the *Temple Scroll* mentions women during their menstruation. However, he adds, after "women during their menstrual uncleanness," the following words: "and after giving birth." After having given birth, women are excluded from the community.

From being in a state of blood purification, parturients have become unclean, as in the days of her menstruation. Literally, the "days of the secretion of her menstruation" have become "days of the isolation." The texts of Qumran, as well as the LXX of Leviticus, offer an interpretation of the Hebrew text of Lev 12. The Septuagint, however, opened the way for identifying "blood of purification" with "unclean blood" and hence "uncleanness."

Conclusion

I conclude that the concept of blood-purification and the doubling of the purification periods in the case of a baby girl are traces of a perceived threat from other religions and other gods.

Let me now return to my initial question, "Why are women in some churches and religious communities still excluded from ordination?" and to my initial intuitive answer: "That 'female blood' is one of the major reasons why 'women are not to being ordained.'" The argument that

---

70. Cf. Lawrence H. Schiffman, *The Eschatological Community of the Dead Sea Scrolls* (SBLMS 38; Atlanta: Scholars Press, 1989), 38–39.
71. Cf. ibid., 39.
72. Cf. ibid.
73. Ibid.
74. 11QT[A] vol. XLVIII, l.14–16. See Yigael Yadin, *The Temple Scroll*, vol. 2, (Jerusalem: IES, 1983), 210–11

women are impure because of their menstrual blood is correct. As we
have seen, however, the holy books also render the hands unclean. Moreover, menstrual blood is not the only item on the list of things that render
a person unclean. Male semen—once out of the body—is on the list too.
Drinking wine or ale, wearing an improper dress, improper washing, and
even having a physical blemish disqualifies priests to the status of layper-
sons.[75] Menstrual blood can therefore not function as an argument
against ordination. This conclusion can be reached by analyzing the
Hebrew text. According to Jensen—following Dorothea Wendebourg—
the Christian reinterpretation led to considering menstruation as cultic
impurity. I would like, however, to nuance this view. In the Septuagint
version of Lev 12:4 we read, for the very first time, the notion of "unclean
blood" as a translation for the Hebrew "purifying blood." The Septuagint,
of course, became the Christian Bible, but only in so far that it became
the Christian Bible can we call this reinterpretation "Christian."

The only argument left against ordination of women is the capacity
of fertility that is given with womanhood. Inasmuch as woman is capable
of giving life, she is on the border of life and non-life, and she should
therefore—according to Leviticus—be kept far away from the sacred.
We have shown, however, that this rule presupposes the existence of
pagan fertility religions in which women and most likely women priests
play the main role. Even Hauke refers to this practice and states that the
threat of referring to Canaanite female clergy was the religious reason for
keeping women from the offices of priest and levite. He writes: "Sexuality is not deified. . . . Since the Canaanite female clergy was made up
largely of prostitutes, eliminating female office was an important measure against the fertility religion."[76] Arguing against the ordination of
women on the basis of her fertility proves to be very unfruitful and leads
even to the affirmation of the opposite. Her fertility affirms her fitness
for ordination. Commenting on the context of the *Apostolic Constitutions,* Van der Meer says, "And in the special material of the *Apostolic
Constitutions* the Greek female deities emerge, thus here too, as in the
writings of Epiphanius, the female priesthood is considered bound up
with the veneration of female deities."[77] It seems that female deities are a
threat in "old" and "new" biblical days. And I wonder, what then is left as
a real argument against the ordination of women?

---

75. Milgrom, *Leviticus 1–16,* 753. Cf. Lev 10:9; 21:23; Exod 28:43; 30:20.
76. Hauke, *Women in the Priesthood?* 215.
77. Van der Meer, *Women Priests in the Catholic Church?* 52.

4

Purity and Impurity in Halakic Sources and Qumran Law

Mayer I. Gruber

Exodus 19:15 and Lev 12:1–8 both seem to suggest that women as such are sources of pollution, who threaten the purity of men and sancta. Elsewhere, I have argued that in both its biblical and rabbinic contexts Lev 12:1–8 is not necessarily a misogynic text.[1] Here I shall show that Qumran exegesis both (1) shares the concern of contemporary feminism in responding to the question of possible misogyny and (2) shares with the exegeses I proposed an attempt to find a nonmisogynic rationale for an enigmatic law.

Just as Qumranic exegesis of Lev 12:1–8 appears to face head-on the feminist critique,[2] so with respect to Exod 19:15 do both Qumranic law and rabbinic halakah appear to face head-on the feminist critique. Moreover, both Qumranic law and rabbinic halakah read Exod 19:15 and other texts referring to sexual intercourse in a thoroughly philogynic mode. Let us begin with Exod 19:15 in its larger biblical context, which is Exod 19:10–15:

---

1. Gruber, "Women in the Cult," 43; republished in Mayer I. Gruber, *The Motherhood of God and Other Studies* (University of South Florida Studies in the History of Judaism 57; Atlanta: Scholars, 1992), 56 n. 13; "Breast-Feeding Practices in Biblical Israel and in Old Babylonian Mesopotamia," *JANES* 19 (1987): 68; republished in Gruber, *Motherhood*, 78; cf. Martin North, *Leviticus,* trans. J. E. Andersen, Old Testament Library, (Philadelphia: Westminster, 1965), 97: "The cultic inferiority of the female sex is expressed in giving the female birth a double 'uncleanness' effect"; cf. also Bernard J. Bamberger, "Leviticus," in W. Gunther Plaut, ed., *The Torah: A Modern Commentary* (New York: Union of American Hebrew Congregations, 1981), 86, at Lev 12:15.

2. Probably the classic example of premodern exegesis that demonstrates a response to feminist critique of Hebrew Scripture is the compilation of lists both in late antiquity and in the later Middle Ages of names for women who appear in Hebrew Scripture simply as "daughter of" or "wife of." See Tal Ilan, "Biblical Women's Names in the Apocryphal Traditions," *JSP* (1993): 3–7.

The LORD said to Moses, "Go to the people and sanctify them[3] today and tomorrow. Have them wash their clothes. Have them be ready for the third day, for on the third day the LORD will descend upon Mt. Sinai in the sight of all the people. You shall cordon off the area around the people, saying, "Beware of going up the mountain or touching the border of it. Whoever touches the mountain shall certainly be put to death: no hand shall touch him/her, but he/she shall be either stoned or shot by an arrow; whether human or animal he/she shall not live." When the ram's horn is blown [indicating that the period of quarantine has ended] they may [again] ascend the mountain." Moses descended from the mountain to the people, and he sanctified the people,[4] and they washed their clothes. He said to the people, "Be ready for the third day; [you; i.e., second-person masculine plural] do not go near a woman."[5]

Now it might be assumed on the basis of v. 15, which is commonly assigned to E and which addresses the men, that (1) women were excluded from being present at the giving of the Torah/Decalogue at Mt. Sinai;[6]

---

3. Driver suggests that this "sanctification" would be accomplished by Moses' enjoining the Israelites both (1) to perform ablutions to remove impurity and (2) to abstain from anything that would render them impure; this exegesis of v. 10 is reflected both in the third-person account of the actions undertaken by Moses upon his descent from Mt. Sinai in v. 14 (see next note) and in the direct speech attributed to Moses in v. 14b: "Do not go near a woman." See Samuel R. Driver, *Exodus* (Cambridge Bible; Cambridge: Cambridge University Press, 1911), 172.

4. Here it is stated that Moses carried out the order given in v. 10 in which he was told to "sanctify them"; this had to have included ablutions to remove impurity; the additional requirement—namely, that Moses instruct the Israelites to abstain from activities that would render them impure, such as sexual intercourse—is referred to in v. 15. Qimron contends that 1QSa 1:25–27, where it is stated, "And if there is a meeting of all the congregation for judging, or for the council of the *Yahad*, or for a gathering for war, they shall warn them to abstain from sexual intercourse (literally, "they will sanctify them") for three days," is based upon Exod 19:19 [*sic*; obviously he means v. 10]. Qimron also observes that in both the biblical text and the Qumran document the verb *qiddeš* has the nuance of "warn them to abstain from sexual intercourse" and that "for three days" in the Qumran text is a paraphrase of "today and tomorrow" in Exod 19:10; Qimron's proposed nuance of *qiddeš* seems to have been anticipated by Moses Nahmanides (1194–c.1270 C.E.) in his Pentateuch commentary at Lev 19:2. See Elisha Qimron, "The Biblical Lexicon in the Light of the Dead Sea Scrolls," *DSD* 2 (1995): 319–21.

5. All translations of biblical and other ancient texts in this chapter are the work of Mayer I. Gruber.

6. Drorah O'Donnell Setel, "Exodus," in The Women's Bible Commentary (ed. C. A. Newsom and S. H. Ringe; London: Westminster John Knox, 1992), 33: "The prohibition in Ex. 19:15 can be interpreted as an injunction against sexual intercourse prior to

(2) women qua women are a source of impurity; and (3) heterosexual intercourse defiles men because women as such are a source of pollution.[7] On the other hand, it is not impossible that "do not approach a woman" is E's euphemistic, albeit male-oriented, expression for "engage in sexual intercourse." It would seem that the corresponding female-oriented euphemism for "engage in sexual intercourse" is *hayetah le'iš* ("be unto a man"), which is attested in Ruth 1:12–13: "Turn back my daughters for I am too old to have intercourse (*mihyot le'iš*) for if I thought that there was hope for me [to conceive] even if I had sexual intercourse tonight and I actually bore sons, would you wait for them to grow up?"[8]

Regardless of whether or not Exod 19:10, 15 intended to suggest that it is women who defile men who engage in sexual relations with them, it is significant that the much maligned (as misogynist) Qumran sectarians and the much maligned (also as misogynist) rabbis of Mishnah-Tosefta and the Talmuds have taken pains to neutralize Exod 19:15 and to incorporate their provisions into a law found in Lev 15:18, which declares unequivocally that it is the male who by emission of semen defiles himself and his sexual partner and that her becoming defiled is solely a result of physical contact with her partner's ejaculate. The entire pericope in Lev 15:16–18, in which semen is mentioned three times and woman only once, reads as follows:

> As for a man, if he has a seminal emission, he shall bathe his entire body in water but remain unclean until the evening [after the lustration]. As for any cloth or leather on which there is a puddle of semen,[9] it shall be washed in water, and it will remain unclean until the evening. As for a woman with whom a man has sexual intercourse

---

the revelation or it can be seen as a clear statement of the exclusion of women from the event altogether"; cf. Plaut, *The Torah*, 849.

7. Cf. Setel, "Exodus," 33:

> Originally, ritual purification may have been an act of renewal, acknowledging the beneficial nature of activities that continually rendered individuals ritually impure. Later, negative understandings of ritual impurity are due to a variety of factors. One was the reattribution of the life-giving female powers, present in birth and menstruation, to a male deity. This was done, in part, by using ritual purification as a demonstration of women's subservience to male authority, both divine and priestly.

8. Cf. Harold Louis Ginsberg, "Studies in Hosea 1–3," in *Yehezkel Kaufmann Jubilee Volume* (ed. M. Haran; Jerusalem: Magnes, 1960), 53 n. 11. Ginsberg holds that in all cases the Heb. *hayetah le'iš* means "she got married."

9. Heb. *šikhbhat-zer`a*; cf. *šikhbhat hattal*, "the puddle of dew" in Exod 16:13–14. Most likely, biblical Heb. *šikhbhah* (puddle) is related by metathesis etymologically and semantically to modern Heb. *šepikah* (ejaculation [of semen]; lit., pouring/spilling

[which includes] a puddle of semen, they [both the man and the woman] shall bathe in water, but they shall remain unclean until the evening.

The defiling nature of a man's semen is reflected also in Deut 23:11–12, where we read: "If any man among you has become unclean[10] by a nocturnal seminal emission,[11] then he should exit to an area outside the camp; he may not enter the camp.[12] Now it shall come to pass:[13] before evening he shall bathe in water, and he may enter the camp when the sun has set." Common to both Lev 15:16–18 and Deut 23:11–12 are the following ideas: (1) a man's semen is an impure substance; and (2) purification of persons/objects who have been defiled by semen is accomplished in two stages: (*a*) bathing in water and (*b*) the onset of evening (so Lev 15) = sunset (so Deut 23).[14]

In his commentary on Exod 19:15 the quasi-canonical Hebrew biblical exegete R. Solomon Isaaki, commonly known by his acronym Rashi (1040–1105),[15] reflects the philogynic tendency in rabbinic halakah and biblical exegesis:

[of semen]). The interchange of the consonants *p* and *b* is well known as, for example, in *šapak hemah* = Akk. *imta tabaku* = pour out venom/poison; on the latter expressions, see Mayer I. Gruber, *Aspects of Nonverbal Communication in the Ancient Near East* (vol. 2; Rome: Biblical Institute Press, 1980), 536–37.

10. Note that Deut 23:11 shares with the J strand of the flood narrative in Gen 7:2, 8 the euphemistic and paraphrastic "not clean" (i.e., two words) to the adjective *tame'* (impure) found in other strands of biblical literature; for the perception of the paraphrastic usage as euphemistic, see *Pesiq. Rab Kah.*, 4:2.

11. Qimron and Martínez argue that the appearance of the same term in a clear context in 11QT 45:7 (quoted below) confirms the meaning of "seminal emission" for *miqreh* in both Deut 23:11 and 1 Sam 20:26. See Elisha Qimron and Florentino García Martínez, *The Temple Scroll: A Critical Edition with Extensive Reconstructions and Bibliography* (Beersheba: Ben-Gurion University of the Negev Press, 1996), 298–300.

12. Cf. NJV "reenter."

13. Heb. *wehayah*.

14. See Ellens, this volume.

15. Born in 1040 C.E. in Troyes, the capital of the provence of Champagne in northern France, Rashi died there in 1105 C.E. There Rashi headed a yeshivah named Geon Ya'aqov (the Pride of Jacob, i.e., the Pride of Jewry; the phrase occurs in Amos 6:8; 8:7; and Nah 2:3). This name indicated that Rashi saw his academy as a legitimate successor of the famous academy of the same name allegedly established at Sura in Babylonia in 219 C.E. The latter academy was regarded by Judaism as the legitimate successor of the Sanhedrin (a combination supreme legislature, supreme executive, and supreme court) presided over by the high priest in the Second Temple era. The authoritative codes of halakah—*Arba'ah Turim* (Four Columns) by Jacob b. Asher (d. 1340) of Toledo and *Shulhan Aruk* (The Set Table) by Joseph Qaro (b. Toledo, Spain, 1488; d. Saphed, Palestine, 1575)—both declared in division *Orah Hayyim* (Daily Life), ch. 285,

DO NOT APPROACH A WOMAN throughout all of these three days so that the women may immerse [in the *mikveh*, i.e., the pool containing 40 *se'ah* of rainwater][16] on the third day and be pure to receive the Torah. For if they engage in sexual intercourse during [the aforementioned] three days, it is possible that the woman may expel semen after her immersion and go back to being unclean [as she was from the time of her partner's ejaculation until her immersion]. However, once she has waited three days [after her last intercourse] the semen has already putrefied and is no longer fit to impregnate,[17] and it is pure so that it cannot defile the woman who expels it.

The rabbinic source, which is the basis for Rashi's exegesis of Exod 19:15, is *m. Šabb.* 9:3: "What is the scriptural proof that a woman who expels semen on the third day [after intercourse] is clean? [The answer is] what is stated in the Bible [in Exod 19:15]: 'Be ready for the third day.'"[18]

---

that a Jew may fulfill the obligation to read twice each Sabbath the weekly portion of the Pentateuch in Hebrew and once the rendering of that portion in the official (believed to have been divinely inspired) Aramaic translation (Targum) by substituting Rashi's Hebrew commentary for the Aramaic translation. The aforementioned codes thus give the biblical commentaries of Rashi canonical status, which, in many circles, they retain to this day.

16. There is abundant archaeological evidence that biblical and rabbinic Heb. *se'ah* (referring to a liquid or dry measure of volume) corresponds to 7.3 liters. See Stern, "Measures and Weights," 16:380. On this basis 40 se'ah, the minimum amount of rainwater necessary for a *mikveh*—a pool of water—should be the equivalent of 292 liters. (The term *mikveh* is found in Gen 1:10; Exod 7:19; and Lev 11:36). However, *b. 'Erub.* 4b equates 40 *se'ah* with 1 square cubit by 3 cubits. Moreover, modern halakic authorities, like their ancestors in the ancient Near East, disagree as to the length of the cubit (Heb. *'ammah*) in ancient sources. Consequently, Sinclair explains that in modern times halakic authorities fix 40 *se'ah* at anywhere from 250 liters of water to 1000 liters of water. See Daniel Sinclair, "Miqveh," in *The Oxford Dictionary of the Jewish Religion* (ed. J. Zwi Werblowsky and G. Wigoder; New York: Oxford University Press, 1997), 469–70.

17. Concerning the physiological basis for this assumption, cf. Robert G. Edwards, *Conception in the Human Female* (London: Academic Press, 1980), 559: "Human spermatozoa may remain motile in the oviduct for several days, and retain their fertility there for at least 48 h[ours]."

18. The reading "clean" is found in Ms. Kaufmann A 50 and Ms. Parma de Rossi 138, which are generally regarded as two of the most authoritative medieval mss. of the Mishnah. This reading is supported also by m. *Miqw.* 8:3 = *t. Miqw.* 6:6 and is brilliantly restored in *m. Šabb.* 9:3 on the basis of conjecture by Obadiah of Bertinora (d. 1510) in his standard commentary on the Mishnah. This reading is also presupposed by the commentary of Rashi on *b. Šabb.* 86a and the Naples edition of the Babylonian Talmud (see the discussion in David Halivni, *Sources and Traditions: Tractate*

Unlike rabbinic halakah, which sees in Exod 19:15 a special stringency designed to assure that all Israelite men and women would be pure and thus enabled to participate in the giving of the Torah at Mt. Sinai, Qumranic law sees in Exod 19:15 a general principle, which applies to every seminal emission.[19] Significantly, the Qumranites' homogenizing exegesis,[20] which Brewer calls "nomological exegesis,"[21] agrees with Lev 15 and later Tannaitic halakah and biblical exegesis in seeing the male ejaculate as the source of defilement of both a man and his sexual partner. By transferring the phrase "three days" from Exod 19:15 to Lev 15 and Deut 23, the Qumranites arrived at the following stipulations:

As for a man, if he has a nocturnal emission, he may not go to the entire sanctuary[22] until he shall complete three days: he shall wash his

---

Shabbat (New York: Jewish Theological Seminary, 1982), 245 [in Hebrew]). The assumption behind the reading "clean" is that human sperm retain their fertility within the female reproductive tract for a maximum of forty-eight hours. The assumption behind the widely attested reading "unclean" in the standard printed editions of *m. Šabb.* 9:3 (supported, inter alia, by Ms. Paris 328–29 of the Mishnah) and also in the standard printed editions of *b. Šabb.* 86a and of *y. Šabb..* 9:3 (cf. other Tannaitic views presented in *b. Šabb.* 86a–b) is that human sperm may retain their fertility for longer periods of time; cf. Edwards, *Conception,* 559: "They [human spermatozoa] have been reported to survive for even longer [than 48 hours] periods in the uterine glands or in the cervix, and they can survive in the female reproductive tract and retain their fertilizing ability in some mammals for exceedingly long periods."

19. For the idea that the three days in 11QT derives from Exod 19:15, see Yadin, *Temple Scroll,* 1:287–89.

20. For this apt term, see Jacob Milgrom, "The Scriptural Foundations and Deviations in the Laws of Purity of the Temple Scroll," in *Archaeology and History in the Dead Sea Scrolls: The New York University Conference in Memory of Yigael Yadin* (ed. L. H. Schiffman; JSPSup 8; JSOT/ASOR Monographs 2; Sheffield: Sheffield Academic Press, 1990), 93; for the demonstration of the application of homogenizing exegesis in Qumran purity laws, see Hannah K. Harrington, *The Impurity Systems of Qumran and the Rabbis: Biblical Foundations* (SBLDS 143; Atlanta: Scholars Press, 1993), 59, 62, 262, 289.

21. David Brewer, "Nomological Exegesis in Qumran Divorce Texts," *RQ* 18 (1998): 561–79.

22. One is inclined to accept the view of Levine that *kol hammiqdaš* (the entire sanctuary) in 11QT 45:8 is synonymous with kol `ir hammiqdaš (the entire Temple City) in 11QT 45:11–12 and that both terms refer to the *temenos* and not to the entire city of Jerusalem. See Baruch Levine, "The Temple Scroll: Aspects of Its Historical Provenance and Character," *BASOR* 232 (1978): 14–15; so also Lawrence H. Schiffman, "Exclusion from the Sanctuary and the City of the Sanctuary in the Temple Scroll," *HAR* 9 (1985): 307, 317–18; "Laws Pertaining to Women in the Temple Scroll," in *The Dead Sea Scrolls: Forty Years of Research* (ed. D. Dimant and U. Rappaport; Leiden: Brill , 1992), 211. Broshi explains, "The total area of the temple compound described in the Temple Scroll was, coincidentally, precisely the size of Jerusalem in the second

clothes, and he shall bathe on the first day, and on the third day he shall wash his clothes, and he shall bathe,[23] and the sun will set; afterwards he may go to the Temple. (11QT 45:7–10)

If a man has intercourse with his wife [producing] a puddle of semen, he shall not go to the entire Temple City where I cause My name to dwell three days.(11QT 45:11–12)

A man shall not have intercourse with his wife in the Temple City [thereby] defiling the Temple City by means of their impurity (*beniddatam*).[24] (CD 12:1–2)

---

century B.C. [i.e., according to Broshi, there]"—"160 acres." See Magen Broshi, "The Gigantic Dimensions of the Visionary Temple in the Temple Scroll," *BAR* 13, no. 6 (1987): 36–37; cf. Jacob Milgrom, "The City of the Temple," *JQR* 85 (1994): 125–28. 23. Following Yadin, Harrington takes note of the repeated emphasis in 11QT of the idea that a person who had undergone immersion in a *mikveh* is unclean until evening; this emphasis points to an early date for the concept of *tebul yom*, which the Qumran sect rejected (Harrington, *Impurity Systems*, 64; cf. Yadin, *Temple Scroll*, 1:331–32). The concept of *tebul yom* is the idea reflected in rabbinic halakah, according to which a person who has undergone immersion in *mikveh* while it is yet day is regarded in some but not all respects as no longer impure; concerning the halakic concept in question, see Jacob Neusner, *From Scripture to 70: The Pre-Rabbinic Beginnings of the Halakah* (University of South Florida Studies in the History of Judaism 192; Atlanta: Scholars Press, 1998), 160–62, esp. 160: "When the Written Torah refers to washing, bathing . . . what accomplishes the purification is sunset. . . . But [the rabbinic] sages take the view that the immersion has affected the uncleanness, removed some of its virulence, even while not wholly effecting cleanness. The halakah of Tebul Yom asks, in what way is the Tebul Yom clean and in what way is he unclean?" Since sperm may remain viable in the female reproductive tract for up to the three days, *b. Sabb.* 86b points out that many of the Israelites at Mt. Sinai may have been in the legal category of *tebul yom.* This assertion may be a not so subtle polemic against the Qumran sect! 24. In rabbinic Heb. *niddah* acquires the specialized meaning of "menstruating woman"; cf. in biblical Heb. Ezek. 18:6; however, in biblical Heb. (see, e.g., Lev 20:21; Ezek 7:20; Ezra 9:11), as here in Qumran Heb., the word can mean simply "impurity," in this case impurity engendered by a male; see Levine, "Temple Scroll," 14; cf. Martha Himmelfarb, "Sexual Relations and Purity in the Temple Scroll," *DSD* 6 (1999): 18. Typical of biblical Heb. *niddah* in its basic meaning of "impurity" is in the expression *mê niddah* as "a liquid substance for [the removal of] impurity" in Num 19:9, 13, 20, 21; 31:23; for a survey of possible etymologies of Heb. *niddah*, see Moshe Greenberg, "The Etymology of Niddah '(Menstrual) Impurity,'" in *Solving Riddles and Untying Knots: Biblical, Epigraphic, and Semitic Studies in Honor of Jonas C. Greenfield* (ed. Z. Zevit, S. Gitin, and M. Sokoloff; Winona Lake, Ind.: Eisenbrauns, 1995), 69–77.

As we have seen, 11QT shares with Lev 15 and Deut 23 and rabbinic halakah the view that it is the male by his ejaculation who has the capacity to defile a woman through sexual intercourse and not the woman qua woman who defiles the man through sexual intercourse; from this, two important conclusions must be drawn. First, the assumption that woman qua woman is a pollutant, which is a linguistically plausible interpretation of Exod 19:15, is shared neither by rabbinic halakah nor Qumran law; hence the failure of either of these sects to accord equality to the sexes is to be sought elsewhere than in the belief that women as such were regarded by these groups as pollutants.[25] Second, as already demonstrated by Sara Japhet,[26] the argument so widely accepted by Qumran experts that the Qumran sect encouraged male celibacy because men would become polluted by having intercourse with women is clearly contradicted by 11QT 45:7–12.[27]

Moreover, 11QT 45:10 appears to take it for granted that members of the sect would normally visit the temple as couples as, in fact, many

25. Cf. Wegner, *Chattel or Person*, 18; see also Judith R. Baskin, "Woman as Other in Rabbinic Literature," in vol. 2 of *Where We Stand: Issues and Debates in Ancient Judaism*, pt. 3 of *Judaism in Late Antiquity* (ed. J. Neusner and A. J. Avery-Peck; Leiden: Brill, 1999), 177–96; Mayer I. Gruber, "The Status of Women in Ancient Judaism," in vol. 2 of *Where We Stand: Issues and Debates in Ancient Judaism*, pt. 3 of Judaism in Late Antiquity (ed. J. Neusner and A. J. Avery-Peck; Leiden: Brill, 1999), 164–67. In fact, as suggested already by Neusner (*The Tosefta Translated from the Hebrew: Third Division: Nashim [The Order of Women]* [New York: Ktav, 1979], x–xi), it is the treatment of women as a caste, rather than the perception of women as sources of pollution, that accounts for their exclusion from all but the outermost area of the temple court in (1) Second Temple practice as witnessed by Josephus, *Ant.* 15.11.5; *J.W.* 5.5.2–3; (2) Mishnah-Tosefta (see, with Schiffman, "Laws Pertaining to Women," 211): *t. Sukkah* 4:1); (3) Qumran law exemplified by 11QT 39:7 where, as Schiffman explains, "a woman shall not enter there" refers to the middle court of the temple; moreover, Schiffman shows that 11QT 40:6 indicates "that women were permitted to enter the outer court" of the temple; see "Laws Pertaining to Women," 211; so also Himmelfarb, "Sexual Relations and Purity," 21.
26. Sara Japhet, "The Prohibition of the Habitation of Women: The Temple Scroll's Attitude toward Sexual Impurity and Its Biblical Precedents," *JANES* 22 (1993): 69–87.
27. Yadin, *Temple Scroll*, 1:288–89; Elisha Qimron, "Celibacy in the Dead Sea Scrolls and the Two Kinds of Sectarians," in vol. 1 of *The Madrid Qumran Congress: Proceedings of the International Congress of the Dead Sea Scrolls, Madrid 18–21 March, 1991* (ed. J. Trebolle Barrera and L. Vegas Montaner; STDJ 11:1; Leiden: Brill, 1992), 287–94; Philip Davies, "The Dead Sea Writings, the Judaism(s) of," in *The Encyclopaedia of Judaism* (ed. J. Neusner, A. J. Avery-Peck, and W. S. Green; Leiden: Brill, 2000), 1:190–92. Interestingly, Wenham raises and rejects the possibility that Lev 15:18 itself stems from "an aberrant pro-celibacy tradition in Israel" ("Why Does Sexual Intercourse Defile," 432–34).

Jews did during the late Second Temple era according to the testimony of Josephus (*Ant.* 15.11.5). This text, like a famous rabbinic text,[28] also takes it for granted that notwithstanding Lev 18:19 and 20:18 Jews might engage in menstrual intercourse: "They [i.e., man and woman][29] should not go to My Temple in her menstrual impurity[30] and [thereby] defile [it]."[31] A very important passage in the *Damascus Document* (CD), which clearly shares the cultic terminology of 11QT, reads, "A man should not have intercourse with a woman in the Temple City so as to defile the Temple City through their uncleanness" (CD 12:1–2).

As suggested by Japhet[32] and later demonstrated by Lawrence Schiffman,[33] "the Temple City" in these documents designates, not the city of Jerusalem, but only the enlarged *temenos*,[34] which is the functional equivalent of "the Temple Mountain" in rabbinic halakah. Therefore, there is no reason to conclude that the Dead Sea Scrolls prohibited

---

28. See the *baraitha* quoted in *b. Ber.* 22a: "Men who have experienced an abnormal genital discharge and men who have had intercourse with menstruating women are permitted to chant Torah, Prophets, and Hagiographa out of a scroll and to chant from memory Mishnah, Talmud, midrash, *halakot,* and *aggadot.* However, men who have experienced an emission of semen are forbidden." See the discussion in Gruber, "Status of Women," 166–67. Insofar as the bulk of Hebrew law from Exod 21 through the latest rabbinic *responsa* is casuistic rather than apodictic, the various corpora, including the Qumran law books, must deal more with the consequences of what people *tend to do* rather than with what they *should or should not do* according to the ideology of one or another ancient or modern Hebrew sect.

29. Note that the author of this legal text contrasts "they" (common plural) with "her" (feminine singular) in reference to the rare case where the common impurity of the man and his female sexual partner derives from *her* menstrual impurity; see next note.

30. The more likely possibility, on any day of the female partner's menstrual cycle, is that the two persons would become impure because of *his* emission of semen, hence the preoccupation of the Qumran texts with the more likely situation, especially among Jewish persons who would have been indoctrinated with the law found in Lev 18:19; 20:18; and elsewhere according to which menstrual intercourse is one of the most grievous of sins.

31. With Qimron and Martínez, I understand *wtm'w* to stand for *wtm'whw* (*Temple Scroll,* 63).

32. Japhet, "Prohibition," 86.

33. Schiffman, "Laws Pertaining to Women," 211.

34. It is likely that Gk. *temenos* (the primary form in Gk. is *temènios*) ultimately derives, possibly via Akkadian *temmenum* (foundation stone) from Sumerian *TEMEN,* meaning "foundation stone," which is the epicenter of the sacred space of a temple complex; for demonstration that the primary meaning of Akk. *temmenum* (my transliteration is based upon W. von Soden, *AHw,* p. 1346) is "foundation(s)," see Richard S. Ellis, *Foundation Deposits in Ancient Mesopotamia* (New Haven: Yale University Press, 1968), 147–50. Ellis explains there that secondarily the Akkadian term came to designate clay and stone cylinders and prisms and even stelae (Akk. *narû*; see Ellis, *Foundation Deposits,* 145–47) that marked the foundation(s), i.e., the epicenter

sexual intercourse within greater Jerusalem outside the *temenos*.[35] Since, however, the specific Judaic system responsible for both CD and 11QT shared the expansion of the *temenos* beyond the physical boundaries of the Temple Mount of the late Second Temple period, it is understandable that the legislator who composed CD 12:1–2 would have to anticipate the possibility that members of the sect might forget that the prohibition of sexual intercourse extends beyond the confines of the Temple Mountain and includes a large part of the inhabited area of Jerusalem in the late Second Temple period. A married couple who belonged to the sect and who lived in Jerusalem might indeed find that their bedroom was located within sacred space as defined by 11QT.[36] It is most likely that in CD 12:1–2 the legislator addresses this distinct possibility. The possible conclusions that they might have to draw from CD 12:1–2 are that (1) they need to relocate, (2) they need to give up lovemaking or at least do it somewhere else, or (3) they need to change their religious affiliation to a different Jewish sect (something that Josephus tells us he did [*Life* #2])—one that allows intercourse in their neighborhood.

The texts analyzed above demonstrate beyond a shadow of doubt that the lawyers responsible for CD and 11QT, like the sages of rabbinic halakah and like Leviticus and Deuteronomy, regard both male semen and menstrual blood as sources of pollution. Moreover, neither Leviticus nor Deuteronomy nor the rabbinic sages nor the authors of the Qumran law corpora regard either of the two sexes as a source of pollution per se.

---

of the sacred space, as early as the reigns of Rim-Sin of Larsa (1822–1763 B.C.E.) and Shamshi-Adad I of Assyria (1813–1781 B.C.E.). Ellis explains that when Neo-Babylonian kings such as Nabopolassar (625–605 B.C.E.) and Nabonidus (555–539 B.C.E.) sought to locate the *temmenum* of a temple in order to rebuild the temple in its proper sacred space, the aforementioned foundation deposits successfully guided these kings and their architects and builders to the *temmenum*.

35. An important functional analogy to the expansion of the Jerusalem *temenos* to include what was in late Second Temple times almost the entire inhabited area of Jerusalem is provided by Ezek 45 and 48. There the city of Jerusalem, which is renamed "Yahweh is there," stretches from the Mediterranean Sea on the west to the Dead Sea on the east. Within that area, whose circumference is 18,000 cubits (Ezek 48:35), there is a square space of 500 square cubits for the sanctuary surrounded in turn by space for houses for the priests. Medieval manuscripts of Rashi's *Commentary on the Book of Ezekiel* include two schematic maps, which give graphic expression to Ezekiel's scheme; see illustrations 4 and 5 in Mayer I. Gruber, "The Sources of Rashi's Cartography," in *Letters and Texts of Jewish History* (ed. N. Simms; Hamilton, New Zealand: Outrigger, 1990), 61–67; see Menahem Cohen, ed., *Mikra'ot Gedolot 'Haketer': Ezekiel* (Ramat Gan, Israel: Bar-Ilan University Press, 2000), 324–25 (in Hebrew); see also the reconstructions of Ezekiel's maps in the standard critical commentaries.

36. Cf. Broshi, "Gigantic Dimensions," 36–37, quoted above, n. 22.

In fact, both CD and the rabbinic law corpora take it for granted that members of their respective sects routinely engage in the abominable (from their shared biblical perspective) practice of menstrual intercourse!

The picture that emerges from the preceding is that neither the rabbinic sages nor the Qumran lawyers saw women qua women as sources of pollution who threatened either the temple or the social order. It should not be surprising, therefore, that the sages of Qumran, who exegeted any possible misogyny out of Exod 19:15, would have been embarrassed by Lev 12's suggestion that baby girls pollute their birth mothers more than baby boys. As demonstrated by Joseph Baumgarten, it is this feminist (my adjective, not his) issue that is addressed in 4Q265 and Jub 3:8.[37] Baumgarten shows that both of these texts teach that the parturient's respective periods of impurity after giving birth to a son or a daughter recapitulate the periods of time that Adam and Eve had to wait between their respective births and their entry into paradise. In addition, he shows that both of these texts perceive paradise as the prototype of the temple.[38] It follows, therefore, that both texts teach that the presence of both men and women in God's temple is part of the primeval order, at least according to the much maligned Qumranites.[39] So too, Second Temple practice[40] and Mishnaic halakah,[41] no less than the much maligned Priestly strata of the Pentateuch,[42] also could not conceive of the temple without both men and women.

---

37. Joseph Baumgarten, "Purification after Childbirth and the Sacred Garden in 4Q265 and Jubilees," in *New Qumran Texts and Studies: Proceedings of the First Meeting of the International Organization for Qumran Studies, Paris 1992* (ed. G. J. Brooke and F. García Martínez (Leiden: Brill, 1994), 3–10.

38. The relevant passage, the fragmentary lines 11–17 with Baumgarten's extensive restorations, reads as follows in my translation, which differs considerably from Baumgarten's: "In the firs[t] week [Adam was created (cf. Gen. 1:26) and he had no (contact with) holiness until] he was brought to the Garden of Eden (cf. Gen. 2:8). (And the LORD God) took a bone [from among his bones] for the woman (cf. Gen. 2:23), [but she h]ad [no name] until she was brought to [him in the second week (of Creation) for] the Garden of Eden is holy, and every young shoot within it is holy. [Therefore, it is written (Lev. 12:2–5), when a woman has given birth to a male] she shall be unclean seven days; according to (the number of) days of her menstrual impurity she shall be unclean. And [thirty days she will remain in her blood] of purity. But if she gives birth to a female, she shall be unclean [two weeks according to (the degree of impurity of) her menstrual impurity" (Heb. *keniddatah*; cf. *niddatah* "her menstrual impurity" in 11QT 45:10 quoted above), and she shall rem]ain in her blood of purity. [She may not touch] any holy thing [and she may not go to the sanctuary until the completion of her days of purification;] (Lev 12:4)." See also the discussion in Himmelfarb, "Sexual Relations and Purity," 25–27.

39. See Baumgarten, "Purification after Childbirth," 6–9. Moreover, Baumgarten observes that in accord with the Qumran law found in CD 12:1–2 and 11QT 45:11–12,

which prohibits sexual intercourse within the "Temple City" (see above), Jub 3:8 places the consummation of the marriage of Adam and Eve during the time of Adam's and Eve's "impurity preceding their entrance into the garden" (p. 7). Finally, Baumgarten observes that Jub 3:8 imagines that Adam and Eve abstained from sexual relations during their brief sojourn in the garden of Eden = sanctuary and resumed sexual relations only after the expulsion and the return of the couple to the land of their creation (p. 8). The relevant passage from Jub 3:32–34 reads as follows: "On first of the fourth month Adam and his wife went out from the Garden of Eden, and they dwelt in the land of Elda, in the land of their creation. And Adam named his wife Eve. They had no son until the first jubilee but after this he knew her." This translation is taken from O. S. Wintermute, "Jubilees," in vol. 2 of *The Old Testament Pseudepigrapha* (ed. J. H. Charlesworth; London: Dartmann, Longman & Todd, 1985), 60–61.

Baumgarten suggests that 4Q265 and Jubilees share the view that the newborn boy or girl, like the mother, is impure for seven and fourteen days respectively ("Purification after Childbirth," 6). Zimmerman argues most convincingly that precisely because Hebrew Scripture itself assumes that the infant boy, like his mother, is unclean for seven days, the rite of circumcision is postponed by Lev 12:3 and Gen. 17:12 to the eighth day after birth (Frank Zimmerman, "Origin and Significance of the Jewish Rite of Circumcision," *Psychoanalytic Review* 38 [1951]: 110–11). In fact, explains Zimmerman, rabbinic halakah in *b. Sabb.* 135a asserts that the postponement of the circumcision to the eighth day applies only to Israelite women who are unclean during the first seven days after parturition. Examples of women who are not unclean for seven days and whose children are to be circumcised on the second day after birth are Gentile women who converted to Judaism after the birth of the child and Israelite women who gave birth by caesarean section. Interestingly, it appears that the boy and girl cease to be impure, not by immersion in water, but by the arrival of a specific date. In fact, this is precisely what Hebrew Scripture in Lev 12:2 seems to say with respect to both menstruants and parturients; so already Frymer-Kensky, "Pollution, Purification, and Purgation," 413 n. 9.

Milgrom argues that "if a minor impurity such as seminal discharge requires ablution ([Lev.] 15:16), all the more so the major genital discharges"(*Leviticus 1–16*, 746). This talmudic-style a fortiori argument is, however, based on a modern phallocentric understanding of what is a major and a minor impurity. In fact, the *baraitha* found in *b. Ber.* 22a quoted above (n. 29) and its parallel in *t. Ber.* 2:12 (see the discussion in Gruber, "Status of Women," 166–67, and the literature there cited) reflects the view that menstrual flow is far less polluting than a seminal emission. Medieval Christian thought, which regarded original sin as a sexually transmitted disease, insisted that Adam and Eve had their first intercourse only after they had contracted the disease of original sin. In contrast, medieval Jewish exegetes, such as Rashi, who denied the doctrine of original sin, took pains to show that, in fact, Adam and Eve had consummated their marriage in the garden prior to their eating of the forbidden fruit (see Rashi at Gen 3:1, 20; 4:1). See Gary Anderson, "Celibacy or Consummation in the Garden? Reflections on Early Jewish and Christian Interpretations of the Garden of Eden," *HTR* 82 (1989): 121–48; Eleazar Touito, "The Historical Background of Rashi's Commentary on Gen. 1–5," in *Rashi Studies* (ed. Z. A. Steinfeld; Ramat Gan, Israel: Bar-Ilan University Press, 1993), 103–4 (in Hebrew).

40. See above, n. 28.

41. See Gruber, *Motherhood,* 64–65; "Rashi's Cartography," 155–56; cf. Judith Hauptman, *Rereading the Rabbis: A Woman's Voice* (Boulder: Westview Press, 1998), 227–28.

42. See Gruber, *Motherhood,* 49–68.

5

The Woman in Childbirth of John 16:21
A Feminist Reading in (Pro)creative Boundary Crossing
Kathleen P. Rushton

[W]omen and men have encoded different concepts of creativity and procreativity into the metaphor itself. Highlighting how . . . "gender informs and complicates both the writing and reading of texts," the childbirth metaphor provides a concrete instance of genuine gender difference in literary discourse as constituted both by the readers and the writers of a given text . . . But women's use of the childbirth metaphor demonstrates . . . a subversive inscription of women's (pro) creativity that has existed for centuries.

—SUSAN SANFORD FRIEDMAN,
"CREATIVITY AND THE CHILDBIRTH METAPHOR"

Birth, an undeniably female activity, enshrines "symbolic, emotional and ultimately political significance" in a philosophical tradition that privileges mind over body, idea over matter, "the word over the bloody, shitty mortal flesh."[1] This insight of Sara Ruddick pinpoints the immense power of actual birth as "a physically innovative act" creating new life as well as its (pro)creative potential for evoking female energy, presence, and power metaphorically. Birth evokes the female body in the messiness of embodiment, in the reality of female flesh and blood. Undoubtedly, many would place the main emphases of Christian philosophical traditions within Ruddick's category of privileging the mind over the body. In contrast, others would understand that the Hebrew and Aramaic traditions of Israel hold significantly different emphases concerning the body and its representations.[2] While those differences surely exist, both

---

1. Sara Ruddick, *Maternal Thinking: Towards a Politics of Peace* (London: Women's Press, 1990), 48.
2. Daniel Boyarin, *Carnal Israel: Reading Sex in Talmudic Culture* (Berkeley: University of California Press, 1993), 5.

scriptural testaments are somewhat cagey in their use of birth images, particularly in relation to the birth giver and the female body.

In this chapter, I want to examine factors that may have surrounded the Johannine community's original reception of a particular biblical birth image, the woman in childbirth of John 16:21: "When a woman is in labor, she has pain, because her hour has come. But when her child is born, she no longer remembers the anguish because of the joy of having brought a human being into the world" (NRSV). I will consider this simple image alongside other biblical birth imagery and the biblical construction of mother. I have argued extensively (in other writings) that this parable functions in the Johannine text to make meaning of the death-glory of Jesus and the struggles of discipleship.[3]

Among the associations that this metaphor evokes is the Isaian daughter of Zion. The story of this "suffering one"—the "barren one who bursts into song"—progresses from abandonment, childlessness, and suffering to joy at the birth of her children and a new creation drinking from her bosom (Isa 54:1; 66:11). Through a feminist sequential reading of Isa 40–66,[4] we discover this female character to be as extensive and as prominent in the Isaian text and as rich in meaning as the "servant of God."[5] We can see her again as she is evoked in a strand of Johannine meaning-making of the death-resurrection of Jesus. In the androcentric and patriarchal Johannine symbolic universe, the power of metaphor enables the image of the woman in childbirth in John 16:21 to reach beyond the limit of the few words it uses to describe natural birth. The bloody, messy phenomenon of natural childbirth is presented in the text itself as a bloodless, *unmessy* event with no emphasis on suffering. Theological language incorporates this birth image into the themes and concerns of the gospel, presenting a parallel to the Johannine portrayal of the death of Jesus—a violent,

---

3. See my doctoral thesis, "The Parable of Jn 16:21: A Feminist Socio-Rhetorical Reading of a (Pro)creative Metaphor for the Death-Glory of Jesus" (Ph.D. diss., Griffith University, Brisbane, Australia, 2000); also see my article, "The (Pro)creative Parables of Labour and Childbirth (John 3:1–10 and 16:21–22)," in *The Lost Coin: Parables of Women, Work and Wisdom* (ed. M. A. Beavis; The Biblical Seminar 86; Sheffield: Sheffield Academic Press, 2002).

4. On this complex character, see Katheryn Pfisterer Darr, *Isaiah's Vision of the Family of God: Literary Currents in Biblical Interpretation* (Louisville: Westminster John Knox, 1994), 13–45.

5. John F. Sawyer, "Daughter of Zion and Servant of the Lord in Isaiah," JSOT 44 (1989): 89–107.

bloody, and excruciating event, yet bloodless and without explicit references to suffering.[6]

The image of John 16:21 both resists and is absorbed by the world of the text. It is singular among biblical birth images because it is the most complete in the mentions of these specific elements: (1) an embodied woman, (2) pain (λύπη),[7] (3) childbirth, (4) a human person (offspring), and (5) joy after childbirth. In contrast, other biblical birth images do not have, or only imply, some of these five elements. In fact, as we shall see, many are not birth images at all. The Fourth Gospel uses the birth image to make theological meaning of the death-glory of Jesus, who is named the Logos/Sophia (1:1), the Christ/Messiah (1:20, 25, 41), the Chosen One (1:34, see footnote h in NRSV),[8] Son of God (1:34, 49), the Savior of the world (4:42), and the Holy One of God (6:69). Such namings align Jesus with God, and by implication birth, a uniquely female activity, is associated with the divine in the Johannine symbolic universe.

This chapter raises questions about the rhetorical effect of how God is presented in relation to such biblical birth imagery, how the Bible constructs and uses motherhood, and how patriarchy and androcentrism have influenced our interpretations. Reference will be made to the post-biblical Christian tradition of the "churching" of women, which illustrates the ongoing ambiguity of views towards women who give birth. However, primarily, I seek to develop a possible backdrop to the rhetorical reception of John 16:21 by briefly exploring relevant biblical texts. These texts show that the birth imagery of the biblical tradition predominately enshrines *male* creativity. The woman-in-labor image of John 16:21 invites a reading against the grain of the text. The conclusion of this chapter will evoke such a reading.

The discussion undertaken in this chapter is relevant to the theme of this volume on purity/impurity because John 16:21 projects a paradoxical image of a life-giving transformation from pain and sorrow to joy and fulfillment—an image that evokes further paradoxes in its cultural and

---

6. Interestingly, the only mention of blood is in another extraordinary scene evocative of birth when blood and water flow from the side of Jesus (John 19:34).

7. In the biblical tradition, the term λύπη is not applied to birth pain; see Rushton, "The Parable of Jn 16:21," 117–21.

8. I follow this variant for the reasons given by Raymond E. Brown, *The Gospel According to John*, vol.1 (Garden City, N.Y.: 1966, 57). JB and NJB follow this. The majority of Greek textual witnesses read o (ui/o\j (cf. NA27) and render it "Son of God," see, RSV, NRSV, NIV, NAB. Also see, F–M Braun, *Jean le théologien II: Les grandes traditions d'Israel, L'accord des Ecritures d'après le quatrième évangile* (Paris: Librairie Lecoffre, 1964), 71–73.

religious contexts. The event of childbirth itself, within the biblical traditions of Israel, places woman under the prescriptions of purity/impurity
codes. This continues in Christian interpretation and practice prompting
us to ask: What is the rhetorical effect of a birth image (John 16:21)
evoking a birth image (the Isaian "daughter of Zion")? How does this
intensified metaphor make theological meaning of the death-glory of
Jesus? Exploration of this metaphor requires some caution on at least two
fronts. First, any attempt to ascertain the context in which it was interpreted in the late first century must be tentative. Second, we do not know
the extent to which impurity/purity codes describe women's actual experience in the religion of Israel and in later rabbinic Judaism and Christianity. However, we do know that, because these codes are found in sacred
texts, they are prescriptive and shape later interpretation and practice.

Birth and Birthless Images in Biblical Traditions

The birth imagery from Genesis to Revelation—whether set forth to
evoke birth pains or any other of the various strands of the metaphor—
requires an approach that distinguishes between several facets of the
image.[9] Not all birth images are in fact actual *birth* images. All of the
"elements" of woman, birth pains, a birth, and an offspring are neither
present nor even necessarily a part of the message the imagery intends to
express.[10] Certainly, birth pains are accentuated in scriptural passages
and emphasized in the history of interpretation.[11] For example, Katheryn
Pfisterer Darr has drawn attention to the necessity of taking seriously the
particular trope—the woman in travail—used as a birth image within Isaiah.[12] The woman in travail most often functions stereotypically within a

---

9. Conrad Gemf, "The Imagery of Birth Pangs in the New Testament," *TynBul* 45
(1994): 120. Gempf remarks that modern scholarship seems to blur together the several distinct facets of the image.
10. Among studies that focus on birth pain are Gempf, "Birth Pangs"; Dale C. Allison, *The End of the Ages Has Come* (Philadelphia: Fortress, 1985); and Robert H.
Gundry, *Mark: A Commentary on His Apology for the Cross* (Grand Rapids: Eerdmans,
1993). Gundry approaches the topic through Mark 13:8. Birth itself in a particular
passage is the focus of Stanley Porter, "What Does It Mean to Be 'Saved by Childbirth' (1 Timothy 2:15)," *JSNT* 49 (1993): 87–102. Etienne focuses on birth in general
in the Christian Scriptures; see Anne Etienne, "Birth," *Ecum Rev* 34 (1982): 228–37.
Very few works focus on the specific image as employed in the Scriptures.
11. Gempf has categorized birth pains as used in the Scriptures as (1) intense pain,
(2) helpless pain, (3) productive pain, and (4) pain that must run its course ("Birth
Pangs," 121–30).
12. Katheryn Pfisterer Darr, "Like Warrior, like Woman: Destruction and Deliverance
in Isaiah 42:10–17," *CBQ* 49 (1987): 564–66; see also Darr, *Family of God*, 39–41.

simile to evoke a specific behavior or emotion. The trope may suggest the behavior of persons who are not in reality giving birth but whose dire circumstances evoke responses that resemble those of a woman in labor.[13] The cries of anguish, panic-stricken faces and helpless hands evoke fear, pain, panic, consternation, and intense distress. Darr points to three such analogies of an "inability-to-give-birth" metaphor in Isaiah in 26:18 (Proto-Isaiah), 37:1–3 (Deutero-Isaiah) and 66:7–9 (Trito-Isaiah).[14] These three texts, taken together, represent an evolving motif that contributes to the reader's construal of Isaiah of a unified literary whole.

But many birth images have a far more limited—or particularized—purpose: they always must be defined in relation to the needs and context of the new subject matter. The birth pains described in the cited texts above, for example, contribute an analogy for intense suffering, helplessness, and even humiliation. Therefore, Darr argues that it is impossible to apply such to God when, in Isa 42:14, God says, "Like a travailing woman I will blow; I will both gasp and pant."[15] In her view this simile differs from others that are applied to human beings rather than to God. She emphasizes that these words of God have a pronounced auditory character rather than a visual one. In a similar fashion Darr links the warrior (v. 13) and the travailing woman similes, which, she argues, share "a markedly auditory quality."[16] This interpretation, which gives attention to specific divine behavior (violent, voluminous breaths) and its effects (laying waste mountains and drying up grass) differs from those of Phyllis Trible and Leah Bronner, who emphasize the gender of God, the divine pain, and the new realities that God births.[17] Such interpretations, in Darr's view, carry the birth-pains analogy beyond its intended and limited auditory purpose.

---

13. "Therefore all hands will be feeble, / and every human heart will melt, / and they will be dismayed. / Pangs and agony will seize them; / they will be in anguish like a woman in labor. / They will look aghast at one another" (Isa 13:7–8 NRSV); "Therefore my loins are filled with anguish; / pangs have seized me, / like the pangs of a woman in labor; / I am bowed down so that I cannot hear, / I am dismayed so that I cannot see" (Isa 21:3 NRSV); and Isa 42:14. Cf. Ps 48:5–7; Jer 22:23; 30:6; 49:24; 50:43; and Mic 4:9–10.

14. The interpretation of 66:7–16 is undoubtedly complex. For example, Darr argues persuasively that vv. 7–9 is part of three incidences in Isaiah in which a proverb of King Hezekiah (Isa 37:3b = 2 Kgs 19:3b) is developed to constitute an "inability-to-bring-to-birth" metaphor (*Family of God*, 205–24). For a similar image, see Hos 13:13.

15. Darr, "Like Warrior, like Woman," 567–71.

16. Ibid., 564.

17. Phyllis Trible, *God and the Rhetoric of Sexuality* (London: SCM Press, 1992), 64; and Leah Bronner, "Gynomorphic Imagery in Exilic Isaiah (40–66)," *Dor le Dor* 2 (1983–1984): 77.

Birth imagery is also found in eschatology, where it is often descriptive of pain. Birth itself is not part of the imagery.[18] In Rom 8:22 pain and groaning are emphasized along with the notions of waiting (vv. 19, 23) and frustration (vv. 20, 23). The juxtaposition of birth pains (v. 22) and adopted children (v. 23) results in mixed metaphors. Birth pain as in the latter instance and in 1 Thess 5:3 tends to suggest that the pain of childbirth is a negative image. In Gal 4:19 the emphasis is again on the pain and not the birth. Thus, within biblical literature at least one category of metaphor exists in which the appeal to the analogy of birth is governed by the controlling image of pain and not birth itself.[19]

In another category in the Jewish and Christian traditions, birth rather than pain is the controlling image. Such emphasis does not, of course, negate the pain.[20] As opposed to the analogy that focuses on birth pain alone, this second category of images may be termed "productive" in that a new dynamic emerges: once pain erupts, it suggests a process, a cycle of reoccurring waves of pain that must run their course. The evolving image of John 16:21 stands in this tradition. As noted above, the evoked image of the "daughter of Zion," the "suffering one" of Isaiah, intersects with the woman in childbirth of John 16:21. However, the "daughter of Zion" in the climactic final poem of Isaiah is a complex female character who differs markedly from a woman often envisaged as "passive" while enduring childbirth. A more complex interplay of metaphorical meanings is at work.

Thus, varied biblical traditions distinguished and emphasized different facets of birth imagery basically reducible to five metaphoric elements: the embodied woman, pain, the childbirth process itself, offspring, and joy after childbirth. (Only the Isaian "daughter of Zion" and the woman of the image of John 16:21 actually contain all five elements.) From this birth imagery arise recognizable constructions or motifs of motherhood and of the longing of women to give birth to children. One of these is the motif of the barren woman. The "daughter of Zion" stands as part of a rich tradition which, in line with the changing circumstances of the religion of Israel, continued to reinterpret the barren woman motif.

---

18. In Mark 13:8 and Matt 20:7–8 birth-pain imagery is used to signal the beginning of strife, earthquakes, and famine.

19. Gempf makes this point ("Birth Pangs," 129–30).

20. Or does it? From a feminist perspective, such an assertion raises interesting questions about an image—drawn from female experience—that is in texts written and interpreted by men.

The Barren Women Traditions

The Isaian "daughter of Zion" is hailed as "barren one" (Isa 54:1). This description and her story align her with the biblical motif of the barren woman that Mary Callaway has traced from Genesis to the Gospel according to Luke.[21] The barren woman who conceives miraculously is a recurring theme in the Scriptures.[22] Certain characteristics can be identified. First, the creative role is understood to lie with God, who is, as Esther Fuchs describes, "the sole proprietor and master of human life."[23] She demonstrates that these biblical tales are contrived ideologically to define and promote motherhood as a patriarchal institution. A woman is seen as having no control over her reproductive capacity. God, an often andromorphized character in the narrative, has control. Secondly, "a literary constellation of male characters" surrounds and determines the fate of the woman's reproductive potential in order to enhance their patriarchal interests and status.[24] Thirdly, a sense of vulnerability and emptiness taunts the childless woman whether she is a barren wife or a widow, whereas pregnancy, and pregnancy alone, moves her to security and ultimately to pride when she gives birth to sons. Finally, the virtuous woman is defined as one who accepts that God opens and closes wombs (Isa 66:9; cf. Gen 20:18; 15:3) and who praises God when she is miraculously with child. The inference is that God's fertility gives children—or more precisely, sons—progeny of miraculous interventions.[25]

---

21. Mary Callaway, *Sing, O Barren One: A Study in Comparative Midrash* (SBLDS 91; Atlanta: Scholars Press, 1986).
22. Sarah (Gen 16–18; 21:1–7), Rebekah (Gen 25:20–26), Rachel (Gen 29:31–30:24), the mother of Samson (Judg 13:2–24), Hannah (1 Sam 1:1–2:10); and the woman of Shunem (2 Kgs 4:1–37). Biblical annunciation scenes show three major thematic components: the barrenness of the wife, a divine promise of future conception, and the birth of a son. The birth of John the Baptist (Luke 1:5–80) is in this genre, as is a birth in 4 Ezra 9:43–45 and the *Prot. Jacobi* 1–5. For outlines of four types of these scenes, see Esther Fuchs, "The Literary Characterization of Mothers and Sexual Politics in the Hebrew Bible," in *Feminist Perspectives on Biblical Scholarship* (ed. A. Yarbro Collins; Atlanta: Scholars Press, 1985), 119 f. Also on the sterile matriarch, see J. Cheryl Exum, *Fragmented Women: Feminist (Subversions) of Biblical Narratives* (JSOTSup 163; Sheffield: Sheffield Academic Press, 1993), 120–30; on infertility and Jewish attitudes in the period 332 B.C.E.–200 C.E., see Tal Ilan, *Jewish Women in Greco-Roman Palestine: An Inquiry into Image and Status* (TSAJ 44; Tübingen: Mohr-Siebeck, 1995), 111–14.
23. Fuchs, "Mothers and Sexual Politics," 119.
24. Ibid., 129.
25. Rachel Adler, "A Mother in Israel: Aspects of the Mother Role in Jewish Myth," in *Beyond Androcentrism: Essays on Women and Religion* (ed. R. M. Gross; Missoula:

In the biblical tradition, the motif of the barren woman more often than not coincides with that of motherhood. The mother in Hebrew Scriptures focuses on the well-being of her children. She is depicted as highly protective of them and single-mindedly devoted to them. This, of course, means her male children. While fathers are portrayed as being in conflict with their sons, the protective mother often intervenes on their behalf. This active promotion of the interests of her (male) children does not extend to those of her daughters.[26] In contrast, the motif of the mother-daughter is virtually nonexistent in the Hebrew Bible.[27] As important and strong a figure as the mother in Israel may appear up to the birth of her sons, she almost invariably fades from any central role in the ensuing course of events.[28]

This brief overview of the barren woman who becomes a mother and the four characteristics showing her subordination to patriarchal control and suffering (as outlined) previously demonstrates that the barren woman motif functions to enhance the status of males in a patriarchal symbolic world. While the literature of rabbinic Judaism's systematic vision of an ideal reality is not a description of any historical society and, in the main, traverses periods later than that which is the concern of this study, it nonetheless offers us a glimpse of another paradigm.[29] Judith Baskin's review of haggadic reflections on barren women demonstrates that these biblical narratives as well as their related rabbinic formulations and commentaries yield "suggestive insights into the dilemma of suffering

---

Scholars Press, 1977), 243–44. Rashkow points out, for example, how Genesis is marked by the desire for male children and the lengths to which women are depicted as going in order to make that possible (Gen 16:2; 30:3). See Ilona N. Rashkow, "Daughters and Fathers in Genesis . . . Or, What Is Wrong with This Picture?" in *The New Literary Criticism and the Hebrew Bible* (ed. J. Cheryl Exum and D. J. A. Clines; JSOTSup 143; Sheffield: Sheffield Academic Press, 1993), 250. The blessing of sons is specifically mentioned in Gen 4:1; 17:19; and 30:21–24. Rashkow suggests that the prizing of sons, joy at their birth, and the emphasis on father-son relationships "is most obvious in the covenant between the deity and Abraham (Gen. 17:9–10), the implicit symbolism of circumcision powerful in its patriarchal reverberations."

26. No mother intercedes on behalf of the daughter of Jephthah (Judg 11:34–40).

27. Rashkow comments that "[in]scribed within Genesis is something more than a general disregard of woman: the *daughter* is specifically absent. Since the daughter's presence is normal and necessary to the biological realities of family, her narrative absence is significant and calls attention to itself" ("Daughters and Fathers," 250–51).

28. Adler sees that although the mother in Israel is "a valid and useful prototype, it is nevertheless one-sided and incomplete, lacking in a creative aspect. . . . Woman is the created, not the creator, the named and not the namer" ("Mother in Israel," 249).

29. For a helpful summary of the literature and approximate periods, see Michael L. Satlow, *Tasting the Dish: Rabbinic Rhetorics of Sexuality* (BJS 303; Atlanta: Scholars Press, 1995), 13–15.

and the efficacy of prayer, as well as examples of the ways in which biblical models could become paradigms and symbols of empowerment in women's lives."[30] For Rachel Adler the "powerful mythic strain" in such biblical models "makes possible broader and more varied female roles than does the weak, family-devoted mother of Western stereotypes."[31] Therefore, within the male and patriarchal world of the motif of the barren woman who becomes mother lie openings for readings that empower women.

From Israel's experience of the exile arose the Isaian reinterpretation of the barren woman tradition in the figure of the "daughter of Zion." Significantly, in her casting in Isa 51:1–3 is found the only reference to Sarah in the Jewish Scriptures outside Genesis. In the time of the exile, when the descendants of Abraham and Sarah were reduced to a small group of exiles, they are exhorted to look back to a particular time when Israel was few in number (51:2). In their desolation, they are to recall Israel's creation by God from Abraham and Sarah. God will create Israel anew from the few of the exile. Isaiah 51:1–3 evokes creation through this couple. However, from a feminist perspective, it is significant to recognize Sarah's preeminence. The memory of the land promised to Abraham is important for Israel's identity. However, in the situation of the exile, the birth motif evoking Sarah in the construction of the "daughter of Zion" becomes the central symbol of the promise. Birth from Sarah/"daughter of Zion" "could transcend the physical land and give them a common identity."[32] The inference is that a woman could give birth—create a nation—anywhere.

The parable of the woman in childbirth of John 16:21, through evoking the Isaian daughter of Zion, stands in the biblical tradition of the barren woman. In this tradition the male divine and human characters exert control over the childless woman. However, the tradition also offers a possible paradigm of women's empowerment. In their struggles the Johannine Christians may have appropriated and reinterpreted the suffering of the barren one, the "daughter of Zion," and recast her transformative story to make meaning of the death-glory of Jesus.

---

30. Judith R.Baskin, "Rabbinic Reflections on the Barren Wife," *HTR* 82 (1989): 101.
31. Adler, "Mother in Israel," 249.
32. Callaway, *Sing, O Barren One*, 81.

Birth Givers in the Biblical Traditions

The patriarchal view found in the recurring motif of the barren woman who gives birth to a male child is further underscored by examining how birth and the birth giver are related to the divine. When God does give birth, this is depicted in poetic metaphor (Deut 32:18), or God's word alone creates (P creation account). When God acts in a more concrete way, forming the *adam* out of the earth, God blows breathe into the *adam's* nostrils (J creation account in Gen 2:7). Blood is absent from biblical creation stories. God acts as a male might act. The depiction contrasts with the prominence of blood in other creation myths.[33] As Lori Hope Lefkovitz states, the tradition "has resisted establishing an affinity between God's work and maternity, as God's labors have been masculinized."[34] According to Adler, the role of birth giver, which is "too important to be rejected yet too anthropomorphic to be taken by God, is passed on by J to the creature fashioned in God's image, and thus man gives birth to woman"—also a bloodless event.[35]

The appropriation of the female birth role by the male in the Hebrew myth involves a reversal of the Sumerian myth of Enki and Nin-hursag. The power of the goddess to give birth without travail or pain is given to *adam*. Eve's subsequent childbirth is not an original event.[36] Eve and her daughters cannot reproduce the original birth—all that they are capable of is a messy, painful, and inexact imitation. Writing from the perspective of the *absence* of pregnancy rituals within the history of Judaism and in modern Judaism, Lefkovitz remarks that while circumcision marks the sign of God's covenant and celebrations marked the weaning of Isaac, the details of the first birth to the first matriarch and the first patriarch are omitted. She asks: "When did Sarah go into labor? Did she scream? . . . More realistically: Did the aged mother come near to death? Did she greet her baby with pleasure or depression? Did her milk come easily?"[37] In contrast, when the Sumerian or Assyrian woman gave birth, "she reproduced an act of cosmic significance. Her midwife recited the myth

---

33. Roslyn Lacks, *Woman and Judaism: Myth, History, and Struggle* (Garden City, N.Y.: Doubleday, 1980), 148.

34. Lori Hope Lefkovitz, "Sacred Screaming: Childbirth in Judaism," in *Lifecycle: Jewish Women on Life Passages and Personal Milestones* (ed. D. Orenstein; Woodstock, Vt.: Jewish Lights, 1994), 8.

35. Adler, "Mother in Israel," 239.

36. Ibid., 240–41.

37. Lefkovitz, "Sacred Screaming," 10. For writing on life cycles and ceremonies, Blu Greenberg remarks, "Imagine for a moment what a glorious celebration the tradition

of the mother goddess' creation of human beings, praying, 'As the Bearing One gives birth / May the mother of the child bring forth by herself.'"[38] Adler comments that the Jewish woman had the promise of Gen 3:16 ("I will greatly increase your pangs in childbearing" [NRSV]).[39]

Karel van der Toorn gives examples of Akkadian, Mesopotamian, and Hittite myths, prayers, and rituals associated with infertility, pregnancy, and birth that were part of the cultural and religious context of early Israel.[40] In the light of these, we cannot rule out that some Israelite women also invoked local worship forms of the mother goddess. The "Queen of Heaven," an Ishtar figure, attracted women (Jer 7:18; 44:15–19). The vast number of small figurines of women (pregnant, nursing a child, or holding up breasts with both hands) excavated in Palestine are linked possibly with the Canaanite goddess Astarte and indicate that Israelite households identified pregnancy and birth as a blessing from the mother goddess.[41]

In the biblical tradition, the birth of the first human is a startlingly bloodless and painless happening that has been sanitized by myth.[42] Childbirth in the tradition is imbued with such paradoxes. On the one hand, childbirth is women's domain at its most mysterious, powerful, and frightening. It is most distinctively female, yet it involves the power to create, projecting the birthing mother into the very image of the divine who creates.[43] She, like the matriarchs and barren ones before her, longs for and prays for the birth of her own (hopefully male) child. It is both a blessing and a command ("Be fruitful and multiply, and fill the earth" [Gen. 1:28 NRSV]).[44] On the other hand, the tradition's focus has been on interpreting the birthing process as a curse. Its dangers are

---

would have developed by now had Jewish men been the ones to give birth during these past four millennia!" Blu Greenberg, "Female Sexuality and Bodily Functions in the Jewish Tradition," in *Women, Religion, and Sexuality: Studies on the Impact of Religious Teaching on Women* (ed. J. Beecher; Geneva: WCC, 1990), 10.

38. Adler, "Mother in Israel," 241. See De Troyer, this volume.

39. Adler, "Mother in Israel," 241.

40. Karel van der Toorn, *From Her Cradle to Her Grave: The Role of Religion in the Life of the Israelite and the Babylonian Woman* (trans. S. J. Denning-Bolle; Sheffield: Sheffield Academic Press, 1994), 78–91.

41. On the other hand, if these figures depict human persons, it could well point to magical practices; see ibid., 90–91.

42. No birth account of Jesus appears in the Fourth Gospel, as in the Matthean and Lukan accounts.

43. Lefkovitz, "Sacred Screaming," 7–8.

44. The legal duty of male Jews to procreate finds its origin in Gen 1:28; 9:1, 7; and Gen 35:11. See Baskin, who points out how the rabbinic tradition appropriates the command in Gen 1:28 to both male and female and narrows it to the male ("Women

acknowledged.[45] According to Adler, in the biblical tradition as well as in the later rabbinic tradition, the birth role of the female is diminished, while the nurturant and compassionate one of woman is augmented.[46]

In addition, the pure/impure Priestly legal sources specify the postpartum mother as impure (Lev 12:1–8).[47] Childbirth excluded a woman from the sanctuary for thirty-three days when a male child was born, and sixty-six days for a female child (Lev 12).[48] Not only did certain factors surrounding this practice originate from the religion of the Hebrew Bible—or more precisely from the Priestly Code—but also, as Judith Romney Wegner insists, such stipulations on women must be set within the context of the political, literary, and cultural history of Israel. Within that particular cultic context, Lev 12 details a set of rules that relate to

---

as Other," 103–4). She questions why the extraordinary measures taken by the daughters of Lot (Gen 19:31–36) and Tamar (Gen 38) to fulfill this mandate as well as Rachel's cry, "Give me children, or I shall die" (Gen 30:1 NRSV), are ignored.

45. For example, Tobit reminds his son Tobias, "Remember her, my son, because she faced many dangers for you while you were in her womb" (Tob 4:4 NRSV).

46. Adler, "Mother in Israel," 237–55.

47. For a historical overview on the *niddah* (the menstruant woman) and the laws of family purity by a woman who observes the ancient ritual, see Blu Greenberg, "Female Sexuality," 25–29. See also the influential essay of Rachel Adler, "Tumah and Taharah—Mikveh," in *The Jewish Catalogue* (ed. M. Strassfeld et al.; New York: Jewish Publication Society, 1972), 167–71. For her later contrasting position as a feminist Reform theologian, see Adler, " 'In Your Blood, Live': Re-visions of a Theology of Purity," in *Jewish Women on Biblical Themes in Contemporary Life*, vol. 2 (ed. and intro. Debra Ornstein and Jane Rachel Litman; Woodstock: Jewish Lights Publishing, 1998: 197–206). From the perspective of cross-cultural anthropology, Eilberg-Schwartz argues that the stigma centered on menstrual blood allows ancient Israelite religion to make a crucial distinction between men's and women's capacities for holiness (Howard Eileberg-Schwartz, *The Savage in Judaism: An Anthropology of Israelite Religion and Ancient Judaism* [Bloomington: Indiana University Press, 1990], 177–94). The uncontrolled blood that flows from women's genitals has the power to contaminate. Its antithesis is the blood of circumcision, which is drawn intentionally from men's genitals and has the power to create covenant. According to Eilberg-Schwartz, who critiques Mary Douglas's work in this area as insufficient, the symbolism of the body and its fluids embedded in rules and categories is constitutive of the social structure within which it is held. The symbolism of Israelite purity links men with fertility and control and women with death and disorder. This constructs a culture in which men dominate women. Later developments in rabbinic and postrabbinic Judaism intensify the symbolic meaning and polarization, for in the *tohorat ha-mishpahah* (purity of the family) that remained after the destruction of the Second Temple, when the system of body contamination and purification fell into disuse, purity laws applying to men atrophied while those applying to women were elaborated and made more stringent.

48. Judith Romney Wegner, "Leviticus," in *The Woman's Bible Commentary* (ed. C. A. Newson and S. R. Ringe; London: SPCK, 1992), 40. See De Troyer, this volume.

women who have given birth as well as similar rules governing menstruation—all in order to maintain priestly standards of *male* holiness and purity.[49] Male perceptions of woman as the source of life and death in her capacity to give birth, as well as her cyclical menstruation where she bled without dying, generated elaborate rituals with striking parallels in other similar traditions. Since these rituals "enjoy cross-cultural ubiquity,"[50] one cannot limit their cause to the prescriptions of Israel alone. Roslyn Lacks explains that "woman's blood—like her voice—stirs profound ambivalence in the hearts and minds of men" everywhere; the idea that "blood speaks" infuses not only biblical narratives but other tribal rites and the practice of capital punishment in modern times.[51]

Thus, the religion of Israel, as a patriarchal tradition, defined woman as "Other" than male, that is, as other than fully human, based on its cultural perception of woman's sexuality.[52] Such a perception, defined in laws and rituals, begins in biblical times and continues throughout the rabbinic era, controlling her sexuality and limiting her identity (or nonidentity) to "Otherness." Named "as objects in a male-constructed version of reality," women became vehicles for birthing males.[53] As Judith Plaskow points out, women's capacity to bear children "would be [her] avenue to social prestige and control."[54] But her one potential for prestige was also her curse: on the cultural level, women's sexuality was devalued and contained. As Plaskow puts it so well, the desire to control female sexuality "is the chief source of male anxiety about women and thus also the source of the central vocabulary and symbolism for the construction of women's Otherness."[55]

In summary, at the divine level, the role of God as birth giver was not only masculinized but bloodless. In the myth of human beginnings *adam*, an assumed male character, is instrumental in the first human "birth"—a bloodless and painless event. Blood and birth pain, so integral to women's experience of childbirth, are absent from these biblical constructions at both divine and human levels. In contrast, flowing blood and childbirth subject woman to the stipulations of pure and impure

49. Wegner, "Leviticus," 37. See her helpful background on pp. 36–44, esp. 40, which explains *tame'* (impure or cultically unclean) and *tahor* (pure or cultically clean).
50. Lacks, *Woman and Judaism*, 151.
51. E.g., see ibid., 150–51.
52. Plaskow provides us with a penetrating insight into this phenomenon. See Judith Plaskow, *Standing Again at Sinai: Judaism from a Feminist Perspective* (San Francisco: Harper & Row, 1991), esp. 171–74.
53. Ibid., 174.
54. Ibid.
55. Ibid.

codes that function to protect male holiness and purity. This tension between the *male* divine/human appropriation of birth as a painless and bloodless event and the female experience of a bloody childbirth (which renders them impure) informs the religious and cultural worlds in which Johannine Christianity arose.

The Reception of John 16:21 in the Johannine Communities

It is impossible to know exactly what elements informed the meaning-making processes of those late first-century readers/hearers of the Fourth Gospel. Certainly, as Raymond Brown reminds us, "their minds were imbued with biblical images and phrases, so that scriptural motifs naturally oriented their interest and understanding."[56] Such biblical images and characters, as redefined through Jesus, could assume new metaphorical meanings in this gospel.[57] For example, the biblical image of the "daughter of Zion," as evoked by John 16:21, was recognized as familiar, yet understood also as in some way redefined through Jesus. Consequently, the birth imagery too—especially the motif of the barren woman and biblical constructions of birth givers and motherhood—appears to have been open to new interpretations.

As we attempt to explore how the birth image of John 16:21 may have been received in the Johannine communities, we must also keep in mind the cultural and religious roots that provided the "central vocabulary and symbolism for the construction of women's Otherness."[58] The historical context, with its legislative prescriptions arising from biblical restrictions, was a major, if not primary, influence on the reception of John 16:21. Late first-century readers/hearers most certainly recognized the metaphoric tie between the images of the "daughter of Zion" and the woman in childbirth of John 16:21 and, arguably, linked them together as the most complete birth image—the only actual birth images—in both testaments. Given the reluctance of biblical traditions to link the divine, explicitly or implicitly, with images of a female birth giver, there could have been surprise, even shock, at the use of John 16:21 evoking

---

56. Raymond E. Brown, *The Death of the Messiah: From Gethsemane to the Grave: A Commentary on the Passion Narratives in the Four Gospels*, vol. 1 (Garden City, N.Y.: ABRL, 1994), 15.

57. Judith Lieu, "Scripture and the Feminine in John," in *A Feminist Companion to the Hebrew Bible in the New Testament* (ed. A. Brenner; Sheffield: Sheffield Academic Press, 1996), 229, 239.

58. Plaskow, *Standing Again at Sinai*, 174.

the "daughter of Zion" as a meaning-making image of the death-glory of the Johannine Jesus.

However, such communities were familiar with the particularly Jewish practice of reinterpreting scriptural motifs to accord with the changing conditions of their lives. Therefore, an important connection could have been made in another area: Sarah and the birth of her child were traditionally associated with the exilic retelling of the barren woman motif in the "daughter of Zion" story. The "deliverer" of her child is the deliverer of her people. The evoking of the Sarah/daughter of Zion story anew in the gospel image of the woman in childbirth may have been used to stress that in the struggle to understand Jesus' death, and perhaps their own persecutions, the Johannine Christians understood that God (in their present situation) would create God's people anew. As a consequence, there is continuity with their religious matrix through the blessing of birth: the birth of a son through Sarah/the birth of a people through the "daughter of Zion"/the new birth through Jesus' death and resurrection. Thus the image evoked through the parable of the woman in childbirth not only explains the death-glory of Jesus as linked to biblical history, but its recurring pattern of childbirth metaphors and their meaning is replicated in Johannine discipleship. Birth still happens through women even in exile and in the changing physical and religious environment in which the people then found themselves.

It is now pertinent to return to the heritage of the prescriptions of the Priestly purity codes regarding childbirth. If, in studying First Testament times, we find it difficult to see how these codes were applied in practice, we must consider further factors relating these codes to Johannine Christianity. In the first place, the first hearers/readers of the parable of John 16:21 would have been influenced by the accumulating traditions of fifty or sixty years of early Christianity. In addition, earliest Christian sources are silent on the observance of birth and menstrual purity regulations. Some recent writers suggest that early Christianity's emphasis on asceticism marks a departure from the positive value ascribed to marriage and sexual intercourse in Jewish circles.[59] However, in early Christian texts two distinct strands of Christian life appear. On the one hand, the

---

59. Ross Shepard Kraemer, *Her Share of the Blessings: Women's Religions among Pagans, Jews, and Christians in the Greco-Roman World* (New York: Oxford University Press, 1992), 143–44, 154–56, esp. 155; Patricia Moss, "Unraveling the Threads: The Origins of Women's Asceticism in the Earliest Christian Communities," *Pacifica* 10 (1997): 137–55.

Asceticism is also found in Judaism; see Kraemer, "Monastic Jewish Women in Greco-Roman Egypt: Philo on the Therapeutrides," *Signs* 14 (1989): 342–47.

ascetic strand, according to Ross Shepard Kraemer, was "most appealing to women who either could not, or would not, accept the traditional standards of worth for women in their culture."[60] On the other hand, another strand is found in the Pastorals; it advocates marriage, social conformity, hierarchy, and structure. Nevertheless, Kraemer suggests, it is to be expected that Christians would reject purity regulations along with circumcision and food purity laws.[61] Leviticus 15:19–30 (governing menstruation and other flows of blood) and Lev 12 (on childbirth) are found in that portion of the law given to Moses after the golden calf incident in Exod 32 (at least according to the chronology of the text). Christians came to view this portion of the second presentation of the law as temporary and not binding on them.[62]

An important factor to remember is that purity/impurity regulations and laws portray not "Judaism," but the religion of Israel, which in the first century C.E. produced two offspring: rabbinic Judaism and Christianity.[63] Any claims about how these regulations and laws were understood in the late first-century C.E. context of Johannine communities need to be stated cautiously. On the one hand, according to Jacob Neusner, the reinstitutionalization of life in the land of Israel did not begin until after the Bar Kochba crisis.[64] Therefore, it is unlikely that these regulations and laws as specified in later rabbinic writings were current practice.[65] On the other hand, the Johannine communities in their late first-century C.E. context are influenced clearly by their Jewish

60. Kraemer, *Her Share of the Blessings*, 155.

61. Ibid., 143.

62. Ibid., 236–37 n. 67.

63. Wegner, "Leviticus," 37. Further, Hoffman illustrates how circumcision "provides an excellent index of the extent to which both Judaism [that is, incipient rabbinic Judaism] and Christianity were anxiously staking out ideological turf in city after city of the Roman Empire" (*Covenant of Blood*, 112). In this "mutual religious ambivalence . . . [a]ttracted and repelled by each other . . . [they] established an historical trajectory much like the fabled DNA spiral: swirling around each other in mutual orbit, never coming quite close enough to coalesce, but at the same time, neither one managing to extricate itself from the pull exercised by the other" (111).

64. For references to his studies, see Wayne A. Meeks, "Breaking Away: Three New Testament Pictures of Christianity's Separation from the Jewish Communities," in *"To See Ourselves as Others See Us": Christian, Jews, Other in Late Antiquity* (ed. J. Neusner and E. S. Frerichs; Chico, Calif.: Scholars Press, 1985), 102 n. 24.

65. When the institutional power of the priests was lost in 70 C.E., this vacuum, which the rabbis aspired to fill, was not achieved without struggle. The exact date of their gaining control is hard to determine, but Shaye Cohen suggests it was not earlier than the seventh century C.E. See his *From the Maccabees to the Mishnah* (LEC; Philadephia: Westminster, 1987), 221.

matrix, yet they are also in the conflictual ferment of issues of self-iden-tity.[66] Nevertheless, as Shaye Cohen points out, the separation of Chris-tianity "from Judaism was a process not an event" in which the "'cutting edge' of sectarianism was not theology but practice."[67]

We cannot be sure how the codes outlined above impinged on the lives of the Christian women in the Johannine communities. Neverthe-less, earliest Christianity, including traditions of Johannine Christians, feasibly would have been influenced by the paradoxes of the religious and biblical world that surrounded them and that produced a female-gendered image such as that of John 16:21. There is certainly evidence, as we shall see, that the ongoing history of Christianity, in its many man-ifestations, carried ambivalence towards women and childbirth.

The "Churching" of Women

Since this chapter is primarily concerned with exploring how late first-century readers may have heard the parable of John 16:21, one of my main foci as an interpreter of scriptural texts is with the rhetorical effect of these sacred stories on women's lives and well-being. While I seek ways in which biblical imagery such as John 16:21 invites a reader to read against the grain of the text and to explore its context of origin, I am also concerned with how the reception of such a text has been shaped by the history of interpretation. My research confirms my hunch that John 16:21 evoked the Isaian "daughter of Zion." The evidence obtained through various methodological approaches, which are beyond the scope of this chapter to detail, has led me to ask why the potential of this female parable has been obscured or ignored in the Christian tradition

---

66. Sean Freyne, "Vilifying the Other and Defining the Self: Matthew's and John's Anti-Jewish Polemic in Focus," in *"To See Ourselves as Others See Us": Christian, Jews, Other in Late Antiquity* (ed. J. Neusner and E. S. Frerichs; Chico, Calif.: Scholars Press, 1985), 117–43.

67. Shaye Cohen, *Maccabees to the Mishnah*, 228, 168. He argues that "in ancient Judaism sectarian alienation, whatever its origins, generally expressed itself in polemics against the central institutions of society (notably the temple), its authority figures (notably the priests), and its religious practices (notably purity, Sabbath, and marriage law). . . . Faith in Christ surely led the early Christians to distinctive ritual (baptism, Eucharist) and practices (possession by the Spirit . . .), and to distinctive interpretations of some of the Jewish observances (the feast of the Passover, the feast of Pentecost, prayer)" (124–73). The Christianity of the early second century C.E. was in the main a separate religion. More than likely the Christians of the Johannine com-munities had been expelled from their local synagogues (John 9:22; 12:42; 16:2), which does not mean, however, that at that point all Jews everywhere expelled Chris-tians. Synagogues were controlled locally. There was no central authority.

for so long. The Christian tradition has certainly been influenced by factors described to this point. It has also continued and developed ambivalence to woman as birth giver, as illustrated by the long history and the widely practiced rite of the blessing or "churching" of women after childbirth, "a pious and praiseworthy custom" that had no officially obligatory character and disappeared only in the 1950s and 1960s.[68]

According to Susan Roll, the "notion that the act of giving birth to a child somehow set a woman temporarily outside the church community in spite of her baptism has deep historical roots in the early Christian church."[69] Roll finds that references to this practice of the "churching" of women begins in the early church with Origen (185–254), who is later than the periods that have been discussed to this point. Nevertheless, this indicates that the practice extends back into the early church. Roll's research finds evidence of this practice to be constant throughout the centuries and to be widespread both geographically and denominationally. Her study of much later texts, councils, synods, and rituals—including Reform, Anglican, and Catholic pastoral practices related to women after childbirth—points to an ongoing dichotomy between churchmen's discomfort with the idea of purification and the persistence of popular and ecclesial belief in the value of the rite. The fact that such a rite persisted until as recently as the 1950s and 1960s demonstrates a continuing ambivalence towards birth and women's sexuality.[70] This tendency reaches back into early Christianity.[71]

Earlier I alluded to a God/Creator who is portrayed as masculine and to Adam's part in the first human birth. One of the consequences of the divine/human male-birthing paradigm is the role of the male priest as heir to this birthing power. As Roll describes, the churching rite formulated by clerical men persisted for about ten centuries and inserts symbolically the male priest into a birth role; she comments: "For hundreds of years . . . the woman [was] led into the church holding the end of the priest's stole, symbolically an umbilical cord by which she was born from a state of alienation and impurity into the communion with God and the church, given birth by the sacerdotal power of male priesthood."[72]

---

68. The words quoted are from the Tridentine Roman ritual, see Susan K. Roll, "The Churching of Women after Childbirth: An Old Rite Raising New Issues," *Questions Liturgiques/Studies in Liturgy* 76 (1995): 206. See also her contribution to this volume.
69. Roll, "Churching of Women," 206.
70. I remember after Sunday mass in a small Aotearoa, New Zealand, country parish church the churching of my mother after the birth of my brother in 1954 and very evasive answers to my questions as to what was happening.
71. See Dresen, this volume.
72. Roll, "Churching of Women," 227.

Further, the same priest had usually baptized the child. Roll comments, "In both cases the priest acts as the agent of birth on a spiritual level, implicitly surpassing the natural, flesh-and-blood birthgiving which is the province of women."[73]

Consistent in Judaic-Christian belief and practice is the conviction that these rites are ambivalent about the role of the female as birth giver. As we have seen, this is evident in a God portrayed as male appropriating the female role of birth giver, in the part of *adam* in the first birth, in the purity/impurity codes of Leviticus, and in the long history across various traditions of Christianity, as exemplified in the "churching" of women after childbirth. This background has consciously or unconsciously informed the reception and the history of biblical interpretations of John 16:21.

Directions for a New Reading

In no way do I deny or underrate the depth of ambivalence that surrounds woman as birth giver and that is found implicitly, and often explicitly, deeply entrenched in the variations of impurity/purity codes and the traditions of both biblical testaments. This heritage extends through centuries of practice in Christian churches. Missing is woman's view. To introduce this, I would like first to return to the quotation of Susan Stanford Friedman with which this chapter began, for she aptly captures what a feminist rhetorical reading seeks to achieve when reading a biblical text such as John 16:21, immersed as it is in an androcentric/patriarchal context and the prescriptions of its worldview(s) and world(s) of origin. Friedman highlights how "women and men have encoded different concepts of creativity and procreativity" into the birth metaphor itself."[74] Furthermore, she asserts that "women's use of the childbirth metaphor demonstrates . . . a subversive inscription of women's (pro)creativity that has existed for centuries."[75] This "subversive inscription of women's (pro)creativity that has existed for centuries" invites a feminist reader to read against the grain of the text to hear women's voices in the openings and ambiguities of the text.

Even in the prescription of male-written and male-centered texts that are not necessarily descriptive of woman's actual experience and

---

73. Ibid.

74. Susan Standford Friedman, "Creativity and the Childbirth Metaphor: Gender Difference and Literary Discourse," *Feminist Studies* 13 (1987): 50–51.

75. Ibid.

meaning-making, woman's role as birth giver exudes power and mystery.[76] Perhaps a feminist reading of the woman in childbirth of John 16:21—as a meaning-making image for the death-glory of Jesus—would, in fact, reveal a boundary-crossing in the sociocultural and religious world of the late first century. Flowing female blood and the female birth giver herself were perceived to defile. In contrast, the flowing blood of the male Jesus saves. Paradoxically, this metaphor of meaning making that straddles cultural and religious ambiguities and prescriptions has the potential to cross those boundaries not only in its world of origin but in the ongoing layers of the Christian tradition. It has the potential to redefine Jesus' and God's activity in imagery, asserting that the female person in her body may, does, and must image God.[77] From the perspective of a present-day reader, Luise Schottroff insists that any feminist reading of such a parable must be underpinned by a theory of parables that regards the activity of the woman in the parable as participative action in the sphere of God's action.[78] In the case of the parable of John 16:21, that activity is childbirth. Childbirth, an undeniable female activity of "symbolic, emotional and ultimately political significance" evoking female presence and power—as used in this parable—can make theological meaning of the death-glory of the Johannine Jesus.[79]

---

76. This context does not provide enough space for me to detail the pitfalls in appropriating a birth metaphor for feminist purposes; see my discussion of the ethics of reading such a metaphor in my doctoral thesis, "The Parable of Jn 16:21," 64–66, and my article, "(Pro)creative Parables."

77. On the reluctance of the Judaeo-Christian traditions to do this, see the essays in Kari Elisabeth Børresen, ed., *The Image of God: Gender Models in Judaeo-Christian Tradition* (Minneapolis: Fortress, 1995).

78. Luise Schottroff, *Lydia's Impatient Sisters: A Feminist Social History of Early Christianity* (trans. B. and M. Rumscheidt; Louisville: Westminster John Knox, 1995), 51–57.

79. See n. 1.

6

Doctors, Philosophers, and Christian Fathers on Menstrual Blood

Jennifer Schultz

> Nothing is more filthy, unclean than a menstruant; whatever she will have touched, she makes it unclean, and still of whose filth is cleansed by the baptism of Christ, through the cleansing of sins.
>
> —JEROME, *COMM. IN ZACHARIAM LIBRI III*

When Jerome wrote these heavy-handed words in the late fourth century—words cited and censured by modern feminists—he reflected the world in which he dwelt. In the late antique period, Christian male writers propagated and perpetuated an inherent androcentrism rooted in ancient Greco-Roman perceptions of the female somatic experience. Laboring with notions as ancient as Hesiod, these men refigured this ideology, adding dimensions previously not found. Jerome's words reflect the embedded cultural construction of menstruation as reprehensible fluidity; they exemplify the acceptance of a distinct Christian menstrual taboo—a taboo that Leslie Dean-Jones has claimed was almost nonexistent in ancient Greece.[1] And while no other early father of the church goes so far as to equate menstruation with sin nor writes with such venom, by the third century of the Common Era questions regarding the status of the menstruant begin to enter texts, texts that arguably introduce this taboo. In his *Apostolic Tradition*, Hippolytus of Rome, writing about 215, includes the menstruant in his canons as one person denied baptism, a denial he neither explains nor justifies.[2] No more than fifty years later, Dionysius of Alexandria turns to the Matthean story of the

---

1. Leslie Dean-Jones, *Women's Bodies in Classical Greek Science* (Oxford: Clarendon, 1994), 245–47.
2. All citations are from the Dix (1969) edition of the *Apostolic Tradition*. See Gregory Dix, ed., *The Treatise on the Apostolic Tradition of St. Hippolytus of Rome* (London: SPCK, 1969). Hereafter cited as *Trad. ap.*

hemorrhaging woman to legitimate the exclusion of the "impure" menstruant not only from the Eucharist celebration but from the church edifice itself.[3]

From the apostolic age to the writings of Gregory the Great, disputa-
tions on purity pervade the writings of the Fathers. These men argue
against the incorporation of Jewish purity laws in order to distinguish
between "New and Old Israel," between their construction of the Jewish
time of law and the Christian time of grace. Purity comes to be defined
over against Mosiac law; purity, they insist, emanates from the heart,
from righteous action and thought, and not from bodily fluids. Yet, some
of the Fathers establish two categories of purity—one spiritual and one
biological—when addressing Christian women. And, with the exception
of Hippolytus and Jerome, all their discussions of woman's menses return
to the gospel story of the hemorrhaging woman of twelve years' issuance
found in Mark 5, Luke 8, and Matt 9. However, when one compares this
woman with the menstruant a problem arises: the woman of the gospel
is pathological *not* menstrual. As we will see, this rhetorical move parallels ancient understandings about menstruation. The boundaries between the pathologically ill woman and the menstruant can be collapsed;
ancient medical authors, followed by church fathers from Dionysius to
Gregory I, considered menstruation an illness.[4] This categorization permits the Fathers to employ this story as the intertext by which they can
legislate for or against the menstruant.

When Hippolytus and Dionysius execute canons shunting the
menstruant from sacramental life, are they perceiving woman's flux as a
malady or impurity? Or both? The complete absence of explanation
regarding Hippolytus's canon indicates a cultural norm or understanding
regarding the menstruant. Dionysius, also embracing the same cultural
assumptions a few decades later, substantiates his canon with the gospel
story, which in turn leaves no room for questions. And in their respective
desires to institute coherent and cohesive rituals, both men formalize a
boundary around the pure church, a boundary not to be transgressed by
menstrual blood. Pollution cannot commune with Christ Jesus: the two
are grossly incompatible. And, in a century in which rapid expansion and
solidification of hierarchy in the church are taking place, these men offer
another argument against women's performing official functions for the

---

3. All citations of Dionysius are from the extant fragments in vol. 6 of the Ante-
Nicean Fathers series. Hereafter citations will be by fragment numbers and chapters
contained within. See Dionysius, *Extant Fragments* (ed. A. Roberts and J. Donaldson;
ANF 6; Grand Rapids: Eerdmans, 1884).
4. See Ellens, this volume.

church: biology becomes one more weapon in the arsenal men employ. Biology determines the discourse that defines female interaction in the third-century church.[5]

Within the past fifteen years, using the history of medicine, feminists have exposed how medicine and society form a circle of mutual interchange and dependence when theorizing about women. Medicine influences society just as society influences medicine. Thus, the history of medicine and natural philosophy, indeed, serve as more than a heuristic device. They expose the cultural assumptions—the foundations upon which Hippolytus and Dionysius construct the Christian menstruant as inferior and as unfit for baptism or receiving the Eucharist.

Medical and natural philosophical discourses become the tools by which I unearth the archaeology of menstruation. This archaeology reflects my work as a historian of theology as I search to get behind these two canons to find the foundations of ancient Christian understandings of female physiology. This essay will first outline ancient medical theories about menstruation and how these theories about woman and her body affected her interaction with pagan religions.[6] I will then examine Hippolytus's and Dionysius's canons against this background in correlation with the writings of other early church fathers.[7] In the end, we will witness how these two men created a taboo in their move to deny women the opportunity to commune with the Divine.

The "Way" of Women

Ancient medicine always equated the female somatic experience with inferiority. Gynecological treatises primarily concerned themselves with woman as reproducer, how the uterus "frequently" contracted diseases, and as Dean-Jones has shown, how the social affected the empirical.[8]

---

5. See De Troyer, this volume.
6. I will not deal directly with Judaism in this chapter. The chapters preceding this one more than amply deal with menstruation in ancient Judaism. My primary concern here is these two canons viewed through the lens of ancient medicine, which is predominantly written by pagan authors.
7. Cf. Roll, this volume.
8. Lesley Dean-Jones, "Menstrual Bleeding according to the Hippocratics and Aristotle," *TAPA* 119 (1989): 178. King explains the term *gynaikeia*, "which can mean women's sexual organs, menstruation, women's diseases, or therapies for these diseases." Menses itself is also called *ta hôraia* (ripe things), *hê physis* (nature), or *ta kata physin* (the natural things). See Helen King, *Hippocrates' Woman: Reading the Female Body in Ancient Greece* (New York: Routledge, 1998), 23, 29. Hippocrates, *Mul.* 1.20; 1.58; 3.230; *Coac.* 511; *Superfoetation* 34; *Aph.* 5.39; *Epid.* 1.19; 6.8.32; 7.123.

From the fifth century B.C.E., doctors and natural philosophers posited that the body consisted of four elements in descending order—fire, air, water, earth—which, in turn, instilled the body with four primary qualities: hot, cold, wet, dry.[9] Doctors and philosophical groups as diverse in their doctrines as Anaxagoras, Pythagoras, Aristotle, Plato, the Stoics, and the Epicureans all espoused this theory as the basic principle of human life.[10] In this construction, the male body, the first point on the continuum of positive and negative, consisted of the highest elements, fire and air. Thus, it was warm and dry. At the opposite side of the spectrum, water and matter (earth), cold and wet, constituted woman. The writings of the Hippocratic authors (fifth century B.C.E.) equate woman with this cold wet nature. The authors believed that woman's spongy flesh explained this inherent wetness and that she was one tube, from mouth to vagina.[11]

Because of this wet nature, women did not sufficiently absorb nourishment; in compensation, a healthy woman menstruated heavily (about a pint) for two to three days monthly.[12] Empedocles (fifth century B.C.E.), like the Hippocratic writers, believed that menstruation purified the womb through the release of blood and that women bled at the waning of the moon.[13] Hippolytus writes that Pythagoras equated the father

9. In his *Horatory Address to the Greeks,* Justin Martyr attributes Empedocles with introducing this notion (see 1.5).

10. William W. Fortenbaugh et al., eds., *Theophrastus of Eresus: Sources for His Life, Writings, Thought, and Influence* (Leiden: Brill, 1992), vol. 2: frgs. 331b; cf. Hippolytus *Haer.* 7.17.

11. King, *Hippocrates' Woman,* 27–28. The writers also stated that a woman would experience a sore throat before the onset of her period because of this "one tube"; see ibid., 28.

12. Ian M. Lonie, *The Hippocratic Treatise "On Generation," "On the Nature of the Child," "Diseases IV"* (New York: de Gruyter, 1981), 8; *Mul.* 1.6. The Hippocratic writers, followed by Aristotle, believed the entire uterus filled with blood during the month. One author claimed that a healthy woman lost "two Attic kotlys," or about one pint monthly (*Mul.* 1.6; 1.78). Five hundred years later, Soranus also agrees with this amount (*Gyn.* 1.20). All citations of Soranus come from the Temkin translation: Soranus, *Gynecology* (trans. O. Temkin; Baltimore: Johns Hopkins University Press, 1956). Also see Helen King, "Bound to Bleed: Artemis and Greek Women," in *Images of Women in Antiquity* (ed. A. Cameron and A. Kuhrt; London: Croom Helm, 1983), 135–36; King, *Hippocrates' Woman,* 30; Dean-Jones, *Women's Bodies,* 88–94.

13. Martin R. Wright, *Empedocles: The Extant Fragments* (New Haven: Yale University Press, 1981), frgs. 57(65), 58(67). Cf. Soranus also states that Diocles believed similarly (*Gyn.* 1.21). Parmenides is perhaps the only writer who attributes menstruation to nature hotter than man's (Aristotle, *Part. an.* 2.2.647b29–31). All citations from Aristotle are from Jonathan Barnes, ed., *Aristotle: The Complete Works* (Princeton: Princeton University Press, 1982).

with hot, dry qualities and the mother with cold, wet (*Haer.* 1.11). In the medical philosophical writings of Aristotle—who frequently adopted and adapted the Hippocratic theories of generation—woman's cold, wet nature produced a residue, menstrual blood, a quasi-semen that "needs working up to purify it" (*Gen. an.* 1.20.728a26–29). Aristotle concluded that woman, because of her coldness, lacked the ability to concoct semen; he defined woman qua woman as a deformed male (*Gen. an.* 1.20.728.16–29; 4.1.7.765b1 ff.).[14] Although recognizing the menses as essential to woman's health, Aristotle, following the Hippocratic writers, pathologized menstruation (*Hist. an.* 7.2.782b7–9).[15] Considered generally unhealthy, menstrual blood was considered to be an unused but necessary sustenance and was also thought to be the matter from which the fetus formed during conception (*Gen. an.* 1.18.725a1 ff.; 1.19.727b ff.). From the earliest Greek writings, menstruation, then, becomes a paradox: unhealthy in general but healthy for women and necessary for conception.

The theory that menstrual blood derived from a pathological imperfection continued in the Hellenistic and Imperial eras and in the medical and philosophical treatises of Roman-Hellenic authors—it continued to be viewed as both healthy and unhealthy at the same time, a concoction of coldness and unabsorbed food. Herophilus, the great anatomist of third-century Alexandria, believed that the menses were healthful to women who were "meager and pale, who later on after menstruation have a good color and are well nourished." Although therapeutic for women, menstrual blood was considered harmful to those who came into contact with the substance (Soranus *Gyn.* 1.27–29).[16] Theophrastus, following his mentor Aristotle (and other Peripatetics), attributed all things in the uterus to menses, which subsequently contributed only a formless matter to conception.[17] And in the Hellenistic and Imperial eras, authors start describing menstrual blood as something more, as quasi-magical, dirty, and potentially polluting. The Greek Sophist Aelian, in his *Nature of Animals*, bluntly asserted that woman is definitely polluted; he even collapsed the boundaries between certain women

---

14. Galen, often reiterating the Hippocratic authors and Aristotle, claims that women are imperfect creatures, functionally mutilated (*On the Affected Parts of the Body* 14.2.296 ff.).

15. King, "Bound to Bleed," 112–33. Cf. Dean-Jones, "Menstrual Bleeding," 177–92.

16. Other than this quotation inside Soranus, we have virtually no comments by Herophilus regarding menstruation. Cf. Dean-Jones, *Women's Bodies,* 250; Heinrich von Staden, *Herophilus: The Art of Medicine in Early Alexandria* (Cambridge: Cambridge University Press, 1989), 299–300.

17. Fortenbaugh et al., *Theophrastus of Eresus,* frgs. 376a, 376c, 377.

and animals (*Nat. an.* 1.54). In his treatise *Greek Herbal,* Dioscorides, writing in the first century C.E., registered the duality associated with menstrual blood: it affected infertility and eased maladies such as gout (2.97).[18] Writing later in that century, the great Roman encyclopedist Pliny classified menstruation as a "pernicious mischief which occurs in greater quantity every three months." Often reflecting earlier Greek viewpoints (and popular conceptions), Pliny wrote that menstrual blood has the ability to kill, maim, rust steel, drive dogs insane, and dim mirrors, and from its presence, a "horrible smell fills the air." Thus, the negative recorded, he continued that this blood is a matter of generation (*Nat.* 7.15.63–67).[19]

From the second century C.E., a more sober explanation of the menses can be found in the master treatise of the famous doctor Soranus of Ephesus: *Gynecology,*[20] which might have been known to Hippolytus since his contemporary, Tertullian, esteemed Soranus as a "most accomplished authority in medical science" (*An.* 6). Writing in Rome, Soranus explained that menstruation was called *katharsis*: "excreting blood like excessive matter, it effects a purgation of the body" (*Gyn.* 1.19). Calling menstruation the first function of the uterus, Soranus believed that menstrual blood cleansed the woman (*Gyn.* 1.28; 3.6). He asserted that "those women have menstruated in right measure who after the excretion are healthy, breathe freely, and are *not perturbed*" (*Gyn.* 1.21, emphasis added).[21] Lastly, he averred that menstruation was natural but harmful for all and was only helpful for conception—menstruation was cathartic, cleansing, but not healthy (*Gyn.* 1.27–29). While variation between authors can be identified, one constant remained throughout six hundred years: the cold, wet, female somatic experience renders woman

---

18. For quotations from Dioscorides, see Robert T. Gunther, *Dioscordies: Greek Herbal* (trans. J. Goodyer; New York: Hafner, 1959); cf. Howard Clark Kee, *Medicine, Miracle, and Magic in New Testament Times* (Cambridge: Cambridge University Press, 1986), 44.

19. Celsus, also in the first century C.E., as von Staden points out, contrasts the Hippocratic writers when in describing female genitalia, he "consistently uses associations which suggest 'impurity and . . . the ascetically disagreeable.'" Celsus parallels the vagina with the man's anus. Cf. von Staden, *Herophilus,* (274–79); King, *Hippocrates' Woman,* 89.

20. Ann Ellis Hanson, "The Medical Writers Woman," in *Before Sexuality: The Construction of the Erotic Experience in the Ancient Greek World* (ed. D. M. Halperin, J. J. Winkler, and F. I. Zeitlin; Princeton: Princeton University Press, 1990), 32. Cf. Dean-Jones explains that medical interest in the phenomenon of menstruation declined in this period (*Women's Bodies,* 349).

21. Soranus reports that a woman bleeds more in the spring (*Gyn.* 1.22). Clement of Alexandria agrees (*Paed.* 1.6).

inferior, and this inferiority is evidenced by her bleeding. Menses is cathartic, but it is unhealthy and, therefore, pathological. It is impure by nature, unconcocted because of insufficient heat, magical, and dangerous, and regardless of all these negatives, it contributes matter to generation, nourishes the fetus in utero, and actually becomes breast milk.

The Practice of Everyday Life

How did such medical theories affect everyday life in ancient Greece and Rome? Do literature and religion reflect this notion of woman as lesser and unclean, ailing because of blood discharges? While classical authors do not frequently, if at all, correlate menses and pollution, the later Greek writers Heliodorus, Porphyry, and Achilles Tatius, as von Staden pointed out, "display awareness of the notion that menstrual blood has polluting effects."[22] In his *Leucippe et Clitophon*, Achilles Tatius (no earlier than the second century C.E.) speaks of how two lovers cannot unite because the woman had her period and cannot be approached (4.7.7–9). In a very recent analysis, Ann Carson has shown how the woman of mythology—and by assumption and construction, a woman living in ancient Greece—was often understood to be malleable, leaking and flowing, her matter mutable, transgressing all boundaries.[23] The need to distinguish boundaries in the ancient Greek world might be best summarized by Plato, who had registered the significance of distinguishing boundaries—of filtering, sifting, winnowing, separating better from worse—a separation transacted through purification (*Soph.* 226A ff.). Moreover, many nonmedical writers, including epigraphers, of the ancient Mediterranean, employed the same language for ritual purity and purification as medical writers used regarding the bodily evacuations of pus, vomit, menses: *kathartic/katharos*.[24] The mystery cults, along with the cults of Artemis (the pure virgin) and Apollo, affixed stringent boundaries to ensure temple purity. But, it is the Oriental cults, moving westward during the Hellenistic era, that instilled a heightened sensitivity toward temple and ritual purity. A fragment of Theophrastus couples

---

22. von Staden, "Women and Dirt," 14.
23. Ann Carson, "Dirt and Desire: The Phenomenology of Feminist Pollution in Antiquity," in *Constructions of the Classical Body* (ed. J. I. Porter; Ann Arbor: University of Michigan Press, 1999), 77, 79. Cf. King, *Hippocrates' Woman*, 94. Aristotle writes that what is wet is not determinable by any limits of its own and that cold unites things (*Gen. corr.* 2.2.329b29–31).
24. von Staden, "Women and Dirt," 15. Cf. Hippocrates, *Morb. sacr.* 148:55 ff.; Soranus, *Gyn.* 1.19.

physical and mental purity as requisite for all people sacrificing to a god.[25] During this time, purity from menses began to appear as a condition for entering the sanctuary of non-Greek cults.[26] Inscriptional evidence illustrates this elevated concern with bodily function and female fluidity. A second-century B.C.E. inscription from the temple of Isis, Sarapis, and Anoubis, in ancient Megalopolis, explicitly states, "Let the one who wants to sacrifice enter the temple precincts, purified (*katharizonta*) on the ninth day after childbirth, on the forty-fourth day after an abortion; on the seventh day after menstruation; seven days after bloodshed; on the third day after (eating) goat and sheep."[27] As Dale Martin shows, Plutarch speaks of purity in the discourse on medicine (*Is. Os.* 351e–384c).[28] Plutarch himself explains, citing Plato with regards to purity, that "no surplus left over from food and no excrementitious matter is pure and clean" (352d). (Menstrual blood was considered *both* leftover food and excrementitious matter.) Similarly, an extant stele (second or third century C.E.) from the cult of Mens, the Phrygian god of the moon, in the Attic region, reads: "No one impure (*akatharton*) is to enter, but let them be purified from garlic and swine and women. When members have bathed from head to foot on the same day they are to enter. And a woman, having washed for seven days after menstruation. And (likewise) for ten days after (contact) with a corpse."[29]

In these examples, female impurity seems contained and confined to the individual; however, the biological fluids manifested in the female uterus are a cause for exclusion from sacrificing. Woman, not man, seems

---

25. Fortenbaugh et al., *Theophrastus of Eresus,* frg. 584a. Epictetus states that since the gods are pure, men have a tendency to be pure and clean when approaching them (*Diatr* 4.10). Selvidge inaccurately claims that un/clean as a category "had little presence" in Greco-Roman culture (Marla J. Selvidge, *Women, Cult, and Miracle Recital: A Redactional Critical Investigation of Mark 5:24–34* (Lewisburg, Pa.: Bucknell University Press, 1990), 72, 74.

26. Robert Parker, *Miasma: Pollution and Purification in Early Greek Religion* (Oxford: Oxford University Press, 1983), 101–2.

27. G. J. M. J. Te Reile, "Une Nouvelle Loi Sacreé en Arcadie," *BCH* 102 (1978): 325–31. I am greatly indebted to John Kloppenborg for bringing these inscriptions to my attention. Shaye Cohen claims that Greco-Roman cults did not as a rule regard menstruation as a source for impurity that had to be distanced ("Menstruants and the Sacred," 287). Perhaps this is true of some cults, but the sacred laws from other Oriental cults in Greece and Rome might suggest otherwise.

28. Dale Martin, *The Corinthian Body* (New Haven: Yale University Press, 1995), 157.

29. G. H. R. Horsley, ed., *New Documents Illustrating Early Christianity: A Review of the Greek Inscriptions and Papyri Published in 1978* (North Ryde, Australia: Macquarie University, 1983), no. 6, 920–21.

"singularly susceptible" to impurity predominantly because of her repro-ductive parts.[30] If von Staden is correct—that medical terminology and religious language coincide—we find how the medical impinges on the religious: in the medical, *katharsis, katharos*; in the ritual, *kartharizonta, akatharton*. Emissions from the uterus—lochia or menstrual blood—are defined as impure, polluting agents. These two inscriptions, separated by centuries and differing sacred laws, signify the belief that menstrual blood, caused by a biological process, is a pollutant for woman.[31] For over four hundred years (and well into the Common Era), fears of pro-faning the temple persisted. But, no allusion or equation of (im)mortality and menses exists in these inscriptions. Regardless, the seeping menstru-ant, impure by lack of physical integrity, which medical writers deny her because of her cold, wet nature, must not touch the sacred.[32] And these notions will quickly seep into the nascent church.

The Enigma That Is Hippolytus

The controversial Hippolytus was born c. 160 C.E. Reputedly a pupil of Irenaeus, Hippolytus calls himself a high priest in the very first pages of his *Refutation of All Heresies* (*Haer.* 1.1). The early church historian Eusebius does not grant him such a title, simply pronouncing Hippoly-tus as "head of a church somewhere" (*Hist. eccl.* 6.20).[33] As a presbyter under Zephyrinus, bishop of Rome (197–217), Hippolytus finds himself at odds with the bishop and his contingent over christological issues. Calling Zephyrinus an "ignorant, illiterate individual," Hippolytus undertakes writing his polemical *Apostolic Tradition* in response to "inno-vation" in Roman Church practice (*Haer.* 9.6).[34] Fracturing the Church

---

30. G. H. R. Horsley, ed., *New Documents Illustrating Early Christianity: A Review of the Greek Inscriptions and Papyri Published in 1979* (North Ryde, Australia: Macquarie University, 1987), 110. Cf. von Staden, "Women and Dirt," 20. Dean-Jones posits that the prohibition against the new mother and child was probably to prevent a death in the sanctuary since both were in danger during and immediately after parturition (1994: 246).
31. See De Troyer, this volume.
32. Ibid.
33. All citations from Eusebius's *Ecclesiastical History* are from Eusebius, *Ecclesiastical History* (trans. R. J. Deferrari; New York: Fathers of the Church, 1953). Cf. Jerome, *Vir. ill*, 61.
34. All citations of the *Refutation of All Heresies* (*Haer.*) come from Hippolytus, *Refu-tation of All Heresies and Fragments* (ed. A. Roberts and J. Donaldson; *ANF* 5; Grand Rapids: Eerdmans, 1884). The text of the *Apostolic Tradition* that has reached moder-nity is, as Mitchell explains, a maze since neither the text nor the content is secure. See Leonel L. Mitchell, "Development of Catechesis in the Third and Fourth Century:

of Rome with his teachings on the Trinity and subsequently disenfran-
chised by the majority, Hippolytus sought the bishop's seat at Zephyrinus's death. When the people chose Calixtus, a former slave, Hippolytus
entered into another theological debate with his enemy—the "impostor
and knave"—disputing the orthodox stance regarding penance (*Haer.*
9.7). According to some modern scholars, it was at this point that his
followers named him the antipope.[35] In the 220s, Hippolytus penned
several treatises, most importantly his *Refutation of All Heresies.* During
the persecutions of 235, Hippolytus, along with Pontianus, then bishop
of Rome, entered the catalog of saints.

   The Apostolic Tradition begins with an appeal to apostolic authority, to
the traditions of the Roman Church (*Trad. ap.* 1.1–1.4). Under these
auspices, Hippolytus sets to paper an elaborate process for the person
seeking conversion to Christianity. After outlining the roles of various
church members, he begins a section on the catechuminate (the time
between decision to convert and actual baptism) with an extensive list of
candidates to be denied outright: no painters, actors, charioteers, harlots,
"sodomites," eunuchs, and only *some* female concubines (*Trad. ap.*
16.9–16.25). The person who wishes to become a Christian must rely on
a sponsor, someone who will vouch for his or her decision and reasoning
(*Trad. ap.* 16.1–16.2). Three years of instruction begin, during which
time the catechumens are segregated from the faithful, the women from
the men (*Trad. ap.* 17.1; 18.1–18.2).[36] Just prior to Paschal, the Sunday
Easter celebration, the clergy assess whether these people lived according

---

From Hippolytus to Augustine," in *The Faithful Church: Issues in the History of Catechesis* (ed. J. H. Westerhoff; Wilton, Conn.: Morehouse-Barlow, 1981), 50; A. F. Wallis,
The Latin Version of Hippolytus' Apostolic Tradition (ed. F. L. Cross; StPatr 1,1; Berlin:
Akademie Verlag, 1957), 157. While the text itself has little influence on later Roman
practice, it finds a secure position in the East—in languages as various as Coptic, Arabic, Greek, and Ethiopic—and in the "Church Orders": the Egyptian *Apostolic Church
Order* (c. 350 C.E.); the Arabic *Testamentum Domini* and *Canons of Hippolytus*; the
Ethopian *Canons of the Apostles.* See Dix, *Apostolic Tradition,* xxxvii; Geoffrey J. Cuming, *Hippolytus: A Text for Students/With Introduction, Translation, Commentary, and
Notes,* 2nd ed. (Bramcote, England: Grove Books, 1987), 5. Lastly, many scholars have
questioned the validity of his chain of apostolic practices; Hippolytus is inaccurate and
adds his own inventions to the text. Gregory Dix, *The Treatise on the Apostolic Tradition of St. Hippolytus of Rome, Bishop and Martyr* (London: SPCK, 1969), xxxvii;
Henry Ansgar Kelly, *The Devil at Baptism: Ritual, Theology, and Drama* (Ithaca, N.Y.:
Cornell University Press, 1985), 82.
35. Cumings claims that this title was inappropriately given to Hippolytus by J. J. I.
Dollinger in 1853 (*Hippolytus,* 5).
36. Tertullian decries heretics who do not separate the faithful from the catechumens
but makes no mention of male/female segregation (*Praescr.* 41).

to Christian mortality (*Trad. ap.* 20.1), and the sponsor again bears witness (*Trad. ap.* 20.2). From that moment, with the catechumens now assembled with the *electi* (the elected), daily exorcisms occur until, finally, the bishop conducts an exorcism to guarantee personal purity, *katharos* (*Trad. ap.* 20.3). If the bishop finds a demon still possessing a person, he will "put him aside because he did not hear the word of instruction with faith" (*Trad. ap.* 20.4). On Thursday, each person will bathe, and "if a woman be menstruous, she shall be put aside and baptized another day" (*Trad. ap.* 20.6). No other extant early baptismal liturgy explicitly denies the menstruant. Is the menstruant impure, ill, dirty?[37]

Since this canon exists without a frame of reference, perhaps Hippolytus's other works can elucidate why he dismisses this woman. In the *Refutation*, he describes the heretic Simon Magnus and his allegory of paradise conceived as a quasi-womb of the world. In his description of that "world" uterus, Hippolytus tells the story of Simon recapitulating Soranus's and Galen's anatomical writings on woman's uterine cavity (*Haer.* 6.9). Expounding on the Valentinian system of the emanation of the *æons*, he explains the procreative attributes of Sophia (divine wisdom) as a "formless and undigested substance" (*Haer.* 6.25). Aristotle, Herophilus, Soranus, and Galen (to name but a few in a linear fashion) all consider menstrual blood to be the formless and undigested substance of generation; it is the formless matter/material acted upon by sperm, the nourishment for the fetus, the substance for breast milk. In his attack on the Sethians, Hippolytus rails against their interpretation of the incarnation, an interpretation set in generative language that, through his rhetoric, appears in the language of pollution: defiled womb, impurity of womb, polluted and baneful womb. He condemns the Sethian idea that during the incarnation the Spirit, becoming a serpent, enters the womb of the Virgin. He concludes, explaining the belief that the Word, "after the foul mysteries of the womb, went forth" (*Haer.* 5.14). Regardless of his vitriolic denial of such "perversion" of doctrine, the language that frames his disputation betrays an implicit disgust for the female soma, for the activities of the womb. Although Hippolytus makes no comment on the substance of generation as nourishment or breast milk, the force

---

37. In 1957, Werblowsky posited a correlation between the person still possessed and the menstruant. Thirty years later, Cohen, in a footnote, addressed this question and concludes no correlation can be found. Cf. R.K. Zwi Werblowsky, "On the Baptismal Rite According to St. Hippolytus," in *Studia Patristica* 2:2 (ed. Kurt Aland; Berlin: Akademie-Verlag, 1958), 93-105; Shaye Cohen, "Menstruants and the Sacred," n. 56. I am inclined to disagree with Cohen, if only because the terms used for the possessed resembles that of menstruation and ritual purity.

of Hippolytus's rhetoric illustrates not only his knowledge of ancient medical theories about women's physiology but also his apparent detestation of matter/menstrual blood, the agent of those mysteries, and thus, by definition, menstruation itself. In the chapter "On the Doctrine of Truth," Hippolytus explains how God created the world, man, and woman from the primary elements (fire, air, water, earth). He then avers that angels are of fire, "and I maintain that female spirits are not present with them" (*Haer.* 10.29). Ancient medical understandings resonate through this statement: man is hot; woman is cold. Thus, cold (and wet) women would not be among the fiery, male angels. These passages illustrate an extensive knowledge of ancient medical theory about woman's body, all implicitly used to deny her access to baptism, to entering into communion with God.

Returning to baptism, Hippolytus explains the power of the water in his *Discourse of the Holy Theophany*. Hippolytus begins the treatise by explaining that the most exquisite gift (from God) is the element water, "for with water all things are washed and nourished, and cleansed and bedewed"; he calls baptism the fountain of "life," a fountain that "gushes with healing" (*Theo.* 1.7). Indeed, he is not alone in equating baptismal water with healing; his contemporaries Clement of Alexandria and Tertullian both agree. Tertullian even calls the water pure in itself, endued with "medicinal virtue through the intervention of the angel" that cleanses the spiritual and corporeal alike (*Bapt.* 3, 4).[38] Thus, the Christian world of Hippolytus valued both the religiously cleansing and medicinal powers of water. Like ancient medical authorities before them, physicians of the third century often prescribed bathing for illness; in the etiology of balance/imbalance prevalent in most ancient medical schools, baths helped to restore a person's elemental constitution to a perfect balance (Celsus, *On Medicine* 1.3.4).[39] With the church fathers, the idea is the same, but the language has changed: the bath, baptism, restores the soul, not the elements, through the body. As Hippolytus explains, the water, concomitant with the Holy Spirit, cleanses the individual internal spirit through the external soma (*Theo.* 8). But can the menstruant wash?

Henry Kelly has posited that perhaps the most likely reason for this canon is that Hippolytus, writing in "bath-conscious" Rome, did not "wish the baptismal water or fountain to be fouled by the candidates'

---

38. Cf. Clement, *Paed.* 1.2; 1.6. Tertullian claims the "authority of water," the material substance that governs terrestrial life acts as agent likewise in the celestial (*Bapt.* 4). All Fathers equate baptism with the remission of sins: Justin, *Dial.* 14.1.2; Irenaeus, *Haer.* 3.12.2; Cyprian, *Epid.* 58.

39. Cf. Dale Martin, *Corinthian Body*, 139–62.

bodies."[40] Pliny corroborates the notion that menstrual blood could foul water; he claims that it is poisonous to the touch and that when a tarlike mixture, bitumen, covers the Dead Sea, only a thread soaked in this blood "can draw it asunder" (*Nat.* 7.15.65–68). The menstruant could invariably poison the bath. From a medial perspective, Soranus stated that it was safer for a woman not to bathe during her period, especially on the first day (*Gyn.* 1.26).[41] If most women bleed for at least three or four days, as Soranus and the Hippocratics before him report, they might not cease purging until the Easter celebration. They would not be able to wash away the (physiologically) impure and possibly poisonous residue since Hippolytus's catechumens did not bathe again prior to the baptism. As we have seen, Hippolytus's argument seems to come directly from ancient medical and popular understandings of the body and, therefore, requires no explanation. And since baptism involves direct contact with the sacred, the menstruant, the profane woman (in a situation akin to pagan ritual), must be interdicted from touching the holy. For as Hippolytus's contemporary Origen claims, the unclean is common, and the holy must be separated from it (*Hom. Lev.* 5.11.8; cf. Acts 10:15).

Hippolytus's understanding, rooted in ancient medical assumptions of woman's cold, wet, and blood-filled body, seems then to lie behind his banning of the menstruant from baptism. Even the symbolism and actual ritual of baptism cannot escape the cultural assumptions about woman's formless seepage. Hippolytus directly contrasts with his contemporary in Africa, Tertullian, who in refuting heretics asks: "Apertures in the lower regions of man and woman . . . why are they not regarded as outlets for the cleanly discharge of natural fluids?" (*Res.* 6.1).[42] The medical and socioreligious ideologies constructed around woman's body and its purgations become religiously coopted, theologized, by Hippolytus. Only the pure can go forth into the baptismal ritual, pure in body (and mind), and Hippolytus does not consider woman's flux as clean or *katharos* (similar to the possessed person) in accordance with medical understanding and the Greco-Roman culture of his day. These forces

---

40. Kelly, *Devil at Baptism*, n. 18.
41. Clement reports that women are to bathe for the health and *cleanliness* (men should only bathe for health), but he does not mention whether they should abstain during their periods (*Paed.* 3.9).
42. But even so, Tertullian registers the inferiority of the female somatic experience when he continues that "woman, moreover, have within them receptacles where human seed may collect; but are they not designed for the secretions of those sanguineous issues, which their tardier and weaker is inadequate to disperse?" (*Res.* 61).

collide and collude against Hippolytus's menstruant. His thought is not entirely Christian. It is representative of the world in which he resides, influenced and affected by variegated forces that reaffirm the normative body—the hot, dry, unleaking and, therefore, superior male. And if woman cannot be baptized on that Sunday, she cannot go forth to the ultimate act of that day, to her First Communion. Even when she is admitted into the community of Christ, she is still denied.

Dionysius and the Holy of Holies

Dionysius does not speak about the baptism of the menstruant. Instead, he answers the question of whether a menstruant can enter the church edifice after she has received baptism. Unlike Hippolytus, an enigmatic figure in the ancient and modern world, much is known about the life of Dionysius. Eusebius gives us ample information about him. Born to pagan parents, he converted to Christianity and became a pupil of Origen in Alexandria. He presided over Origen's catechetical school prior to Bishop Heraclas's death, and in 247 he ascended to the bishop's seat of perhaps the only organized church in Egypt (*Hist. eccl.* 6.29; 6.35).[43] Caught in a scandal for fleeing the Decian persecutions, Dionysius exerted much energy refuting criticisms from other bishops and clergy (*Hist. eccl.* 6.41; 6.45; 7.11).[44] A prolific letter writer, Dionysius displayed great concern for the various ecclesiastical issues confronting Christianity throughout the empire and, concomitantly, exhibited a vast knowledge of pagan literature. Eusebius reports that Dionysius died "in the twelfth year of the reign of Gallienus (264 or 265), having held the episcopate at Alexandria for 17 years" (*Hist. eccl.* 7.28).

Dionysius's disputation on the status of the menstruant appears in a response letter to the bishop Basilides amid issues regarding fasting, marital intercourse, and nocturnal emissions (frg. 5). Of the three canons concerning "sexual pollution," he denies only one group access to the *ecclesia*: menstruants. The married couple, for Dionysius, can judge for themselves (frg. 5, canon 3). Men who experience nocturnal emissions, through the "testimony of their own conscience," can enter: "In these things, therefore, let every one who approaches God be of good conscience and of proper confidence so far as his own judgment is concerned" (frg. 5,

---

43. C. Wilfrid Griggs, *Early Egyptian Christianity: From Its Origins to 450 C.E.* (Leiden: Brill, 1990), 67. That the church was organized but not always unified is attested by the fragments of Dionysius's epistles "To the Alexandrians" and "To Hierax, A Bishop in Egypt." Cf. Eusebius, *Hist. eccl.* 7.22; 7.21.
44. Griggs, *Early Egyptian Christianity*, 86.

canon 4). Uncleanness or impurity is not a factor, only a sound conscience, "proper confidence." He simply repeats the prerequisite for men offered by his predecessors Clement and Origen.[45] The rational male mind can decide issues of physical integrity. However, Dionysius does not grant such an option to the menstruant; he writes:

> The question touching women in the time of their separation, whether it is proper for them when in such a condition to enter the house of God, I consider a superfluous inquiry. For I do not think that, if they are believing and pious women, they will themselves be rash enough in such a condition either to approach the holy table or touch the body and blood of the Lord. Certainly the woman who had the issue of blood 12 years' standing did not touch the Lord Himself, but only the hem of His garment, with a view to her cure. For to pray, however a person may be situated . . . are exercises altogether blameless. For the individual who is not perfectly pure both in soul and in body, shall be interdicted from approaching the holy of holies. (frg. 5, canon 2)[46]

The tone and language of this canon is harsher than the one addressing the ejaculant. The passage begins by offering women the ability to do the righteous and "pious" thing and ends with an unequivocal prohibition. This very prohibition raises the question of why Dionysius does not make the same option for rational choice available to women.

In another fragment, Dionysius states that the brain—and therefore reason—rules the "citadel," while vice and virtue emanate from the heart (frgs. 2.4; 4.11). While ancient authors disputed whether reason and intellect were situated in the head or heart, Dionysius favored neo-Platonic philosophy, which located reason in the head.[47] Galen of Ephesus

---

45. Clement, *Strom.* 1.1; Origen, *Hom. Lev.* 5.3.4–5; *Comm. Matt.* 11.12. On causes for nocturnal emissions, see Galen, *On the Affected Parts of the Body* 7.6; cf. David Brakke, "The Problematization of Nocturnal Emissions in Early Christian Syria, Egypt, and Gaul," *JECS* 3 (1995): 419–60.

46. Cf. Matt 9:20 ff.; Luke 8:43 ff.

47. Plato, *Tim.* 45. Among the pre-Socratic authors, Alcmaeon, Hippon, and Anaxagoras all list the brain as the seat of the intellect. Aristotle, Diocles, and Praxagoras all place it in the heart. See James Longrigg, *Greek Rational Medicine: Philosophy and Medicine from Almaeon to the Alexandrians* (New York: Routledge, 1993), 58–59. Pythagoras believed the intellect was in the head (Diogenes Laertius, *The Lives of the Philosophers* 8.18). The Stoics and Epicureans alike chose the breast/heart: see Cicero, *On the Nature of the Gods* 1.15; Lucretius, *On the Nature of Things* 115 ff.; Julia Annas, *The Hellenistic Philosophy of Mind* (Berkeley: University of California Press, 1992), 61–62. Hein has explained that one way the Alexandrians understood

believed that the rational pneuma (life-giving soul) resided in the brain, the passions in the heart.[48] One Hippocratic author asserted that there is a natural sympathy between the womb and the intellect.[49] As noted earlier, Soranus had stated that one sign that a woman has bled the appropriate amount was that she is "not perturbed" (*Gyn.* 1.21).

Does Dionysius, then, consider woman's rational faculties inferior or flawed, allowing her to be ruled by the passions from which vice flows? Could woman's body affect her reasoning? In accord with his ancient predecessors and virtually all his peers, Dionysius likely assumed, as did Soranus, that a woman was "perturbed" during her menses. According to the Hippocratics and Aristotle, woman's wet, spongy body could affect her mental faculties (she is more emotional) and make her more vulnerable, more susceptible to impurity. For Aristotle, woman's inferior, cold body caused her to be more cunning and devoid of shame and respect.[50]

In classical Greece, the term *hysteriokos* simply meant "uterus"—the physical organ from which *all* female diseases flow forth. In early Christian writings, the term came to signify a lack, or shortcoming, "a defect that must be removed so that perfection might be attained"; furthermore, the term had moral implications.[51] By late antiquity, the term in its cognate form, *hysterema*, had come to denote "deficiency or defect," as the writings of Irenaeus, Hippolytus, *and* contemporary medical writers attest.[52] This deficiency in women, located in and caused by the uterus, often left a woman in a more vulnerable position, a vulnerability to which her mind might fall prey. She was, after all, defined by her defective, formless matter.

---

the symbolic nature of the Eucharist was through the Platonic concept of reality and symbol. See Kenneth Hein, *Eucharist and Excommunication: A Study in Early Christian Doctrine and Discipline* (Frankfurt: Peter Lang, 1975), 311.

48. Margaret Tallmadge May, ed., *Galen on the Usefulness of the Parts of the Body* (Cornell Publications in the History of Science; Ithaca, N.Y.: Cornell University Press, 1968), 45. For an excellent analysis of ancient pneuma (soul), see Dale Martin, *Corinthian Body*, 7–38. As Martin accurately asserts, *pneuma* is considered throughout all society as the "life-giving material for the members of the body" (p. 22). Unlike the modern Cartesian dualism of body/soul, this material was not thought of as a separate entity from the body.

49. Hippocrates *Mul.* 1.38. Cf. Dean-Jones, *Women's Bodies*, 75.

50. Maryanne Cline Horowitz, "Aristotle and Woman," *Journal of the History of Biology* 9 (1976): 209; cf. Dean-Jones, *Women's Bodies*, 244. Aelian, likening the polluted woman to an animal, implies woman's irrationality (*Nat. an.* 1.54).

51. *Hermas* 13.1; *T. Benj.* 11:5; Cf. Arndt and Gingrich, *Greek-English Lexicon*, 849.

52. Hippocrates, *Loc. hom.* 47. Cf. Irenaeus, *Haer.* 1.31.2; Hippolytus, *Haer.* 4.14.7; King, *Hippocrates' Woman*, 213; Paula Fredrickson, "Hysteria and the Gnostic Myths of Creation," *VC* 33 (1979): 287–88.

In regard to woman as *matter*, Dionysius himself (like the Stoics, Epicureans, and Plato) tells us that matter is *generated*: it is opposite to God: impressible, mutable, variable, alterable (frg. 5). As Carson has shown, this impression of matter, corresponding with wetness, finds expression in the medical writers of antiquity; matter, like wetness, does not maintain boundaries; it is mutable, variable, leaking.[53] Woman, as the diametrical opposite of the hot, dry male, is formless to man's form, unbound to his bound, impure to his pure. The deficiency, then, of the uterus might be its inability to control fluidity; women will bleed—and according to the ancients, bleed heavily—and she might do so inside the church. A resonance with Plato's theory of the importance of distinguishing boundaries seems clear (*Soph.* 226a ff.). But why can woman not simply rely on her conscience like the male? The answer seems simplistic: a woman's level of rational ability is determined by her *lack* of physical integrity.[54] And, as Clement reports, sin is irrational (*Paed.* 1.13). For Dionysius, entrance was irrational, a "superfluous inquiry" (frg. 5, canon 2).

Dionysius solidifies his argument through an appeal to the gospel story of the hemorrhaging woman, which also reflects ancient medicine. In his invocation of this story, Dionysius, while slightly more literal than Origen, employs a reading almost identical to that of his mentor.[55] In his *Homilies on Leviticus*, Origen had written that the woman was not bold enough to touch Jesus' flesh because she had not yet been made pure (*Hom. Lev.* 4.8.1); but in his *Commentary on Matthew*, Origen simply repeats the gospel story and notices that others sought to *touch* Christ directly (*Comm. Matt.* 11.7). Dionysius, however, varies from his predecessors and contemporaries outside of Alexandria, particularly Irenaeus and Tertullian. In *Against the Heresies*, Irenaeus mentions this woman but makes no pronouncement regarding purity (*Haer.* 2.23). Tertullian tells this story to show how Christ "desired not only that this woman should touch Him, but that He should heal her." He continues, declaring that since her touch would not contaminate Christ, she correctly assumed he was beyond "all possibility of pollution by an uncleanness." Tertullian, reading this story appropriately, states that this woman did not fall under

---

53. Carson, "Dirt and Desire," 77–79. Cf. Aristotle, *Gen. corr.* 2.2.329b26–33.

54. In the *Republic*, Plato allows for women to achieve the same virtue as men, their respective differences being strength and childbearing; however, in the *Timaeus*, he claims that women are evil-men reborn into that body (*Resp.* 454d–e; 456a; *Tim.* 42, 90).

55. Hein, *Eucharist and Excommunication*, 327.

the prohibitions for the menstruant in Lev 15 (*Marc.* 4.20).[56] For Dionysius, the idea of contaminating Jesus never arises; instead, he concerns himself with what he believes to be the *correct* reading of this miracle story. Informed by medical theory, Dionysius *can* employ this story of the hemorrhaging woman as parallel to a menstruant: both she and the menstruant—following the rationale of the Hippocratics, Aristotle, and Soranus—are unhealthy. Perhaps Dionysius fears that women might read or hear this healing story as a liberating example. Thus, his invocation would demonstrate how the issuing woman exemplifies restraint. If the hemorrhaging woman did not touch his body, then menstrual women should not assume to touch it now.

Indeed, direct Jewish sources appear to have provided little, if any, support for Dionysius's canon. Although Shaye Cohen posits that this canon is a transference of "temple terminology," he also asserts that the exclusion of the menstruant from the synagogue occurred several centuries after this canon.[57] Even if this canon is resonant with Judaism (and *not* derived directly from it as some have posited), Dionysius, as Charlotte Fonrobert states, does not reason from Lev 15.[58] Instead, the prohibition of the menstruant seems more aligned with the pagan cults of the ancient East, of which the Egyptian cult of Isis, Sarapis, and Anoubis is one: only the purified menstruant can enter. But in contrast to the sacred laws of the Hellenistic cults, in the Christian church of Alexandria, men are no longer excluded for any reason; the church excludes only women who commit a sin. And although Dionysius writes extensively on matters of orthodoxy and orthopraxy, he was not known for his innovations.

Ancient medicine (subsequently appropriated by the Fathers) appears to undergird Dionysius's canon on the menstruating woman. Woman's body *can* rule over her. Dionysius takes this notion a step further: it now appears implicit that a woman's rational function *does* need protection from her very own body. This protection equates to a need for guardianship, a guardianship only the male and rational (unperturbed) mind can provide. Dionysius's canon echoes with the words of Clement a few

---

56. Tertullian acknowledges this woman's uncleanness but only to show Christ's inability to be contaminated and that she was not under the Levitical law for menstruants.

57. Shaye Cohen, "Menstruants and the Sacred," 288–89.

58. Charlotte Fonrobert, "The Woman with a Blood-Flow (Mark 5.24–34) Revisited: Menstrual Laws and Jewish Culture in Christian Feminist Hermeneutics," in *Early Christian Interpretation of the Scriptures of Israel* (ed. C. A. Evans and J. A. Sanders; Sheffield: Sheffield Academic Press, 1997), 136n. 36.

decades earlier, words exhorting both male and female to enter the church pure in body, pure in mind, fit to pray before God (*Paed.* 311). Clement, however, had made no pronouncement regarding the menstruant. Again, Dionysius simply takes his predecessors' thoughts a step further; his only originality appears to be his decisiveness on this issue. Nonetheless, the groundwork had been laid by Clement and Origen. Dionysius's entire discourse flows most directly from the thoughts and words of these two prolific authors of Alexandria: Clement and Origen.

The Creation of Taboo

The canons of Dionysius and Hippolytus lend us insight into the marginalization of woman in the early church and to the source of that marginalization. But that source is *not* where most feminist researchers have assumed. Many feminists who have engaged Dionysius's canon level the accusation that he simply continues from Judaic practice or Levitical law. And with regard to Hippolytus, studies of him and his *Apostolic Tradition* remain the domain of men; feminists rarely address his canon. Judaic praxis, I have argued, had little if anything to do with the development of menstrual taboos; rather, the biological assumptions of classical medical theories form the foundation of Hippolytus's and Dionysius's positions on women. Traditional medical theories on woman as cold, spongy, defective, and irrational *are* the cultural assumptions upon which these men formulated their canons. The Hippocratics and Aristotle pathologized menstruation, Pliny made it magical, and Soranus claimed the menses was unhealthy. Together these theories formed a composite picture of the female body as inferior to the male soma. Woman's biology, issuing forth, cannot only influence her mind and affect the entire world within her reach, but it can potentially sully the sacred.

And as the early church writers came to view *all* corporeality as negatively encoded, woman could not escape categorization as the very embodiment of somatic expressions. Menstrual blood unquestionably informs the discourse. And, in the third century of the Common Era, the menstruant finds herself outside the body of the church even before she enters, unable to commune formally and publicly with her God. Inside and outside the ecclesial walls, she could not function in positions of power. Hippolytus and Dionysius and their peers may have formulated the Christian menstrual taboo, but they did not perpetuate it. Like all taboos, it became embedded in the very paradigm of the culture that created it. In the West, for example, the taboo lays beneath the influential *Penitential of Theodore,* written in the late seventh century, which punishes the menstruant seeking to enter the church with a penance of fasting for three days (1.14.17).[59] In the East, the medieval Byzantine canonist Theodore Balsamon observes that "the uncleanness of menstruation banished the deaconess from her role at the holy altar," discontinuing a position established in the early church.[60] Through the canons of Hippolytus and Dionysius—one believed to be from Rome (the West) and one from the East—the pathologized, unclean body of woman, constructed by medicine, dangerous in popular ideology, and impure in ritual, stands opposed to the pure body of Christ, the church, and thus must remain outside. The female body is stigmatized.

---

59. *The Penitential of Theodore* was issued over and against Gregory I's papal decision in favor of the menstruant that was established less than a century before. Cf. Gregory, *Epistle* 10.64.
60. Phipps, "Menstrual Taboo," 300.

7

The Old Rite of the Churching of Women after Childbirth

Susan K. Roll

> My mother had ten children in the course of the 1920s and 30s, and after each of the first few births she went to have the rite of the blessing after childbirth done. Then at one point my father, who understood Latin, read the text of the rite and was outraged. He declared to her, "You're not going to submit to that anymore."

This testimony from a Belgian woman echoes the witness of women now in their seventies, eighties, and nineties who remember the rite of the blessing, or "churching," of women after childbirth. This "pious and praiseworthy custom" in the words of the Tridentine Roman ritual, a ceremony with no officially obligatory character, had remained fairly consistent in its ritual structure, gestures, and symbolic actions from the High Middle Ages until the mid-twentieth century. It fell into disuse by the early 1960s and disappeared in its traditional form in the liturgical reforms of the Second Vatican Council.

A wide gap exists between the way in which liturgical historians describe the intended purpose and meaning of the rite and its purpose as perceived by the women themselves. Over the centuries theologians and pastors have insisted that the true purpose of this rite was a voluntary expression of thankfulness on the part of the mother, explicitly excluding any motif of "purification." Yet a strong consensus existed among women that it was intended precisely as a ritual purification, as if something contaminating and ungodly had occurred in pregnancy and childbirth. This serves as a fascinating case study in pastoral liturgy that testifies both to the persistence of folk belief and to the perceptive awareness of ordinary worshipers of the original intention of a rite.

This is a revised version of Susan K. Roll, "The Churching of Women after Childbirth: An Old Rite Raising New Issues," *Questions Liturgiques/Studies in Liturgy* 76 (1995): 206–29.

A diachronic examination of its ritual shape—readings or psalms, gestures, actions—together with extant interpretations of the rite by (exclusively male) theologians and liturgical historians, sheds light on a number of striking and often unsavory ways in which women's bodies, women's relation to their church communities, and the act of giving birth to a child were perceived. The issue reflects very clearly the global shift taking place in all aspects of theology and ecclesial praxis from women and women's bodies as objects—in this context, objects of pastoral/sacramental care—to women as persons, subjects, and agents of liturgy, and to affirming the goodness and holiness of their bodies.

Childbirth and Ritual Impurity in the Early Church

Several sources for the Eastern churches attest to the practice of forbidding new mothers access to the worshiping community, but a few other sources indicate a firm refusal to continue the practice.

Origen's homily VIII on Lev 12–13, which deals first with the purification of women after childbirth and then with the isolation of lepers, reveals that the Judaic law in Leviticus remained a topic of discussion and apparently a source of ongoing norms in the early Christian church. Seeking to find foreshadowings of New Testament elements in the Old, Origen argues first that the apparent superfluous expression in Lev 12:2, "When a woman conceives and bears a male child" (that is, one could only bear a child as a result of conceiving), points ahead to the Virgin Mary's unique miraculous conception of Christ without male semen, implying that purification is required for all other mothers who can only conceive via sexual intercourse (NRSV).[1]

Origen then poses the question of why a woman who "provides a service" for the world in giving birth to a child should be considered unclean and must make propitiatory sacrifice to God for her purification. He says cryptically that there must be some secret, hidden reason why she must bring a sin offering of two doves. He declares that all birth in the flesh results in impurity and cites proof texts from the Hebrew Bible that indict all humanity of having been born in filth and sin: Job 14:4, Jer 20:14–15; and Ps 51:5. Yet in these passages the original text is not a doctrinal formulation, but rather a cry of pain and lament arising from unbearable guilt from deeds later in life.[2]

---

1. English text from Gary Wayne Barkley, *Origen: Homilies on Leviticus 1–16* (FC; Washington, D.C.: Catholic University of America Press, 1990), 154–59.
2. Barkley, *Origen*, 154–59

While no outlines of a possible Christian rite for purifying new mothers can be extracted from Origen's sermon, one can see an interesting crossover taking place. In Hebrew thought, on the one hand, the need to maintain cultic purity resulted in laws that enforced a temporary isolation of the new mother from the community, while sexual intercourse as such remained a holy act. The presuppositions characteristic of Greek philosophical dualism and Christian ascetic tendencies, on the other hand, presented a fundamental baseness and defilement of human flesh in contrast to the spirit, particularly in the act of generation and birth in the flesh. In the early church this inherent defilement of the flesh extended to the very ontological condition of being born female.

The logical consequences in pastoral practice of the evolution of a negative attitude toward birth in the flesh and to mothers who give birth are reflected in the passage in the *Canons of Hippolytus* (mid-fourth-century Egypt).[3] Canon 18 includes the attending midwife in the purity prescriptions but seems to shift the frame of reference between her and the new mother:

> The midwives are not to partake of the mysteries, until they have been purified. Their purification shall be thus: if the child which they have delivered is male, twenty days; if it is female, forty days. They are not the [to?] neglect the confinements, but they are to pray to God for her who is confined. If she goes to the house of God before being purified, she is to pray with the catechumens who have not yet been received and have not been (judged) worthy to be accepted.

> The women are to be separated in a place. They are not to give the kiss to any man.

> The woman who has given birth stays outside the holy place forty days if the child which she has borne is a male, and if it is female, eighty days. If she enters the church, she is to pray with the catechumens.

> The midwives are to be numerous so that they may not be outside all their life.[4]

---

3. No reference to giving birth or new mothers appears in the *Apostolic Tradition of Hippolytus,* an earlier edition of the *Canons of Hippolytus* dated by scholars to the first half of the third century.

4. Paul Bradshaw, ed., *The Canons of Hippolytus* (trans. C. Bebawi; Alcuin/Grow Liturgical Study 2; Grove Liturgical Study 50; Bramcote, England: Grove Books, 1987), 20. This passage replicates the *Trad. Ap.* 18–19a with regard to catechumens,

Several points to notice here follow. (1) The midwife as well as the delivering mother is considered in need of purification, which implies that she has been contaminated by contact with the blood and the placenta. Yet a pastoral note recommends that there be enough midwives so that each one is not in effect cut off permanently from the community. (2) As in Leviticus, the period of impurity is doubled if the baby was a girl, although the overall period is shorter, and the doubling is the rule also for the midwife. (3) The requirement that the new mother and the midwife remain among the catechumens if they are not yet purified indicates that they were not absolutely prohibited from attending worship. Yet this provision makes clear that giving birth, or assisting at a birth, somehow temporarily nullified her baptism, so that her status was equivalent to those who were not yet "found worthy" of baptism. A parallel exists in the Roman custom of relegating members of the Order of Penitents to a separate section in the assembly, as were the catechumens in this period.

If "purification" is interpreted in this text as "bathing," canon 35 puts the provision in sharper contrast: "The Christian is to wash his hands each time he prays. He who is bound by marriage, even if he rises from beside his wife, he is to pray because marriage is not impure and there is no need of a bath after second birth, except for the washing of the hands only, because the Holy Spirit marks the body of the believer and purifies him completely."[5] Apparently the ambivalence associated with childbirth runs so deep that even the definitive purification by the Holy Spirit in baptism has its limits.

One further note in the *Canons of Hippolytus* states briefly that "a presbyter, when his wife has given birth, is not to be excluded."[6] Since this statement does not appear in the *Apostolic Tradition*, perhaps a question needed to be settled concerning whether the impure state of the wife who had given birth extended to her husband in his service at the altar, considering that worship by the mid-fourth century had taken on a more highly ceremonial character.[7]

Dionysus, bishop of Alexandria, witnesses to the widespread practice in his day by which women who were "impure" (*akathartoi*) due to

---

though the *Apostolic Tradition* makes reference to the segregation of all women within the assembly with no special mention of new mothers or midwives. Bradshaw observes, "The same distinction between the periods of time required for purification after the birth of a male or female child continues to be observed in later Coptic practice."

5. Bradshaw, *Canons of Hippolytus*, 29.
6. Ibid., 16.
7. Ibid., 16 (canon 8). See Schultz, this volume.

menstruation had to stand in the vestibule of the church, specifically in an area reserved for penitents. The bishop expresses admiration for these women and cites canon 44 of the Synod of Laodicea (ca. 365) to the effect that new mothers are not to participate in the "pure mysteries" for a period of forty days. They are still permitted to pray, but only by standing outside the church and listening to the psalms.[8]

Several early witnesses indicate the opposite attitude—that baptism and incorporation into the new covenant annulled the legal prescriptions of the first covenant. The third-century Syrian *Didascalia* argues that those who had converted from Judaism to Christianity should no longer follow the legal prescriptions concerning cultic purity (ch. 26). The Holy Spirit is not absent from them when they would be cultically unclean according to Hebraic law. If they still believe they are unclean, they are denying the power of their baptism and of the Spirit.[9] The *Apostolic Constitutions* (ca. 375) similarly repudiates the necessity of adhering to the Mosaic law once one is baptized.[10] Both texts refer to menstruating women and not to postpartum mothers as such.

A strikingly strong statement in favor of permitting new mothers to attend church as soon as they liked appears in a letter purportedly written by Pope Gregory the Great (+604) in response to Augustine of Canterbury, in a discussion of appropriate pastoral strategy for evangelizing the tribes of England.[11] The author cites the Leviticus text, then argues that if a new mother wanted to go to church immediately after the birth to give thanks, she should not be prevented from doing so. The sin involved has to do with concupiscence, not with the pain of childbirth, which was the curse pronounced upon Eve. If church leaders stopped a woman from entering, they would be indicting her personally of that guilt: "Si itaque enixam mulierem prohibemus ecclesiam intrare, ipsam ei poenam suam in culpam deputamus" (If therefore we were to prohibit a woman from entering the church, we would impute guilt to her because

---

8. "Canonical Epistle of Dionysius Bishop of Alexandria to Bishop Basil," canon 2 (PL 10:1281–1284).
9. See R. Hugh Connolly, ed., *Didascalia Apostolorum* (Oxford: Clarendon, 1929).
10. F. X. Funk, ed., *Didascalia et Constitutiones Apostolorum* (Paderborn, Germany: Schoeningh, 1905), 1:373.
11. *Decima interrogatio Augustini*, followed by *Responsio beati Gregorii papae* (PL 77:1193–1198). According to Müller, the letter was probably written in 731 by Nothelm, later archbishop of Canterbury. See Michael Müller, *Die Lehre des Hl. Augustinus von der Paradieselehre und ihre Auswirkung in der Sexualethik des 12. und 13. Jahrhunderts bis Thomas von Aquin* (Regensburg, Germany: Pustet, 1954), 36n. 10.

of the punishment itself).[12] With regard to menstruation, his position is that women cannot be prohibited from receiving Communion during their period; however; if a woman chooses not to do so out of "great veneration," this is praiseworthy. This suggests that negative associations still hung over the discharge of blood caused by childbirth and menstruation, although the decision was left to the woman herself in her own conscience. The underlying rationale, as the author explains further, is that the Old Testament purity prescriptions dealt with exterior matters; the New Testament, with interior, according to Matt 15:11.

The Medieval Period

Oddly enough, while the above citation from (Pseudo-)Gregory appears in the penitential books from the eighth century, which originated in Ireland and were distributed on the Continent, these reference texts for tariffed penance declare further that women who have given birth may not enter a church. To do so incurs a penance of forty days.[13] Almost all of the medieval penitential books, of which some seventy dating from 600–1200 are extant, stipulate that a woman during her menstrual period as well as a new mother is cultically unclean and may not enter a church or receive Communion. Popular belief supposed that loss of blood attracted the devil.[14]

The *Bigotian Penitential* draws an analogy between the testing of gold in fire and the necessity of the mother's purification after childbirth according to Leviticus. The text echoes Origen's argument concerning purification and the symbolism of the time period: the "seventh day" represents the present age, while the "eighth day," the day of circumcising a male child, points to the future time of perfection; as a result of the son's circumcision, the mother is immediately made clean. Further, in accord with Origen, the time periods symbolize a man who, at the

---

12. PL 77:1194. The Latin text translates to: If therefore we were to prohibit a woman from entering the church, we would impute guilt to her because of the punishment itself. A text variant in two copies reads "in culpam duplicamus."
13. For example, the *Iudicia Theodori* 42 (early ninth century) forbids women from entering a church before they have been purified ("ante mundum sanguinem post partum") and requires forty days' penance if they do so. See Hubertus Lütterbach, "Holy Mass and Holy Communion in the Medieval Penitentials (600–1200): Liturgical and Religio-Historical Perspectives," in *Bread of Heaven: Customs and Practices Surrounding Holy Communion. Essays in the History of Liturgy and Culture* (ed. C. Caspers, G. Lukken, and G. Rouwhorst; Liturgia Condenda 3; Kampen, Netherlands: Kok Pharos, 1995), 67 and n. 35.
14. Lütterbach, "Holy Mass," 78, 79.

Last Judgment, is found worthy because of "manly" resistance to sin, while a man who was "remiss and effeminate" in his actions needs twice as much time to be purified. The *Bigotian Penitential* thus implies that the circumcision of the male child effects the purification of the mother on "the eighth day," in the "pure future world." Nothing is said about a female child or the double length of time.[15]

The *Penitential of Cummean* prohibits intercourse after the birth of a child, for thirty-three days if the child was a boy and fifty-six (not sixty-six) days if it was a girl, but attaches no penance.[16] The *Penitential of Bede* mandates the Levitical requirement for purification, differently if the child is a boy or a girl, but does not impose a penance for failure to do so.[17]

The *Canons of Theodore*, ascribed to the Greek monk Theodore, bishop of Canterbury, and dating from circa 700, is the basis of the regulations found in many of the penitentials. These stipulate that a new mother who reenters the church before her purification period of forty days is completed incurs a penance of three weeks' fasting, the same as a woman who enters a church while menstruating. Here the forty days was the same if the child was a girl or a boy. This reflects a custom that by this time was common in the East, partly due to the influence of the false *Acts of the Council of Nicaea.*[18]

In Germanic sources the first indication of a period of sequestration followed by an injunction to come to church immediately thereafter appears in the ninth century. Otfried, the Frankish author of the poem *Krist,* prescribes that the mother should bring the (male) child to church at the close of the forty-day period, much as in Leviticus.[19]

Extant material from the thirteenth century shows evidence of both mutually contradictory attitudes. The *Decretum of Gratian* (1174)

---

15. Ludwig Bieler, ed., *The Irish Penitentials* (Dublin: Dublin Institute for Advanced Studies, 1975), 200–201.
16. Pierre J. Payer, *Sex and the Penitentials: The Development of a Sexual Code 550–1150* (Toronto: University of Toronto Press, 1984), 25.
17. Ibid., 27.
18. Ibid., 25; and Marian Wisse, "De kerkgang van de moeder na de geboorte van een kind," (unpublished doctoral qualifying paper, Utrecht, 1984), 104–5. Kottje, cited by Wisse, indicates that while it would be easy to attribute the West's introduction to an Eastern custom to Theodore, in fact Irish texts of the sixth century, such as the *Liber ex lege Moysi,* present the Levitical law as normative. See Raymund Kottje, *Studien zum Einfluss des Alten Testaments auf Recht und Liturgie des frühen Mittelalters (6–8 Jh)* (Bonner Historische Forschungen 23; Bonn: n.p., 1970).
19. Adolph Franz, *Die Kirchlichen Benediktionen im Mittelalter* (Freiburg i.B., Germany: Herder, 1909), 219; Peter Browe, *Beiträge zur Sexualethik des Mittelalters* (Breslau [now Wroclaw, Poland]: n.p., 1932), 25.

repeated the position of (Pseudo-)Gregory that new mothers should not be barred from attending church.[20] Similarly, Pope Innocent III had written to the archbishop of Armagh in 1198 that the Levitical law was no longer binding on new mothers and that they were not prohibited from attending church. Yet if a woman chose to stay away for a period of time, she should not be reprimanded.[21] The 1227 synod of Trier stipulated that a new mother should not be denied "reconciliation" with the church even immediately after childbirth, though she was not obliged to commence sexual relations for a period of forty days after the birth. The use of "reconciliation" (*reconciliari*) tends to suggest a distancing from the worshiping community with overtones of negativity.[22] The synod of Cambrai, 1310, instructed church leaders not to purify ("sacerdotes mulieres non purificent") new mothers before a month had passed due to danger of death.[23]

Commonly if a woman had died in childbirth, she was not buried in the church cemetery, yet the synods of Rouen in 1074 and Cologne in 1279 countermanded this policy in favor of giving women who had died before churching a normal burial.[24] At a later period rites existed for the compensatory blessing of the body, which would make a church burial possible.[25] Thus an ambivalent attitude prevailed—Christian women were not held subject to the old Mosaic law because it had been superseded by the new covenant in Christ, yet a powerful perception lingered that childbirth represented a fearful mystery with negative or diabolical potentiality of its own.

20. *Decretum of Gratian* D5, c. 1–2; see Browe, *Sexualethik des Mittelalters*, 26. Wisse cites several others who reiterate (Pseudo-)Gregory's position, including Pope Nicholas in his 866 letter to the Bulgarians ("De kerkgang van de moeder," 108).
21. *Epistles I* 63; see Browe, *Sexualethik des Mittelalters*, 26. Ranke-Heinemann adds that the following year Pope Innocent placed all of France under an interdict because of the French king's invalid marriage. While permitting infant baptisms, the pope explicitly forbade the churching of new mothers (Uta Ranke-Heinemann, *Eunuchen voor het hemelrijk: De rooms-katholieke kerk en seksualiteit* [Baarn, Netherlands: Ambo, 1990], 26; Uta Ranke-Heinemann, *Eunuchs for the Kingdom of Heaven* [New York: Doubleday, 1990], 26).
22. Franz, *Die Kirchlichen Benediktionen*, 218; see also Wisse, "De kerkgang van de moeder," 8; Ranke-Heinemann, *Eunuchs*, 25.
23. Franz, *Die Kirchlichen Benediktionen*, 218.
24. Browe, *Sexualethik des Mittelalters*, 20; and Ranke-Heinemann, *Eunuchs*, 25.
25. One example, found in the Prague *Enchiridion Rituum* of 1716, relates how the deceased mother is brought to the church door. After reciting the antiphon "Si iniquitates" and the "De profunctis," the priest lays the stole on the deceased and leads the body into the chapel with the words "Ingredire in ecclesiam Dei, ut vivas cum Deo in saecula saeculorum." See F. Schubert, "Liturgie und Volksgebrauche," *Theologie und Glaube* 22 (1930): 137–49.

In the East the ritual for the reintroduction of a new mother to the church after a certain period, which can be traced back to the early church, was widespread and had an explicitly obligatory character. According to the *Acts of the Council of Nicaea*, which originated in Egypt, both parents and the baby were to present themselves at the altar. The priest offered a prayer of purification over the mother and a blessing for the baby and then baptized the child. In the Greek church of the Middle Ages, the rite of churching the mother was seen as offering prayer to neutralize the stain caused by conception and birth. The priest would meet the mother and baby in the narthex of the church. Following prayers of praise identical to those that close the daily office, the priest would pray over the mother: "Cleanse her from every sin and from every stain, so that she may be able to share in the sacred mysteries without fault." After blessing the child, the priest would say a further prayer over the mother, invoking Jesus to "wash her of the stain of the body and the contamination of the soul at the close of these 40 days."[26] Then the priest would carry the child forward into the church; the mother would follow. In this Greek ritual the joyful entrance into church is that of the child, not the mother who simply trails behind. A male baby is carried right up to the altar, while a female child is only carried as far as the doors separating the altar from the nave. In case of miscarriage or abortion the woman was required to do penance to atone for the death of the fetus, whether deliberate or accidental, before the act of purification could take place.[27]

The *Manual of Sarum* includes a "Blessing of the mother after birth," which takes place at the church door. The purification motif lies in the ritual placement (beginning outside the church, the priest then leads her in) and symbolism (she kneels at the steps holding a lighted candle, and the priest sprinkles her with holy water). The text used is a prayer of thanksgiving after a safe delivery.[28]

The earliest extant texts of Germanic origin for a blessing after childbirth were used during the priest's pastoral visit to the home and date only from the eleventh century. The rite does not appear in all the handwritten texts from this period. This blessing was administered to the new

---

26. Franz, *Die Kirchlichen Benediktionen*, 220–21.
27. Ibid., 222–23.
28. Natalie Knödel, "Reconsidering an Obsolete Rite: The Churching of Women and Feminist Liturgical Theology," *Feminist Theology* 14 (1997): 111. According to the *Manual of Sarum*, the marriage ceremony also began at the church door (p. 113). J. Wickham Legg, ed., *The Sarum Missal, Edited from Three Earlier Manuscripts* (Oxford: Clarendon Press, 1916, repr. 1969), 413n. 2.

mother in her sickbed, eight days following the birth, and bears the imprint of a blessing of the sick, although one text speaks of a cleansing from every contamination of the body: "Benedicere. . . ancillam istam, ut mundes eam ab omni inquinamento corporis celesti benedictione." (Bless this [your] servant . . . that you wash her of all foulness of body by [your] heavenly blessing). The ritual texts commonly use Ps 128 ("Your wife will be like a fruitful vine / within your house"), Ps 67 ("May God be gracious to us and bless us. . . . The earth has yielded its increase"), Ps 113 ("Praise the Lord! . . . He gives the barren woman a home, / making her the joyous mother of children"), Ps 82 ("Rescue the weak and the needy"), or the prologue to the Gospel of John.[29] John Chrysostom in the East and Augustine in the West both attest to the use of various pre-Christian rites and practices at the childbed and in caring for the newborn.[30]

Bringing the new mother to church for the blessing appears in texts of the Latin church beginning only in the eleventh century. A text from eleventh- or twelfth-century Salzburg mentions in the rubrics that the mother comes to church after forty days after bearing a boy, forty-six days after having a girl.[31] After reading Pss 113; 128; and the prologue of John, the priest extends his right hand to the woman saying, "Aufer a nobis, domine, iniquitates nostras" (Take away our sins), which is the same prayer spoken by the priest at the foot of the altar in the Eucharist. The woman, prostrate, repeats the antiphon "Cor mundum" to Ps 51, a psalm of repentance from grave sin. After an Our Father, the priest prays the collect from the Feast of the Purification of Mary and sprinkles the woman. The twelfth-century Ritual of Wessobrunn cites the passage from Leviticus as the rationale for the rite, prays that the new mother be freed "from every stain of sin and every impurity of heart and body," then continues with the prologue to John, Ps 51, and other texts.[32] The twelfth-century Ritual of St. Zeno cites the Levitical passage in its collect, which continues, "Make this your servant worthy, wash [her] from every defilement of the flesh."[33] A shorter twelfth-century text refers to

---

29. Franz, *Die Kirchlichen Benediktionen*, 209–12. Interestingly of the five texts presented by Franz, two invoke Sarah as a model and only one Mary. Quotations are from the NRSV.

30. Franz, *Die Kirchlichen Benediktionen*, 212–13. The specific reference for Augustine is *Civ.* 6.9.

31. *Codex Vindobonensis* 2090. According to Franz, this is probably a copyist's mistake: XLVI instead of LXVI, the Levitical sixty-six days for a girl (*Die Kirchlichen Benediktionen*, 224).

32. *Codex Monacensis* 22039; see Franz, *Die Kirchlichen Benediktionen*, 224–26.

33. *Codex Monacensis* 16401; see Franz, *Die Kirchlichen Benediktionen*, 227.

"your servant, liberated from a share in the nature of women and purified according to the law."[34]

Many of the available formulas are entitled "The Leading of a Woman into the Church" ("Ad introducendam mulierem in ecclesiam," or "inthronisatio," which recalls the blessing of a bride). Occasionally the formula comes under the heading "Ordo ad purificandam mulierem (Order for the purification of a woman)," as in a pontifical preserved at Trinity College, Cambridge. The unusual Wessobrunn text refers directly back to the prescriptions of Lev 12. More usually the reference is to the purification of Mary in the temple (Luke 2:22–39) and uses the collect for the Feast of the Purification.

Unlike in the parallel Greek rite, the mother is the object in the Germanic rite. In fact, the baby might or might not be present, and there is no mention of the father. The widespread usage of *introductio* tends to echo the notion of *reconciliatio*. Both catechumens preceding their baptism and penitents preceding their formal reconciliation with the church on Holy Thursday had to wait outside the church before being personally "introduced" into the church by the priest, who extended his right hand or, in the case of catechumens, the stole. The practice of sprinkling with holy water also suggests cleansing or purifying. This practice was common in ninth-century Frankish-German church communities, before private confession supplanted the practice for penitents.[35]

Both textual material and illustrations depict the churching in central Germany and Austria in the late Middle Ages as a festive occasion, at least for the nobility and wealthier bourgeoisie. The mother might be finely dressed, accompanied by the midwife and an entourage of family and friends. The priest, vested in either alb or cassock and stole, would meet the mother at the church door. She would be holding a lighted candle, reminiscent of the candles carried in procession at the Feast of the Purification. (Someone else would be holding the baby.) He would sprinkle her with holy water, recite the prescribed psalms and prayers, then lead her with his right hand (in some localities with one end of the stole) into the church and up to either the main altar or a side altar. In

---

34. *Codex Lambacensis* 73; see Franz, *Die Kirchlichen Benediktionen*, 226.

35. See Wisse, who cites from a manuscript version of Herman Wegman, *Geschiedenis van de christelijke eredienst in het westen en in het oosten* (Wisse, "De kerkgang van de moeder," 12; cf. Wegman, *Geschiedenis van de christelijke eredienst in het westen en in het oosten*, 137). In the *Manual of Sarum* the prayer that the priest used when leading the woman into the church was the same as for carrying an unbaptized baby into church. See Marion Hatchett, *Sanctifying Life, Time, and Space* (New York: Crossroad, 1976), 88.

some regions further prayers would be said at the altar, then the woman would be blessed and sprinkled again with holy water and perhaps incensed. A universal custom was for the woman to bring an offering to the church: money for the support of the priest or perhaps goods such as bread, a farm animal, candles, or homespun yarn. A variety of additional local customs accompanied the churching, such as the mother's kissing the gospel book or having it laid on her head, giving the baby ablution wine as a foretaste of the Eucharist, and so forth. In France and Italy, as well as some localities in England, the churching combined with a mass, after which blessed (not consecrated) bread, called *purificatio,* was given to the woman.[36] After the churching ceremony a large crowd of family and friends might return to the woman's home for a festive meal.[37]

While in the Western church the churching of women formally retained the status of a custom, by the late medieval period this custom was so deeply entrenched in Germany that it functioned as a religious duty. If a woman said in confession that she had skipped her churching, she would be required to either make it up (if this did not threaten the seal of confession) or to do penance.

The extant documents reveal no special prayer texts for those who had suffered an abortion or miscarriage. They might have been dispensed, although the *Agenda of Schleswig* (1512) says that a woman in this circumstance should be churched, not with a lighted candle in her hand, but an extinguished one. In Cracow the form for a woman who had had an abortion contained first a formal absolution, then the churching.[38] As the dicta of the synods of Rouen (1074) and Cologne (1279) testify, burying in a church cemetery a woman who had died in childbirth met with some resistance. A further issue was whether a funeral for a woman who had died in childbirth could be held in the church without desanctifying the church building due to the flow of blood, since the funeral might take place on the day of death and without a coffin. The matter of churching the body of a woman who had died in childbirth rested in some cases on the superstition that the woman's soul would never enter heaven unless she had been churched. In 1502 a rite appears in the Lammespringe Ritual for the churching of a deceased mother. In some regions another woman underwent the churching as a

---

36. Wisse, "De kerkgang van de moeder," 13–15. According to Franz, blessed bread was also given to a bride after the wedding night (*Die Kirchlichen Benediktionen,* 252).
37. Franz, *Die Kirchlichen Benediktionen,* 223–36.
38. Ibid., 240.

substitute or proxy for the deceased woman.[39] According to the Ritual of Chur, only a married mother had the right to request the rite.[40] If a mother had borne a child out of wedlock, assuming she were allowed to be churched at all, the priest would wear a purple stole to signify her penitence. Further, he would use Ps 51, which speaks of remorse for sin, and would replace the blessing with a prayer of repentance. An unmarried mother was often required to pay a greater offering.[41]

By the sixteenth century, some evolution had occurred. Newer local rituals tended to use shorter prayers for the churching rite, and a shift in emphasis began to take place from purification to thanksgiving for the gift of a child, for the survival of the mother, and for protection. Yet at the same time, in different areas of the European continent, the custom of churching was showing signs of dying out. Reasons for the decline are unclear. Perhaps there was confusion over the meaning of the rite, or perhaps the mothers were reluctant to remain sequestered at home for forty days. (On the other hand, one side benefit of the custom had always been that farm women could legitimately refuse to resume heavy agricultural labor until they had regained their strength.) Texts found in the rituals of Mechelen (1589), Roermond (1599), and Cologne (1614) clearly point to a sharp decline in the custom, but several synods, including Constance (1567), Ypres (1577), Würzburg (1589), and Hertogenbosch (1612), explicitly encouraged women to continue to undergo the rite of churching.[42]

In England the 1549 *Book of Common Prayer* retained the rite with slight modifications under the explicit title "The Order for the Purification of Women," in contrast to the Reformers on the Continent. The

---

39. Franz adds that in the duchy of Schaumberg it was believed that the graves of women who had died in childbirth should be kept separate because women of childbearing age who stepped over such graves were endangered by the aura and might themselves die in childbirth (*Die Kirchlichen Benediktionen*, 241–45). This was also true in Protestant Breslau, modern Wroclaw, until 1713. See also Hugo Hepding, "Das Begräbnis der Wöchnerin," in *Volkskundliche Beiträge: Festschrift R. Wossidlo* (Neumünster, Germany: n.p., 1939), 151–65.

40. Bruno Kleinheyer, Emmanuel von Severus, and Reiner Kaczinski, *Sakramentliche Feiern II, Gottesdienst der Kirche* (Handbuch der Liturgiewissenschaft 8; Regensburg, Germany: Pustet, 1984), 154.

41. Wisse, "De kerkgang van de moeder," 25. According to Valentin Thalhofer, this special rite was in force in München-Freising until 1864. See Thalhofer, "Aussegnung," in *Weber und Welte, Kirchenlexikon* (ed. J. Bergenröther; 2d ed.; Freiburg i.B., Germany: Herder, 1882), 1713. On June 18, 1859, the Sacred Congregation of Rites in the letter "in Wratislavien," declared that unmarried mothers had no right to the blessing after childbirth.

42. Browe, *Sexualethik des Mittelalters*, 28.

1552 edition retitled the rite as "The Thanksgiving of Women after Childbirth, commonly called the Churching of Women" and abandoned the purification motif, although in popular belief a woman remained in a state of impurity after giving birth and was expected to stay secluded. The 1552 rite no longer began outside the church door; instead, the new mother knelt "at a convenient place near the altar," and the ceremony took place at the baptismal font. Also, the woman was no longer required to wear a black veil. By the seventeenth century the churching ceremony provided an occasion for women to gather together with celebration, feasting, and drinking, sometimes to excess. The scale of the feast varied according to one's wealth and social position.[43]

The Roman Ritual of 1614

The new Roman Ritual, which promulgated the reforms of the Council of Trent and was intended to provide a norm for liturgical practice, drew upon source material, which included the old Gregorian Sacramentary and the *Ordo Romanus* as well as fourteen printed rituals, six from Italy and eight from abroad. Of these, the primary source for the rite "De benedictione mulieris post partum" (the blessing of a woman after child-birth) seems to have been the Ritual of Brescia of the reform-minded bishop Domenico Bollani, dating from 1575. The Brescia text departed remarkably not only from past practice but from at least one of its contemporaries in eliminating overt reference to the motif of purification and penance as the rationale for the rite. While the Brescia rite included a requirement for the mother to make a general confession of sins before being sprinkled with holy water, the verbal content of the rite largely shifted the emphasis to expressing the mother's thankfulness for her survival and health. The classic motif of purification was set aside.[44]

The rite in the *Rituale Romanum,* which prevailed from 1614 up until the last books of the old ritual were printed in 1964, indicates in its preface the complete freedom of the mother to come to church by her own choice to express thanks, while calling the churching a "pious and laudable custom." No time period is specified following the birth. By implication the mother is asking the priest for a blessing on her own initiative. Another sign of a new approach is the use of the liturgical color white.

---

43. Knödel "Obsolete Rite," 111–16.
44. Balthasar Fischer, "Das Rituale Romanum (1614–1964): Die Schicksal eines liturgisches Buches," *TTZ* 73 (1964): 261; and Wisse, "De kerkgang van de moeder," 28–33.

The shape and movement of the rite closely resemble its antecedents, however, with the curious change that the mother, while waiting outside the church, is now kneeling, not standing, normally a sign of penitence and submission (as in the *Manual of Sarum*). The priest and a server with aspergillium meet her at the threshold of the church. The woman is holding a lighted candle in her hand. The introductory "Adjutorium nostrum in nomine Domini" (Our help is in the name of the Lord) is followed by Ps 24, also a newer component.[45] Then the priest extends the left end of his stole for the woman to hold and leads her into the church with the words, "Enter the temple of God, adore the Son of the Blessed Virgin Mary, Who has given thee fruitfulness of offspring." The woman kneels at the altar and prays silently, the priest says a Kyrie Eleison, then a silent Our Father; the priest then invokes protection from "the enemy" for her and prays for the woman. The content of the prayer claims that the childbearing of the Virgin has turned the birthing pain of the faithful to joy and invokes the intercession of the Virgin so that the woman who "comes rejoicing" to the temple may inherit eternal life.[46] The priest then sprinkles the woman again and pronounces the blessing.

When one looks a bit under the surface, traces of ambivalence concerning the goodness of childbirth linger in the new rite. The overall movement, in which the woman is dependent upon the priest to fetch her and lead her into the church, remains. The use of Ps 24 can be interpreted several ways: liturgical historians who prefer to emphasize the abolition of the purification motif point to the use of this psalm elsewhere as a psalm of joyful entrance, as if welcoming a king or a conqueror. If so, this might be very affirming for the struggle and victory of the new mother, but it would also represent a novelty in the mentality surrounding sexuality and generativity in the seventeenth century and is not supported elsewhere.[47] However, the antiphon is "This woman shall

---

45. *The Sacerdotale Romanum*, Venice, 1585, inserts Ps 24 following Ps 51 and before a series of psalms of pleading and thanksgiving (Wisse, "De kerkgang van de moeder," 36).

46. Wisse remarks that this text contrasts strikingly with the more common linking of the pains of childbirth with punishment for the sin of Eve ("De kerkgang van de moeder," 38). By virtue of the childbearing of Mary and the new covenant in Christ, which secures the promise of eternal life for those who have died in Christ, the pains of childbirth are turned into joy. This, of course, is a theological template placed over the fact that giving birth is still unspeakably painful for the mother.

47. By comparison, some African cultures greet a new mother upon her emergence from the home as a conqueror in battle or a successful hunter. See Bénézet Bujo, "Feminist Theology in Africa," *Theology Digest* 36, no. 1 (1989): 27.

receive a blessing from the Lord and mercy from her God, her Savior, for she is of the people who seek the Lord," which seems to reiterate vv. 3–5,

"Who shall ascend the hill of the LORD?
    And who shall stand in his holy place?
Those who have clean hands and pure hearts,
    who do not lift up their souls to what is false,
    and do not swear deceitfully.
They will receive blessing from the LORD,
    and vindication from the God of their salvation.

This clearly points back to an underlying motif of renunciation of evil conduct and of purification as prerequisites for "standing in his holy place," literally the church building.[48]

Pastoral Practice up to the Twentieth Century

The introduction and widespread usage of the *Rituale Romanum* did not, however, wipe out local liturgical usage, and many of these texts retained some reference to purification even into the twentieth century, even when the Jewish custom was explicitly rejected. In some cases this occurred by presenting Mary's willingness to undergo the purification rite (and one text from Liege presents Hannah's dedication of her son to God) as the model for what pious Catholic women were expected, if not legally compelled, to do. In several rituals from the Low Countries, when the churching was followed by a mass, it was the February 2 Feast of the Purification of Mary. In Poland, a woman would use for her churching a "thunder candle" (*Matka Boska Gromniczna*), which had been blessed on the Feast of the Purification, also known as the Feast of the "Mother of God of the blessed Thunder Candle."[49] Where Mary was emphasized, a

---

48. Wisse, "De kerkgang van de moeder," 34–37; and Kleinheyer, von Severus, and Kaczinski, *Sakramentliche Feiern II*, 154. Schuck deals with the meaning of Ps 24 in the context of the churching rite as it was understood at this time. See Johannes Schuck, *Der Segen Gottes: Ein christliches Hausbuch von dem kirchlichen Segnungen und Weihen* (Würzburg, Germany: Fränkische Gesellschaftsdruckerei Würzburg Echter, 1939), 282.
49. Sophie Hodorowicz Knab, *Polish Customs, Traditions, and Folklore* (New York: Hippocrene, 1993), 66. The beeswax thunder candles were kept during the year to be lit during thunderstorms as a prayer for safety and at the bedside of someone who was sick or dying to protect the person from the devil's power, as well as for the churching of a new mother. This custom persisted well into the twentieth century among Americans of Polish origin.

clear implication of the themes of purification and freedom from sin prevailed, and the theme of giving thanks was as good as absent.

The accent in the texts and the pastoral material that accompanied them clearly shifted toward giving thanks, however, and this was more marked in the degree to which the Roman Ritual had influenced the local liturgical books. Several French rituals of the seventeenth and eighteenth century provide for some explanation in the vernacular and indicate some pastoral sensitivity to mothers whose child had died. Right up to the mid-twentieth century, to the extent that the rites were in Latin, the woman was unlikely to comprehend what was being said or why. The character of the ritual action was "ex opere operato" (grace flows from the work performed). The choice of one psalm or another, or the content of the blessing text, would have communicated nothing at all to the mother.

Under the influence of the Enlightenment, local rituals and pastoral material in the vernacular took on an often heavy didactic approach. The German texts generally retained the central ritual movement, by which the mother is led into the church on the priest's stole, and occasionally retained the burning candle, sprinkling with holy water, and reference to Lev 12 as the origin of the rite, which would implicitly, though not expressly, restore the purification motif. These texts present Mary as the model of a dutiful mother who dedicated her child to God. The blessing texts themselves tend to be long, wordy, and directed toward impressing upon the mother the gravity of the responsibility she is undertaking in raising a child. The mother is to give thanks to God for the gift of this child, but at the same time she is repeatedly instructed in her duty to raise the child to be a pious, useful member of society. Her promise to do so becomes a constituent part of the rite. Ironically the custom of churching a woman whose child has died is retained, but both the instructional purpose and the modeling after the example of Mary disappear; one can only give thanks that the mother's life was spared. Both mother and child stand under the almighty power of the Father God, who gives life and takes it away; the earthly father of the child is never mentioned. Different psalm choices—notably Pss 84; 100; 103; 121; and 145—express thankfulness and need for protection. For the first time the Magnificat is used. The overall tenor is on the rite as a "teachable moment." However, since the mother is still to be churched even when the child has died, an underlying element of purification seems to remain.[50]

---

50. Wisse, "De kerkgang van de moeder," 71–87; and Kleinheyer, von Severus, and Kaczinski, *Sakramentliche Feiern II*, 154.

Meanwhile, in the Protestant churches, the rite was retained in the earliest ritual texts though with some modifications. Cranmer's 1549 *Book of Common Prayer* retained the ritual: the woman entered the church herself and knelt "in some convenient place"; the priest comes to her, exhorts her to give praise to God for deliverance from the great danger of childbirth, then prays Ps 121, the Lord's Prayer, and a collect that asks God's help that she may "faithfully live, and walk in her vocation according to thy will." Then "the woman that is purified must offer her Chrysome and other accustomed offerings," and if possible, she is to receive Communion. In 1552 the description of the rite was changed from "purification" to "thanksgiving."[51] Martin Luther, influenced by the argument of (Pseudo-)Gregory, tried to convince his people that there was nothing impure about giving birth. Though Luther did not abolish the rite, he worked to transform its character to one of thanksgiving and intercession.[52]

Pious exhortations and explanations of the rite in the nineteenth and early twentieth centuries were at pains to explain it in terms of the spirit of the times. According to one Irish explanation, its roots are still to be found in the need to purify the woman. Carrying the lighted candle is done because candles are carried in procession on the Feast of the Purification. The priest's stole is white because white is the liturgical color for the purification. The woman waits at the threshold of the church because "she thus acknowledges her unworthiness to enter until she receives the blessing of the priest and is introduced by him." The initiative for this rite is ascribed, or perhaps projected onto, women themselves: "A desire of imitating this humility of the Blessed Virgin [i.e., undergoing the Jewish purification practice] induced the custom amongst Christian mothers of abstaining from entering the church for some time after childbirth. They then asked the blessing of the priest at the church door and made their first visit one of thanksgiving to God for their safe delivery."[53]

In nineteenth- and twentieth-century Germany, the rite's original title of *"Aussegnung"* or less commonly *"Hervorsegnung,"* somewhat negative terms that literally meant "blessing-out" (probably denoting "out of the house"), and in southern Germany *"Fürsegnung"* became more simply

---

51. Hatchett, *Sanctifying Life*, 121; and Buttrick et al., *Interpreter's Bible*, 2:61 n.

52. Rudolf Schwarzenberger, "Der Muttersegen nach der Geburt," in *Heute segnen: Werkbuch zum Benediktionale* (ed. A. Heinz and H. Rennings; Freiburg im B., Germany: Herder, 1987), 280.

53. James O'Kane, *Notes on the Rubrics of the Roman Ritual* (2d ed.; Dublin: Duffy, 1868), 245, 249, 251.

"Muttersegnung" (the blessing of a mother).[54] Customs associated with the rite varied greatly in different regions. In the Rhineland the new mother customarily came to church only at twilight and took a place at the back of the church (associated with impurity), less often by the church doors or in the bell tower. The ceremony took place usually at the altar of St. Anne or of the Virgin Mary. She gave a money offering to the sexton or split it among the pastor, sexton, and other ministers. A reception with coffee and cake might follow, organized by women of the neighborhood including the midwife.

Further into the twentieth century when, according to the reports of women themselves, women increasingly refused to undergo the ritual, often at the price of some social pressure, male theologians were deploying extravagant rhetoric to convince women that the blessing had nothing to do with purification but, instead, expressed great praise and honor for women. The deepest meaning of the rite was to be the mother's own personal "feast of light," a feast of the joy that she had been the "workshop" of the miracle of life, ennobled among women with the highest vocation in the reign of God.[55]

The mother's own experience of her churching consisted, according to a male author, in rejoicing that she had survived her most difficult hours, that she was enabled to experience the deepest secret of life, and that on behalf of "nation, family and church she was able to pay an extremely painful but proud and precious tariff;" furthermore, she must now fulfill her duty to raise a God-fearing and socially useful person.[56] While it might happen that a "bad Catholic" who had neglected to fulfill her Easter duty might ask for the blessing in the belief it would bring her good luck, according to a 1933 moral case study, the priest should not refuse to bless her as if refusing the sacraments to a "public sinner" but should explain its meaning.[57] In theory every mother was to make her churching because her heart would be filled with holy joy and happy thanks because God is Lord of all. She may approach his holy place

---

54. Arx calls *Aussegnung* "a more general bestowal of blessing, which can lead to misunderstandings." See Walter von Arx, "The Churching of Women after Childbirth: History and Significance," *Concilium* 112 (1978): 65.

55. Georg Alfes, *Die kirchliche Weihe des Familienlebens* (Cologne: Bachen, 1998), 22–24.

56. Schuck, *Der Segen Gottes*, 281. The present author translates *Volk* here as "nation": "für Volk, Familie und Kirche eine zwar schmerzhafte, aber stolze und kostbare Steuer entrichten durfte." The tone clearly echoes the then-prevalent ideology of the national-socialist period in Germany.

57. E. J. Mahoney, "Moral Cases: Churching a Bad Catholic," *Clergy Review* 5 (1933): 73.

because she is pure and upright of heart. She would remind all Christians of Mary's entry into the temple; however, Christians were told that this rite qua content and goal had nothing to do with the customs of the old covenant.[58]

The most remarkable male theory of the dignity of motherhood from this period calls it the "priesthood of woman" and calls the blessing rite "ordination" (*Priesterweihe der Mutter*). As a wife she already exercises an ennobling priesthood, but as mother her priesthood is of a much deeper and more godly sort: that of influencing the supernatural life of another. In this view motherhood is pastoral care of children, a priesthood to the next generation, and thus the greatest and most holy task a woman can undertake. The entire fate of the Western world rests upon how she performs this duty. As the ordination to this priesthood, no other rite of the church is as "modern and relevant" as the blessing of the mother. Carrying a burning candle symbolizes her desire to be a bearer of Christ; the antiphon of Ps 24 refers to her status among the chosen people; the priest brings her from a kneeling to a standing position because standing is a sign of priesthood; she holds the end of the stole, sign of ordained ministry, the only time when a woman may do so.[59] Here the notion of purification is categorically excluded as "too Old-Testament, too unredeemed."[60]

Apart from stretching the symbolism and reading into the rite a unique and unsupported interpretation, this notion of motherhood as women's priesthood in service of their children conceals some pitfalls. The woman is to serve the husband and children, but the husband does not serve in a similar way. Single or childless women are entirely excluded, and the extension of this paradigm to a parallel between women's lives and the sacrifice of the mass idealizes women's self-sacrifice and suffering in a way dangerously liable to promote exhaustion and to justify exploitation and abuse.[61]

According to these more modern authors, the origins of the churching rite are "absolutely not to be sought" in the purity laws of Leviticus.[62]

---

58. Hugo Dausend, "Der Mutter erster Gang zur Kirche," *BL* 9 (1934–35): 448–50.
59. Norbert Stenta, "Segnung der Mutter nach der Geburt," *BL* 7, no. 1 (1932–33): 193–96.
60. Ibid., 194.
61. See Teresa Berger, "Liturgie und Frauenseele: Die Liturgische Bewegung aus der Sicht der Frauenforschung," *Praktische Theologie heute* 10 (1993): 90–93. Both Stenta and Pius Parsch used the same term (*Priestertum der Frau*) in the same period.
62. Lucas Brinkhoff et al., eds., *Liturgisch Woordenboek* (Roermond, Netherlands: Romen, 1965), "Kerkgang." Just thirty years previously this had been contradicted by

The notion of purification comes from "false opinions and misunderstandings," not from the opinion of the church, since Christ himself had instituted the sacrament of marriage. The priest leads the woman into church in a manner befitting only princes or bishops because of the church's loving understanding of the mother who has just stood between life and death.[63] In a 1964 ritual, published just as the custom had largely died out, the author locates the origins of the rite in a "related practice in the Old Testament":

> It must be understood clearly that the Jews did not say there was actually any stain of sin on the mother in consequence of giving birth to a child, but merely a restriction imposed by law. With Christ's coming, womankind was elevated and ennobled, and motherhood too was more clearly seen as something honorable, deserving a blessing rather than a purification.[64]

Historically speaking this is simply untrue. But the discomfort and embarrassment with the idea of purification on the part of churchmen going back to the time of (Pseudo-)Gregory, on the one hand, and the persistence of the popular belief that in fact this was what the rite was all about, on the other hand, represent an ongoing dichotomy.

Up to this point every piece of data invoked in the research—textual, ritual, explanatory, exhortatory—has originated from men, persons who will never conceive and bear a child. Even casual conversations today with elderly women who remember the rite often touch a raw nerve. These women are likely to report discomfort, confusion, a feeling that they were being insulted, and more importantly a sense that the act of giving birth was regarded by their church as something shameful, negative, and requiring purification. One regularly hears that a woman did her churching after the first one or two babies, then refused to do it following subsequent births. Even with the advent of texts and explanations

---

Ravanat, who claims that the rite certainly did go back to Leviticus. See F. Ravanat, "Della Benedictio mulieris post partum," *Perfice munus* 4 (1929): 738–42.

63. Wilhelm Cleven, *Fragen um Sakrament und Sakramentalien* (Bonn: Borromäus-Vereins, 1949), 34–36.

64. Philip T. Weller, *The Roman Ritual* (Milwaukee: Bruce, 1964), 430. A similar emphatic rejection of the link between churching and purification was made in a 1974 proposed alternative text for the blessing, but what appears instead is a disturbing motif of dependency of the mother upon the "heavenly Father" to fulfill her duty in her weakness, and trust in the Father's motherly compassion: "Sie legt es voll Vertrauen in den Schoß der ewigen Vatergüte . . . was sie in ihrer Schwachheit nicht vollbringen kann." See Paul Wohlmann, *Buch der Segnungen* (Lucerne: Rex, 1974), 79.

in the vernacular, women dared not ask the priest for an explanation of the rite, and usually none was given them. Social pressure in small communities played a role: young women were sometimes pressured by the local pastor or scolded by older women if they did not do their churching. One woman reported that she was led through the deserted streets of her German village to the church, while other village women peeked from behind the curtains to see what kind of shape she was in after childbirth. Little children were shooed out of the church so they would not be exposed to a rite so closely connected with shameful aspects of sex and pregnancy, or so that adults would not need to explain it.[65]

Commonly women themselves explicitly made the connection between the churching rite and purification. Many understood it as a rite "to ask for forgiveness and purification," to restore one's membership in the church community, or to cleanse the sinfulness of sexual contact between man and woman. Women who perceived it as a purification ritual reacted most strongly against it: "It was as if I had committed murder!" A Dutch woman said, "As a child I saw these women go into the confessional, and then I knew that they had had a child. I connected that with Mary the Immaculate Conception. These women had done something which was wrong."[66]

One can only conclude that the shape of the rite itself, its own gestures and movements, and the symbolic elements employed communicated clearly to the women the ambivalence at best, fear and repulsion at worst, of churchmen toward women's sexuality and childbearing. In effect, the rite represented a reverse symbolic birth: the woman is brought into the church holding the stole, which visually resembles a lead or leash, a symbolic unbilical cord in an act of (re-)birth or restoration by the priest into

---

65. See Wisse, "De kerkgang van de moeder," 133–44; and Grietje Dresen, "Het betere bloed," *Mara* 6 (1992–93): 30–31. Kohlschein tells virtually the same story with regard to his own mother ("Die Vorstellung von der kultischen Unreinheit der Frau. Das weiterwirkende Motiv für eine zweispältige Situation?" in *Liturgie und Frauenfrage: Ein Beitrag zur Frauenforschung aud liturgiewissenschaftlicher Sicht* [ed. T. Berger and A. Gerhards; Pietas Liturgica 7; St. Ottilien: EOS, 1990], 283 n. 52). She was churched after the birth of her first two children in 1934 and 1938 because it was the custom and because the local pastor at that time promoted it. She began to question the necessity for the rite after her third child was born in 1939. When the fourth child was born in 1942 and the new pastor saw no value in the rite, she was relieved not to have to undergo it. My informal inquiries among older women in Belgium, Germany, and elsewhere turned up the same pattern, with one sole exception: a British woman who said, "I was happy the church recognized this great thing I had done in giving birth to a child."
66. Wisse, "De kerkgang van de moeder," 135–37.

her rightful place as a baptized Christian within the ecclesial assembly as represented spatially by the church building. The burning candle represented her return from darkness into light, the light of Christ and the church.[67] The use of Ps 24, if the woman understood the text, would say nothing about childbirth but makes a passing reference to clean hands and pure heart as a prerequisite to entering the sanctuary, which women could not do in any case. In the end, women themselves boycotted the rite by individual choice (a fact that mirrored its largely individual and privatized nature), and thus in the mid-twentieth century, not for the first time in history, the rite fell into disuse.

The Vestiges of the Rite

An "Order for the Blessing of a Mother After Childbirth" still appears in the *Roman Ritual De Benedictionibus* of 1984, to be used in case the mother is not present at the child's baptism. The rite of baptism now includes as part of its conclusion a blessing for the mother, then for the father. The separate blessing for the mother after childbirth (no separate rite exists for the father, though a blessing after miscarriage and one for adoption includes both parents together) contains two sets of texts, one if a priest or deacon presides, another if a lay man (*laicus*) gives the blessing. The greeting expresses an uncommonly incarnational theme: If led by a cleric, "May Christ, who became one of us in the womb of the Virgin Mary, be with you all," or if led by a lay man, "Brothers and sisters, let us bless the Lord Jesus, who in the womb of the Virgin Mary became one of us."

The opening exhortation refers back to the baptism which had already taken place, and addresses the mother with a didactic, instructional approach which, as we have seen, originated in the post-Enlightenment period, as well as the theme of thanksgiving: "that you [the mother] will fully recognize the gift you have received and the responsibility entrusted to you in the Church and that, like Mary, you will proclaim the greatness of the Lord. Today we all wish to join with you in glad thanksgiving." The reading is 1 Sam 1:20–28, Hannah's dedication of her son in the temple; alternate readings are 1 Sam 2:1–0 or Luke 1:67–79, the canticle of Zach. The responsorial psalm is Ps 128 including "Your wife shall be like a fruitful vine in the recesses of your home . . . Behold thus is the man blessed who fears the Lord."

---

67. Dresen, "Het betere bloed," 31.

The ritual offers two alternate prayers of thanksgiving: The first uses the themes of thanksgiving and prayer for protection from evil, while the second speaks of God's "welcoming the simple prayers" of those who turn to God, and prays for reassurance of God's nearness and protection. A clerical minister then blesses the mother, using either a simple or a triple blessing, while the formula for a lay minister says simply, "May the tender love of the Father, the peace of his Son Jesus Christ, the grace and strength of the Holy Spirit preserve you to live by the light of faith and to reach the promise of eternal happiness." While the Roman *editio typica* refers here too to the lay minister as male, *laicus*, the English translation speaks of the lay minister "signing himself or herself." A short form is provided which offers 1 Thess 5:18 as another alternate reading.[68]

Here the entire original ritual shape of the blessing of women after childbirth which prevailed for at least ten centuries is abolished. The new rite is comprised entirely by words spoken and read, or perhaps sung. Ritual gesture and movement consists only in the hand motion of blessing. If the new rite is highly logocentric, then at least it has eliminated the ritual elements which in the past spoke directly to women of purification from sin and contamination. But the very fact that such a rite still exists suggests that the church has not yet come to terms with the fundamental subject/object dichotomy embedded in rites designed and led by males (or perhaps led by females according to the forms prescribed by males) to give confirmation and approbation to women's lives. The idea of the normativity of women's dependency for ecclesial validation remains almost untouched.

In the past two decades local groups of women have undertaken creative and highly original symbolization and ritualization processes to express and raise up their lived experiences of God. Blessing as a motif appears prominently in the published literature, yet it is virtually impossible to find a women's rite of blessing after childbirth which recalls either the themes or the ritual framework of the churching rite. There are naming ceremonies and affirming celebrations of birth and lactation, as well as an abundant bibliography of meditations and rituals on God as Mother. But the newer informal experimental rites do not depend upon

---

68. *Rituale Romanum De Benedictionibus*, Editio typica (Vatican: Typis polyglottis Vaticanis, 1984): 92–99; and *The Roman Ritual: Book of Blessings* (Collegeville, Minn.: Liturgical Press, 1989): 79–85. A slightly earlier Canadian book includes a very simple blessing of both parents and their child in case baptism is postponed: *A Book of Blessings* (Ottawa: Publications Service, Canadian Conference of Catholic Bishops, 1981), 59.

a cleric to pronounce a blessing upon the mother; leadership is more circular and mutual, as among a community of equals. Feminist blessing rituals give no hint of purification. The starting point is fundamentally positive, affirmative of the holiness of creation and of the human body, and expressing genuine joy at the gift of life.

8

The Better Blood
On Sacrifice and the Churching of New Mothers in the Roman Catholic Tradition
Grietje Dresen

The pharmacist no longer automatically places it in a paper bag, but the preference is still for the sanitary napkin to be invisible: it is becoming thinner and thinner all the time and is preferably pleasantly packaged. Since the introduction of the plastic layer, the fear of leaking that accompanied my menstruation during puberty is mostly a thing of the past, but the taboo of menstrual blood has yet to diminish. Why else should the unprecedented absorption capability of that superthin sanitary napkin of the advertisements be illustrated, not with red, but with blue fluid? Menstrual blood is not the only form of "feminine" blood loss that incurs such a fate; other forms also remain conspicuously hidden. Thus most women have no knowledge of the amount of blood that is lost during delivery or miscarriage until the time comes, and they experience it for themselves.

This taboo of feminine blood loss is not just a by-product of, for example, a modern emphasis on hygiene but can be found in numerous times and cultures.[1] In contrast to these often negative assessments of feminine blood loss stands the awe with which the masculine confrontation with blood is frequently clothed. Much more than women, men have the power to intentionally shed blood: as soldier, sacrificial priest, first lover, "blood brother," executioner, perpetrator of violent offenses, or as physician (in those cultures where the healing function is reserved for

---

In memory of Sue Houston-Hall. This chapter is dedicated in remembrance of Sue Houston-Hall who, although seriously ill, corrected this chapter with the greatest attention.

1. Cf. Janice Delaney, *The Curse: A Cultural History of Menstruation* (Chicago: University of Illinois Press, 1988); Buckley and Gottlieb, *Blood Magic*.

men). Practically all of these forms of intentional shedding of blood confer upon the shedder of blood honor or holiness; at the very least they
confer respect and a hint of power.

Such a gender-based double standard for contact with blood is especially developed in religious contexts.[2] Generally, in these contexts, the
blood loss that is a part of feminine fertility is explicitly unclean, while
the intentional shedding of blood, particularly in the form of the sacrifice, is clothed in sacred power. What is the origin of this sharp contrast
between the honorable or even sacred aspects of the contact with blood,
on the one hand, and the thoroughly dishonorable and unclean aspects
of it, on the other hand (blood being a neuter substance in itself, after
all)?

In this essay, I search for an answer to this question. My point of
departure is the Roman Catholic tradition, a tradition that forms a striking example of such an ambivalent recognition and appreciation of
blood. The holy sacrifice of the mass, the remembrance of the body and
blood of Christ, is central to Roman Catholic worship. Christ is supposed to have given his body and blood for the salvation of sinners, and
in the holy sacrifice of the mass, this sacrifice is repeated in the sacred
acts of the priests. To be permitted to perform these holy acts, the ultimate requirement for priests is to keep themselves as far away from that
"natural" body and blood, the body and blood of women. Roman
Catholic priests must still not have the body of a woman nor touch the
body of women; in other words, they must be celibate men. Under certain conditions, female pastoral workers, without the ordination of
priesthood, can preside over a service, but they can never perform the
consecration.[3] While bodily contact with a woman is no longer explicitly
considered as defiling, as was the case in earlier eras, the fact that the
body of women, especially the reproductive function of women, was not
allowed to associate with the divine still affects the assessment of women
in the Roman Catholic Church. The nonordination of women is one
outcome; another is the ritual of *churching*, which was common in the
Roman Catholic community in the Netherlands until the 1960s.

The ritual of churching preceded the first church attendance of a
woman who had recently given birth. During the first weeks after

---

2. In 1991, the Nijmegen Center for Women's Studies, on the initiative of Willy
Jansen, organized an interdisciplinary lecture series around the theme *Bloedbanden,
bloedschande* (Blood Bonds, Blood Shame). In its original form, this chapter was a part
of this lecture series.
3. During the consecration, bread and wine are changed into the body and blood of
Christ by the ritual words and acts of the priest.

childbirth—the time in which she was supposed to lose some blood—a new mother remained outside the church. The ritual of churching marked the end of this period and served traditionally as a symbolic purification. In the first half of this chapter, I will focus on this ritual and on its background. In the second half, I examine the work of various authors in an attempt to come up with an explanation for the aforementioned ambivalence in dealing with blood. Although in anthropological literature, especially in women's studies, menstruation taboos receive much attention, their connection with the other side of the confrontation with blood, blood shed as a sacred act, remains underdeveloped. That is unfortunate, because the extremes mentioned above—of defilement and highest honor—are strongly gendered. The ambivalence of contact with blood casts a sharp light on the gendered balance of power in the cultures in question, particularly on the way in which biological differences between the sexes are observed, valued, and symbolically emphasized.

The Ritual of Churching

The ritual of churching was not obligatory for Roman Catholic women, but until about the middle of the 1950s was rather inevitable—as a social obligation or because the pastor expected the new mother to do so. Some forty days after the delivery, the woman had to report herself to the priest, to be solemnly reintroduced into the church. The woman was not supposed to set foot in the church, and especially not to receive Holy Communion, before the ritual of churching had occurred. A new mother could therefore not be present for the baptism of her child because baptism had to take place quite soon after birth (as a precaution should the newborn die, since unbaptized children would not go to heaven).[4]

At this first solemn visit to church after the birth, the woman had to kneel by the church door, with a burning candle in her hand, and wait for the parish priest. In some parishes, she carried her newborn with her. The priest sprinkled the woman with holy water, read Ps 24 (placing emphasis on the glory of God's kingdom and purity of life), offered her the end of his white stole, and blessed her saying, "Enter the temple of God, worship the Son of the Virgin Mary, who has

---

4. In the late Middle Ages, the idea that unbaptized children would not be permitted to enter heaven (as all the unbaptized would not be permitted) softened to the idea of the so-called limbo, in which innocent children would have to wait until the end of time for their salvation.

granted you fertility."[5] With the woman holding the end of his stole, he led her to the high altar. After kneeling before the holy sanctuary on the high altar, they stood before the altar of Mary. Here the woman kneeled again, still holding the candle, and the priest said some other prayers. The woman offered the burning candle and a bunch of flowers or a small monetary gift Then the priest again sprinkled the woman with holy water and blessed her. Through this ritual she was, as it were, solemnly reintroduced into the church and, especially, dignified to participate once more in Holy Communion.

The original basis for this ritual was the conviction that the woman became impure through parturition, particularly through the blood she lost during and after parturition. Jewish law (Lev 12:1–8) laid down provisions concerning the purification of new mothers. These provisions were thus known to Christianity as a regulation of Jewish law. As a Jewish woman, Mary, the mother of Jesus, also held herself to this law and submitted herself to purification after the birth of Jesus (Luke 2:22). Later Christian tradition believed that Mary, as the mother of God, did not become impure through parturition and that even her virginity remained intact through conception and delivery. That the Virgin, although she did not become impure from normal childbirth or lochia, did not withdraw from being purified was explained and esteemed by the Roman Catholic Church as a sign of fidelity to priestly rule. This explanation served the church well when, in the course of time, it formally abandoned the idea that women became impure through childbirth but held on to the ritual of churching—thus threatening the rite with senselessness.

The official explanation of the ritual of churching became then that this rite referred to the purification of Mary, to which she submitted herself faithfully, even though she did not become impure. The rite was thus interpreted as a remembrance of Mary's faithfulness and as a thanksgiving after birth. The rather progressive *Liturgisch Woordenboek* (Liturgical Dictionary) from 1967 even asserted that the ritual must be seen as a "statement of homage from the church for motherhood"![6] In spite of — or possibly just because of—this explicit denial of the character of purification, most Roman Catholic women continued to experience the rite as purification for these reasons: because of the advice not to go to

---

5. The stole is a long kind of sash, hanging down at both sides from the neck and colored differently according to the liturgical occasion.
6. L. Brinkhoff, ed., *Liturgisch Woordenboek* (Roermond: J. J. Romen & Zonen, 1967), 1311.

Communion before being churched; because she was asked to kneel, waiting for the priest to sprinkle her with holy water; because of the words that accompanied Ps 24 in the folder that she received when she entered the church;[7] because of the way she was introduced into the church, holding the end of the priest's stole; and last, but not least, because of the complex reference to the purification of Mary. And so in the course of the 1950s, more and more women—as if it were something in the air—became irritated by the ritual and rejected it. Why, they wondered, did they have to be reintroduced into the church this way after giving birth?

Rebirth

In general, women participate more faithfully and conscientiously in Roman Catholic rituals than men. The fact that the rite of churching was the first of the ancient Roman Catholic rituals to be given up in the late fifties of the last century tells a tale. Apparently this churching, in spite of all its beautiful interpretations, was experienced by the women involved as profoundly inappropriate and deservedly so, as the following analysis shows.

Let us take a closer look at the symbolism involved in the rite. The priest leads the new mother into the church by a kind of tie. Childbirth placed her, as it were, outside the community participating in Communion, but she is brought back into this community by the priest, connected to him via his stole. Does the ritual not resemble a kind of reverse, metaphorical birth, a symbolic rebirth? Reintroduced into the church by the priest, connected to him by a ritual umbilical cord, the new mother is symbolically reborn, returned into the community. The candle that she carries, symbol of the light of Christ, also symbolizes this: returned from the darkness, she is carrying the light of Christ that is guarded by the church.

The same priest that churched the new mother had, in most cases, baptized her child a few weeks earlier. By being baptized, the child was incorporated into the church in the most fundamental way. Baptism, too, is a rite of purification and rebirth (symbolized by the water) and a transition from the world of darkness into the light (symbolized by the light

---

7. "Alleen wie rein en zuiver leeft in de eenmaal aanvaarde levensstaat mag Gods tempel binnengaan en kan rekenen op Zijn overvloedige genade" (Only those who live cleanly and purely in the estate of life once accepted, may enter God's Temple and can count on his abundant grace").

of the baptism candle). Baptism rites in which the child or adult are entirely plunged into water represent this element of purification and rebirth most explicitly. Through baptism—that is, through the sacramental acts and words of the priest inducing baptism—the child is reborn into the church and receives his or her Christian name.

Thus, within a month after the mother's giving birth, the priest had already performed two symbolic rebirths: he had rebirthed the child in a "better," spiritual way, during a ritual at which the mother could not be present, and he had reintroduced the new mother into the community of Holy Communion. The fact that many new mothers came to experience the rite of churching as completely out of place may reveal that they identified with some of this symbolic appropriation of their labor.

Interpretation and Development of the Rite in Roman Catholic Tradition

The biblical background of the rite of churching is found in Jewish law. Leviticus 12:1–5 (NRSV) states, "The LORD spoke to Moses, saying: Speak to the people of Israel, saying: If a woman conceives and bears a male child, she shall be ceremonially unclean seven days; as at the time of her menstruation,[8] she shall be unclean. On the eighth day the flesh of his foreskin shall be circumcised. Her time of blood purification shall be thirty-three days; she shall not touch any holy thing, or come into the sanctuary, until the days of her purification are completed. If she bears a female child, she shall be unclean two weeks, as in her menstruation; her time of blood purification shall be sixty-six days." The book of Leviticus, in which the purity laws in general play such a central part, stems from the so-called Priestly strand (P). These laws date from around the time of the Jews' exile to Babylon in the sixth century B.C.E. Probably as a result of the loss of the temple and of familiar cultural surroundings, the Israelites placed special emphasis on the symbolic borders of the social body and, as a parallel with those borders, on the boundaries of the human body, on rules of living with respect to purity and just behavior.

Such tendencies to formalism and purism are often found in cultural communities that are displaced or feel threatened.[9] During the time of the exile there was a conspicuous sharpening of both the rules pertaining

---

8. Namely, she shall be ceremonially unclean to the extent to which she is unclean during the time of menstruation. The regulations listed here and the accompanying guidelines can be found in Lev 15:19 ff.

9. Cf. Douglas, *Purity and Danger*. In the third chapter of that book, she discusses Leviticus.

to the circumcision of boys and the rules relating to the purity of women and loss of blood.[10] Leonie J. Archer has posited a relationship between the sharpening of both rules. Circumcision, as a physical sign of cultic inclusion, implied an intentional and controlled shedding of blood. According to Archer, it is not by chance that the passage concerning the circumcision of boys was inserted into the passage on the purification of new mothers. She relates this insertion to the function of circumcision, which

> served as a rite of cultural rebirth by which the male individual was accorded entry into the society and religion of his people. In other words, whilst women, as it were, merely conducted the animal-like repetitive tasks of carrying on the reproduction of the human race, men, by one supreme symbolic act, imposed themselves upon nature and enacted a cultural rebirth. The blood of circumcision served as a symbolic surrogate for the blood of childbirth, and because it was shed voluntarily and in a controlled manner, it transcended the bounds of nature and the passive blood flow of the mother at delivery and during the preparatory cycle for pregnancy, menstruation.[11]

Christianity gave up the practice of circumcision as an outward sign of inclusion into the covenant. Yet in Christianity too consciously shed male blood marks the covenant: "For the ultimate cultic sacrifice and voluntary shedding of blood was seen to have been achieved in the figure of the male, circumcised, saviour Christ. He was the new and eternal Paschal lamb, he was the new Temple and law; through his blood the new covenant was established and by his blood sins were forgiven."[12] To be part of the new covenant, Christians only have to endorse their salvation through the blood of Christ. (We will return to Archer's elaboration of the contrast between the natural blood loss of women and the cultic shedding of blood by men later on.)

The Gospels record no incident in which the loss of female blood is disparaged. When Jesus was touched by a woman who had been bleeding for years and thus was ritually impure, he praised her for her belief, defying the protest of the onlookers (Mark 5:25–34; Matt. 9:18–26; Luke 8:40–56).[13] Yet in early Christianity, predominantly under the

---

10. For a comparison, see also Plaskow, *Standing Again at Sinai*, particularly ch. 5.
11. Archer, "Bound by Blood," 39.
12. Ibid., 41.
13. For these and other examples of Jesus' unconventional interactions with women, including their bodies, see Ruether, "Women's Body and Blood."

influence of gnostic thinking, the body and especially the reproductive functions of women were looked upon with more and more reserve, even rejection.[14] The "work of women," reproduction, was repudiated by many gnostic groups as being the cause of the imprisonment of (elements of) the Spirit into the material body from generation to generation.[15] If people ceased procreating, the continual imprisonment of spiritual elements in matter would end, and ultimate salvation would draw near. The regulations of Leviticus concerning the impurity of women's blood were linked to this dualistic contempt of the body, notably the procreative body.[16] Reminiscences of these purity laws continued to haunt the texts that were developed from early Christianity onwards concerning the church attendance of new mothers and menstruating women.[17]

In Western Christian tradition, an important text concerning the question of whether parturients and menstruating women were impure and could enter the church is found in a response written under the name of Pope Gregory the Great to the English bishop Augustine of Canterbury, the so-called *Responsum beati Gregorii ad Augustinum episcopum*.[18] The letter was probably written in 731 by Nothelm, a subsequent archbishop of Canterbury, who lent it the authority of a pope whose pastoral leadership had played such a decisive role in the Chris-

---

14. Cf. Peter Brown, *The Body and Society: Men, Women, and Sexual Renunciation in Early Christianity* (New York: Columbia University Press, 1988). As a counterpart, the virginal, "closed" body of women was bestowed ecclesiological significance. So Ambrose writes (in a passage with references to Mary, symbol of the virginal procreation that is effected in and through the church as the bride of Christ):

> So the Holy Church, unstained by sexual union but fertile in bearing, is a virgin in respect to chastity, a mother in respect to offspring. And thus she labors to give us birth as a virgin, impregnated not by a man but by the Spirit. The virgin bears us not with physical pain, but with the rejoicings of angels. . . . For what bride has more children than the holy Church? . . . She has no husband, but she has a bridegroom, inasmuch as she . . . weds the Word of God as her eternal Spouse. (*Virg.* 1.31)

For the quotation, see Virginia Burrus, "Word and Flesh: The Bodies and Sexuality of Ascetic Women in Christian Antiquity," *JFSR* 10, no. 1 (1994): 27–51; cf. Grietje-Dresen, *Is dit mijn lichaam? Visioenen van het volmaakte lichaam in katholieke moraal en mystiek* (Nijmegen, Netherlands: Valkhof Pers, 1998), 67.
15. Cf. John T. Noonan, *Contraception: A History of Its Treatment by the Catholic Theologians and Canonists* (Cambridge: Belknap, 1965).
16. Cf. Ranke-Heinemann, *Eunuchs*, ch. 2.
17. For an analysis of the liturgical texts concerning parturients from early Christian times onwards, see the contribution of Susan Roll in the present book.
18. Regarding the question of the authenticity of the letter, see Müller, *Die Lehre des Hl.*, 36 n. 10. The letter is listed in the Patrologia Latina amongst the letters of Gregory the Great: PL 77:1183–1200.

tianization of Europe.[19] In response to the question of whether a new mother could come to church soon after childbirth, (Pseudo-)Gregory answered that she should not be forbidden to enter the church; and the same encouragement applied to women during their menses. Nevertheless, it would be good if women themselves displayed restraint in doing so, he cautioned, thus alluding to some kind of guilt, although not necessarily personal guilt. Even though women might in a strict sense not be considered guilty or impure, because their blood loss was a natural and unintentional given, it would become them to acknowledge the fact that the blood loss itself was a phenomenon of fallen nature, a consequence of original sin.[20]

(Pseudo-)Gregory's response was rather ambiguous, all the more so because it was a woman, Eve, who was held responsible for the fall and the *corruptio* of the original, harmonious natural order. Actually, many churchmen continued to consider the lochia and menstrual blood as impure and new mothers and menstruating women as in need of special treatment. Evidence of this can be found in numerous penitential books and, from the twelfth century onwards, in the manuals for confessors (e.g., in their interdictions concerning marital intercourse during the menses).[21]

In the Latin church, evidence of the existence of actual services and formulae for the reintroduction of new mothers into the church can only be traced back to the eleventh century.[22] Most of the rituals have reminders of the issue of purification, at least in the symbolism used (e.g., elements referring to the Feast of the Purification of Mary and to the introduction of catechumens into the church, such as the holding of the stole). From the Middle Ages onwards then, councils had to state time and again that the ritual was a rite, not of purification, but of thanksgiving to the Lord and a way of following Mary in her faithfulness. In the history of the church, however, such repeated conciliar repudiations of apparently condemnable, but in fact current, practices reveal

---

19. *The Moralia in Job and the Regulae Pastoralis liber* of Gregorius were important handbooks in the Middle Ages.

20. See the tenth question and the accompanying answer in the letter of response mentioned above (*Responsum beati Gregorii*).

21. For the penitential books, see Wisse, "De kerkgang van de moeder"; and Roll, this volume. Written to be used in conversion and pastoral practice from the eighth century onwards, the penitential books converted the moral principles of Christianity into the most concrete examples of crime and punishment. Having intercourse with one's wife while she was menstruating was always considered more or less sinful and could cause the birth of deformed or feeble-minded children.

22. For concrete examples and references, see Roll's chapter in the present book.

the denigrating practice—in this case the interpretation of the rite of churching as a purification—to be persistent.[23]

These ambiguities about purification appeared to be a fixed feature of the ritual of churching. As we saw in the description of the rite practiced in the Netherlands in the 1950s, which was based on the formulae offered in the *Rituale Romanum* of 1614, ambivalence continued to be part of the rite up until its discontinuation (informally by the decision of the women desiring to dispense with this embarrassing "blessing" and formally after the Second Vatican Council and the insertion of the blessing into the baptism rite).[24] For example, when I was searching dictionaries preparing for this chapter, and asked a noted, progressive theologian (who happened to be in the library) whether he knew the French word for "churching," he suggested it would be *purification*.[25] In the aforementioned *Liturgisch Woordenboek* from 1967, the entry for the keyword *kerkgang* (churching) opens with such an explicit denial of the idea of purification that it cannot but raise one's curiosity or even suspicion: "The theological basis of the churching rite is absolutely not to be sought in the idea of purification of Leviticus 12:2."[26] Comparable admonitions can be found in most of the treatises on the subject by male churchmen or theologians.[27] As we have seen, these explicit repudiations conflict with the obvious symbolism in the ritual itself, as well as with the reference to the purification of Mary. Even if women knew that the Roman Catholic Church did not actually deem them to be impure after childbirth, they did connect the imitation of Mary represented in the ritual with an idea of impurity in Roman Catholic tradition, that is, with the impurity or sinfulness associated with sexuality.[28] Lacking any explanation of the ritual except that within the folder given to them (and in which the few Dutch commentaries did speak of cleanliness and purity),

---

23. Ranke-Heinemann, *Eunuchs*, 24–25.

24. *Rituale Romanum auctoritate Pauli PP VI promulgatum* (Vaticanum 1969). See *Ordo Baptismi parvulorum*, nr. 70 and 247–49.

25. As I learned later, the French word for churching is relevailles (Von Arx, "Churching of Women," 65) or, more officially, "Bénédiction d'une femme après ses couches." For formulae from French rituals, see Wisse, "De kerkgang van de moeder," 51–53, 62–68, and 200–206.

26. So Wisse describes in the introduction of her excellent M.A. thesis on the rite of churching that it was precisely this opening sentence in the *Liturgisch Woordenboek*, combined with the experience of being churched that a woman told her of, that raised her curiosity about the subject ("De kerkgang van de moeder").

27. An exception is Von Arx, who explicitly states (in opposition to Franz) that the element of purification is present, one way or another, in most of the rituals (see Von Arx, "Churching of Women," 68; cf. Franz, *Die Kirchlichen Benediktionen*).

28. Cf. Dresen, *Is dit mijn lichaam?*

many women indeed interpreted being churched and ending up in front of the altar of Mary as an act of renewed dedication to the ideal of virginity.[29]

Nancy Jay: Transcending Mortality

The Roman Catholic Church—unlike the Eastern-Orthodox and Anglican churches—has given up the ritual of churching, but the sense of "otherness" evoked by the body and blood of women and the seeming incompatibility of aspects of physical reproduction with the most sacred acts of worship appears to subsist. Men that administer the holy body and blood of Christ must still abstain from bodily association with a woman, and women themselves are declared unfit for mediating the sacred transformation of bread and wine into body and blood of Christ. Sometimes women seem to have internalized this taboo. A female Roman Catholic pastoral worker told me that when she is assisting in services during her menses, she is always painfully aware of her condition. Imagine that the immaculate minister's robes should betray the state she is in: would that not be the ultimate taboo, a bloodstained minister? Rosemary Radford Ruether describes another traditionalist horror vision: "What if she were pregnant at the altar?"[30] Ruether identifies an implicit clerical concern: should a woman assume some priestly functions, she would have to remain unrecognizable as a woman. She would have to insert herself into the existing symbolic universe: "She will learn to preach and do the liturgy in the same way as he does. There is an avoidance of recognizing the way her mere presence as a female in the Christian 'sacred spaces' changes the symbolic and psychic dynamics of relationship to the holy."[31]

What then would change if women stand at the altar? Or maybe we should first ask the preceding question: Why are women—notably pregnant women—declared unfit for conducting the ritual offering? This question is answered by Nancy Jay in her article "Sacrifice as Remedy for

---

29. Ever since I published the first version of this article (in 1992), I have heard from very many women this personal interpretation of the ritual. Some women added that because they interpreted the ritual in this way, it angered them so much, at least afterwards. Why should she be the only one to be purified from the stains associated with sexuality? (Often she had not even been the initiating party in intercourse and had been obliged to fulfill her marital duties.) Cf. Wisse, "De kerkgang van de moeder," 125–40; Roll, "Churching of Women," 225.
30. Ruether, "Women's Body and Blood," 17.
31. Ibid.

Having Been Born of Woman" and in her posthumously published book *Throughout Your Generations Forever* (in which she elaborates the earlier article). Being an anthropologist, Jay handles this question not only with regard to the Roman Catholic sacrifice of the mass but with respect to all religions in which the central acts of worship comprise some kind of blood sacrifice.

In her studies, Jay discovered that in many unrelated and very divergent religions, blood sacrifice is the crucial cultic act. In order to understand this central role of cultic blood shedding and its gender-related features, Jay found it essential to consider the particular kind of social organization and kinship structures in which the sacrificial cult originates. According to Jay, blood-sacrifice religions have prevailed in pre-capitalist societies with some degree of technological development where rights to durable ("real") property are highly valued and where kinship is organized in unilineal, patrilinear descent groups.[32] These qualities can be found in societies with quite divergent features, but in all those societies "the control of the means of production is inseparably linked with the control of the means of reproduction, that is, the fertility of women."[33] It struck Jay that gender is ignored in the great quantity of anthropological literature concerning sacrificial cults, or, in any case, the gender-related aspects of the rituals are dismissed without any reflection upon them. This is all the more astonishing when one recognizes that blood sacrifices are virtually always accompanied by gender-related rules. The most elementary of these rules introduce a sharp contrast between the purity that is required to perform the sacrificial acts and the impurity that is brought about by the processes of physical reproduction, notably by the loss of blood that is part of the female fertility process.[34] In all of the cultures examined, only ritually pure men were allowed to perform sacrificial acts. Jay found only a few exceptions to this rule. But in the few cases where women could play a marginal role in the cult (such as drawing water to be used in the ritual), the selected women were always those excluded from the reproductive process: virgins or women past menopause.[35]

Why were fertile women not allowed to play an active role in the sacrifice ritual? Jay looks for an answer to this question in the patrilineal

---

32. Nancy Jay, "Sacrifice as Remedy for Having Been Born of a Woman," in *Immaculate and Powerful: The Female in Sacred Image and Social Reality* (ed. C. W. Atkinson; Boston: Beacon, 1985), 289.
33. Ibid.
34. Ibid., 284.
35. Ibid. See also Johnson, this volume.

organization of kinship structures in the societies concerned, societies in which blood sacrifice plays such a central part. In these cultures, blood sacrifice implies an essential sealing of the social order. Fatherly descent (with its corresponding rights) is, in contrast to motherly descent, not defined by birth alone. Biological fatherhood can never be as certain as motherhood, no matter how close a watch is kept on the woman whose reproductive faculties are appropriated. A patrilineal society, therefore, displays a tendency to emphasize formal, symbolic fatherhood over biological fatherhood. Although, preferably, these go together, it is symbolic fatherhood that determines one's position, rights, and obligations in a patrilineal society. Biological fatherhood would be too unreliable a base upon which to build a firm social order. In order to lend to a system of lineage based on symbolic fatherhood the luster of being a system intended by the gods, the lineage has to be sealed by a symbolic deed as powerful, definite, and available to the senses as birth.[36] In many divergent cultures membership in the patrilineal descent group is confirmed through participation in blood sacrifice (taken as an offering to the ancestors). Members can be identified not only through anthropological evidence but also by the terminology used to indicate exactly who is eligible to participate in sacrifice, or to share in the same sacrificial meat.[37]

However, in all of these data we do not find an answer to the question of why it is blood sacrifice, and not another ritual, that plays this crucial role in symbolically confirming patrilineal descent. [38] Jay offers

---

36. Jay, "Sacrifice as Remedy," 291; *Throughout Your Generations Forever: Sacrifice, Religion, and Paternity* (Chicago: University of Chicago Press, 1992), 36.

37. Jay, "Sacrifice as Remedy," 292.

38. Jay, "Sacrifice as Remedy." In *Throughout Your Generations Forever* (the title refers to a frequent sacrifice formula in Leviticus), Jay does not explicitly return to this question, at least not in the manner in which it is formulated here. In her book, Jay situates her approach explicitly within the modern structuralist studies of sacrifice of ritual (see particularly chs.1 and 9). That is, developing her questions less from an "external" perspective, she searches to understand social and religious structures of meaning in their internal coherence and effects: "The approach taken here will not focus primarily on symbolic representations of childbirth or childbearing women but on the social contexts of sacrificial ritual, especially on the ways the practice of sacrifice affects family structures, the organized social relations of reproduction within which women bear their children" (*Throughout Your Generations Forever*, xxiv). Questions posed within this approach include the following: "What role does sacrificing (in any particular tradition) play in indexing social groups and their boundaries? What kinds of social structures are so identified? Who is included? Who excluded? What is the relation of women, especially childbearing women, to sacrificial practices? How is intergenerational continuity between males maintained?" (p. 147).

Apparent similarities in meaning systems between unrelated cultures must subsequently also be structurally situated "in common conditions of life, such as the way

two possible explanations. The first explanation she labels "symbolic reasons."[39] The argument in this symbolic reasoning reads like this:

> The only action that is as serious as giving birth, which can act as a counterbalance to it, is killing. This is one way to interpret the common sacrificial metaphors of birth and rebirth, or birth done better, on purpose and on a more spiritual, more exalted level than mothers do it. ... Unlike childbirth, sacrificial killing is deliberate, purposeful, "rational" action, under perfect control. Both birth and killing are acts of power, but sacrificial ideology commonly construes childbirth as the quintessence of vulnerability, passivity, and powerless suffering.[40]

Jay does not elaborate on these symbolic reasons, that is, on the contrast between the valorized and controlled shedding of blood and the inferior, involuntary loss of blood by women.[41]

In the aforementioned article by Archer, this contrast is quite explicitly worked out and in fact represents the core of her argumentation. Archer proceeds from the concept of nature-culture (a conceptual dichotomy that has been thoroughly questioned in anthropological literature during the last decade). She argues that the blood shed by men in the context of a culturally prescribed act receives higher regard than the natural, involuntary blood loss of women. The first signifies the ultimate sealing of the social order (of the social body) and is therefore looked upon as an honorable or even sacred act. The second, female blood loss, ranks as impure because bodily secretions, as "matter out of place" (Mary Douglas), represent disorder and lack of control. Particularly in societies that feel threatened, from within or from without, cultural identity will be reinforced by stressing social cohesion and by increasing the resistance

---

agrarian and pastoral systems of production may lead to a concern for birth- and death-transcending male intergenerational continuity" (p. 149). The titles of Jay's article and book summarize her change of focus very well. The direction and conclusions of both studies remain approximately the same, although in her book (in which she not only analyzes patrilineal sacrificial culture but also a matrilineal and a "mixed" one) her conclusions are much more varied.

39. Jay, "Sacrifice as Remedy," 293. Jay does mention "psychological reasons," but she does not name them and suggests in the subsequent sentence that the "symbolic reasons" that she is going to mention do not quite correspond with those psychological reasons. I would say that within these symbolic reasons, psychological reasons can also be recognized.

40. Ibid., 294.

41. In her book, Jay points to this contrast as the original observation and point of departure for her study of many years concerning the origins and dynamics of blood sacrifice (*Throughout Your Generations*, ix–x).

against internal or external transgressions. By guarding the imaginary boundaries of its social body and keeping everything in its place, a culture maintains the purity of that social body. The increase of attention towards the purity and integrity of the physical body reflects the need for a reliable, stable community. Under such conditions, physical or symbolic transgressions of the ideal of body control (such as sexual disorder or, nowadays, being fat) are regarded as impure and require the transgressor to take up extra endeavors to restore purity.[42]

To comprehend the central function of blood sacrifice in patrilineal organized kinship structures, Jay locates the second explanation in "the formal logical structure of the sacrifice itself."[43] She distinguishes between the two most common modes of blood sacrifice, communion sacrifice (in which, for example, a part of the sacrificial animal is collectively eaten) and expiatory sacrifice:

> Communion sacrifice unites worshippers in one moral community and at the same time differentiates that community from the rest of the world. Expiatory sacrifice integrates by getting rid of countless different moral and organic undesirable conditions: sin, disease, famine, spirit possession, social discord, blood guilt, incest, impurity of descent, pollution of childbirth, and so on, all having in common only that they must be expiated.[44]

In this way, the participants are united, becoming members of one social body, and concurrently they are shielded from everything that could be a threat to that body. Among these threats, the (image of) blood connected with female reproductive power often counts as a severe one. The participants in sacrifice become members of the true community, the community constituted in and through the "better" blood:

> Sacrificially constituted descent, incorporating women's mortal children into an "eternal" (enduring through generations) kin group, in which membership is recognized by sacrificial ritual, not merely by

---

42. Cf. Douglas, *Purity and Danger*; Dresen, *Is dit mijn lichaam?*; Archer, "Bound by Blood," 37–39.

43. Jay, "Sacrifice as Remedy," 294. In her book, Jay develops this explanation in more detail—in both a theoretical manner (*Throughout Your Generations*, ch. 2) and as it applies to different sacrificial cultures, including post-Vatican II Roman Catholic culture (ch. 8).

44. Jay, "Sacrifice as Remedy," 295; and nearly identical in Jay, *Throughout Your Generations*, 19.

birth, enables a patrilineal descent group to transcend mortality in the same process in which it transcends birth. In this sense, sacrifice is doubly a remedy for having been born of woman.[45]

A similar process of transcending both normal birth and mortality was represented in the two rituals of rebirth I described earlier: baptism and the rite of churching, taken as a renewed dedication of new mothers to the church. These rituals of rebirth could only be performed by the priest, whose supreme sacramental power consists in his exclusive right to execute the holy sacrifice of the mass.

Julia Kristeva: Abjection and the Repression of the Maternal Body

In her studies on the function of blood sacrifice, Jay does not elaborate on psychological motives, at least not explicitly. An author who did pay extensive attention to the possible psychological backgrounds of the shudder or "abjection" provoked by the blood of women is the French philosopher and psychoanalyst Julia Kristeva. In *Pouvoirs de l'horreur: Essai sur l'*abjection, Kristeva associates the repugnance to the blood of menstruation and lochia with the aversion towards everything that recalls the earliest, vague but overall sensory experiences acquired in connection with the maternal body. According to Kristeva, the constitution of a separate, personal identity, and especially of one's identity as a *man*—women are supposed to identify themselves more easily with the maternal body—presupposes a partial repression of the propensity to surrender to this total sensory experience. All sensations or persons that recall the experiences of fusion associated with the maternal body will evoke defense because they pose a threat to self-consciousness and to the capacity to distinguish oneself as a separate and unique individual. Everything that reminds us of our symbiotic relation to the maternal body—immediate physical closeness but also the blood of birth and menstruation—evokes "abjection," that is, according to Kristeva, "that state of uncertainty between subject and object that consciousness conceives as abject—state of uncertainty regarding the *identity* of the *self* and the *other*."[46]

---

45. Jay, "Sacrifice as Remedy," 297; *Throughout Your Generations*, 40.
46. Julia Kristeva, "Pouvoirs de l'horreur" *Tel Quel*. 86 (1980): 50. For a detailed presentation of Kristeva's concepts of "abjection" and the repression of the maternal body, notably in Judaism and Christianity, see Grietje Dresen, "Einde van de inquisitie, geboorte van een ander. Verhalen van de liefde in een voorstel tot ethiek," *Te Elfder*

I consider Kristeva's psychoanalytic interpretation of the repressed maternal body as an explanation of the defense mechanism that can be activated through experiences of fusion or loss of self, but I wonder whether it also applies to the shuddering caused by the confrontation with female blood. In the earliest phase of life, in which the child has yet to become aware of its separate being and feels finest in close physical contact with the maternal body, the child has no consciousness of the fact that this body is that of a woman, let alone that this body bleeds during menstruation and after childbirth. The later separation from the mother will certainly be coupled with aggression and abjection, and this aggression will often serve as a personal incentive to control female sexuality, notably female reproductive abilities, in a patrilineal society (cf. Raab). However, the specific revulsion provoked by female blood appears to be, not a direct residue of infancy, but rather a later combination of defensive reactions against experiences recalling the maternal body; it also involves the urge to control that dangerous capacity women have—their power over reproduction—to which their "bleeding without dying" testifies (cf. J. Delaney). Kristeva, though, is not only interested in psychological motivations; she also considers the repression of the maternal body from the perspective of its social function and its significance for patrilineal kinship structure, that is, for the creation of a genealogy from father to son and a community centered around the word of the Father.[47]

Reconsidering the Rite of Churching

Jay's study interrelates the taboo connected with the blood loss of women and the function of sacrifice within kinship structure. This broadening of the perspective (compared with studies that only consider menstruation taboos and rules concerning impurity) is informative with regard to the question I formulated as a guide for this chapter, the question concerning the origins of the remarkable, gendered contrast between honorable and dishonorable contact with blood in certain cultures. As an example

---

Ure 29, no. 2 (1986): 178–212. For more recent introductions of her thinking, see John Fletcher and Andrew Benjamin, eds., *Abjection, Melancholia, and Love: The Work of Julia Kristeva* (London: Routledge, 1990); Kelly Oliver, ed., *Ethics, Politics, and Difference in Julia Kristeva's Writing* (New York: Routledge, 1930; *Reading Kristeva: Unraveling the Double-Blind* (Bloomington: Indiana University Press, 1993).

47. Cf. Julia Kristeva, *Des chinoises* (Paris: Des Femmes, 1974), 23; *Pouvoirs de l'horreur: Essai sur l'abjection* (Paris: Du Seuil, 1980), 110–19.

of such a contrast, I focused on the sacrifice of the mass in Roman Catholic tradition and its connection with the ritual of churching and the general restrictions that regulate the way in which Roman Catholic women can approach the holy.[48]

Jay's studies have thus another focus than studies that seek to interpret menstruation taboos. Jay's point of departure is the central role of blood sacrifice in (precapitalistic) patrilineal societies. She interprets the rules regarding female blood loss in the perspective of the function of blood sacrifice. It would be interesting to broaden her analysis to include other cultures such as the Islamic, in which a similar sharp distinction is found between the purity required for participation in blood sacrifice and the impurity of female blood.[49]

Of the explanations that Jay offers to account specifically for the crucial role of sacrifice (and not some other ritual), the first, "symbolic," explanation appears to me to be the most convincing and elucidatory. In a society based on patrilineal kinship structure, the apparent descent from natural mothers must be exceeded, and symbolic fatherhood and a social order of fatherly descent must be sealed with a deed at least as decisive, unmistakable, and irrevocable as a woman's capacity to give life (to which the female blood testifies). In various cultures that otherwise have little in common, this decisive deed was found in the taking of life, in the intentional and ritualized shedding of blood in blood-sacrifice. Fertile women, and especially women losing blood, were excluded as much as possible from attendance at the ritual of blood-sacrifice, the purpose of which was to seal the bonds between the members of the patrilineal group, mutually and in relation to the ancestors, and to dissociate these bonds from the blood of the female cycle.

The second account that Jay offers as an explanation of blood-sacrifice, localized in the unifying structure of the ritual, clarifies the inner

---

48. See Johnson, this volume.

49. Jay does not elaborate on Islamic sacrifice (a relevant reference though is found in Jay, *Throughout Your Generations*, 149). For a precious anthropological case study and interpretation of the contrast between the impurity of menstruation blood and the holiness of sacrificial blood in Islamic cult, see Carol Delaney's interesting article "Mortal Flow: Menstruation in Turkish Village Society," in *Blood Magic: The Anthropology of Menstruation* (ed. Th. Buckley and A. Gottlieb; Berkeley: University of California Press, 1988). Her conclusions are strongly similar to those of Jay, although she presents an interesting variation of the argument of why men alone may kill: men are supposed to be the ones who give life (women provide only the substratum for the life-giving seed); therefore, men are also the only ones who may take life. The supposed monogenerative power of semen is also the foundation of patrilineal lineage.

structure and social functioning of sacrifice, but this account is less helpful as an answer to the question of why this function is so often fulfilled
through *sacrifice*. At least, for me, Jay's illuminating structural analysis
gave no convincing answer to the question of why this dual function of
both communion and expiation could not be fulfilled by some other ritual in which the shedding of blood plays a less prominent role. In her
latest book, however, Jay elaborates quite extensively on this structuralist
interpretation.[50] The rituals I mentioned at the beginning of this essay
though, churching and baptism, appear to fulfill a comparable function
(of both communion and exclusion from evil) and can certainly be seen
as examples of "birth done better."[51] The specific power of priests to perform these (and similar) varieties of ritual rebirth in the Roman Catholic
tradition ultimately goes back to the role of the priest in the holy sacrifice of the mass, in which Christ's offering is remembered and the
Christian is reborn as a member of the body of Christ.

If we trace the origins of the aforementioned ambivalent appreciation
of blood back to the need of a patrilineal society to "forget" the natural
mother (to summarize it shortly and simply), many questions remain.
One of these questions is, of course, why patrilineal organization of kinship is so widespread, given the fact that motherly lineage is so much
more reliable. I do not venture here to answer this grand question, but
anyone who so ventures must not underestimate (as Kristeva sometimes
does) the role of psychological motives—envy of the role of women in
reproduction, for example, or the psychic consequences of the necessity
of separating oneself from the maternal body. But neither should the role
of psychological motives be underestimated or tabooed, as is the case
with many anthropologists (for fear of projecting Western categories).
The hermeneutical problems concerning the recognition and assessment

---

50. Jay brings this explanation from the "formal logical structure of sacrifice" even
more to the foreground in her book. Other psychologically oriented authors inspired by
Jay's theses have attempted to develop her "symbolic" explanation in more detail (Beers,
using the psychoanalytic concepts of Melanie Klein and Heinz Kohut, among others)
or have attempted to psychologize her structuralist-anthropological explanation (as
does Kelley Ann Raab, in "Nancy Jay and a Feminist Psychology of Sacrifice," *JFSR* 13
[1997]: 75–89). Raab interprets "the unifying logic of sacrifice as communion and expiation outlined by Jay" as a rite expressing the infant-mother differentiation process as a
way of "separating from the mother while still remaining connected to her in some
sense" ("Nancy Jay," 86). Yet this psychological interpretation does not answer the question of why just sacrifice (and not another ritual) more convincingly than Jay does.
51. In her book, Jay does not use this concise summary of her original thesis very
often, due to her change in perspective, but it is still used in the foreword (by Karen E.
Fields; p. xiii) and, for example, in Jay's introduction (p. xxiv).

of psychological motives in another time and culture will not be solved by denying those motives altogether.[52]

With regard to the Roman Catholic tradition, the question remains how the Roman Catholic Church manages to hold up to its premodern roots—witness the emphasis on the sacrificial character of the Eucharist, on priestly celibacy, and on the unsuitability of women for the office of priesthood—while at the same time preserving its worldwide claims of representing universality and eternity. Although this achievement is aided by the universality of "forgetting" motherly descent and by the agelong experience of the church in ritually designing symbolic father-hood, it may not last forever. The nonordination of women is no longer taken for granted, and debates on celibacy as an obligation for priests increase, as do even more subtle arguments over hierarchical/apostolic succession and the exclusive sacramental power of the clergy. In the Netherlands, at least, the Eucharist is celebrated more and more fre-quently within an ecumenical service, with nonordained pastors as cele-brants and with variations of the traditionally unchangeable words and acts during consecration and Communion.[53] Ruether's suggestion, though, that the mere presence of women in the Christian "sacred spaces" would change the symbolic and psychic dynamics of relationship to the holy must remain a suggestion. Within the Roman Catholic spaces, at least, there is little room for a trial. The experiences of female ministers in the Anglican and Protestant churches, however, do not quite support her suggestion.

In the meantime many people—men and women, within or without the churches—are looking for religious expressions that symbolize their growing receptivity towards the processes and cycles of nature. For instance, the Christian interpretation of the feasts of Christmas and Easter appears to be slowly giving way to the return of old, pagan ori-gins: celebration of midwinter and the return of light at Christmas (sym-bolized by the green Christmas tree laden with candles) and the return

---

52. Cf. Grietje Dresen, *Onschuldfantasieën: Offerzin en heilsverlangen in feminisme en mystiek* (Nijmegen, Netherlands: SUN, 1990).The studies of Beers and Raab are not classic examples of recognizing these hermeneutical problems and historical realities.
53. Yet for the Church of Rome the interpretation of the sacrifice of the mass as a recurrence of Christ's offering and the incompatibility of that sacrifice with (the near presence of) the female body is not only of crucial importance in a theological sense but above all with regard to church politics, that is, with regard to the maintenance of ecclesiastical structure and power. Cf. Joseph Blenkinsopp, "Sacrifice and Social Maintenance: What's at Stake in the (Non)-Ordination of Roman Catholic Women," *Cross Currents* 45 (fall 1995): 359–67.

of new life and fertility in spring (expressed by the old custom of Easter bunnies bringing eggs and the new one of decorating with budding hazel branches). It is difficult to predict to what extent the Roman Catholic Church can give in to this turn towards a "pagan," nature-oriented, and maybe more female-oriented type of religiosity without losing its claims to be the representative of a unique and eternal community of universal truth. But one must remember that in Roman Catholic tradition, these "pagan" elements were never quite absent.

Within feminist theology, several authors have recently discussed the history and meaning of the rite of churching.[54] Though critical of the element of purification that lingered on in the shape and symbolism of the old rite (both in Roman Catholic and in Anglican tradition), they do look for a new kind of churching rite as a way to celebrate the profound life experience of giving birth within the context of a faith community. In line with the aforementioned turn towards a more nature-oriented and woman-friendly kind of religiosity, they would welcome a newly styled ritual to celebrate the life event of giving birth. Such a new ritual should not only include elements of thanksgiving (elements that both the Roman Catholic Church and the Anglican Church did not com-pletely neglect, unrecognizable as they often were) but should also be a festive, social event to mark the end of a rather isolated period.[55] Above all, a celebration like this could be part of the various ways in which women and men search for a transformation of worship, of symbolizing their relationship to the holy.[56] "I understand the history and develop-ment of the rite of *Thanksgiving of Women after Childbirth, commonly called the Churching of Women* as a starting point for taking the debate about feminist liturgical theology beyond the issue of inclusive language to incorporating women's occasions into the liturgical life of the whole community," argues Natalie Knödel, speaking from the Anglican tradi-tion.[57] Women themselves should play a central part in these transfor-mations, all the more so with regard to the rite of churching, which traditionally conveyed the church's view of women as being unsuitable for mediating the most sacred. Whether a new rite to celebrate the process of childbirth and new parenthood is viable from the perspective of both the women and the men involved, as well as from that of the churches, is an open question. At least in the Netherlands, the processes

---

54. Roll, "Churching of Women"; Knödel, "Obsolete Rite."
55. Knödel, "Obsolete Rite."
56. Cf. Roll, "Churching of Women," 229.
57. Knödel, "Obsolete Rite," 125.

of secularization and individualization (or individual searching for religious meaning), on the one hand, and Roman Catholic rigorism, on the other, do not create a favorable climate for the development of such a rite. Perhaps new forms will develop from the context of the parishes, provided women can actively represent what they experience to be holy and wholesome.

9

Female Blood Rituals
Cultural-Anthropological Findings and Feminist-Theological Reflections
Anne-Marie Korte

Introduction

"Ironically, contemporary Jewish and Christian feminists are construct-
ing rituals to celebrate women's physiological passages, yet most female-
dominated religions ignore menarche, menstruation and menopause."[1]
This observation made by the anthropologist Susan Starr Sered in her
highly original study on religions dominated by women *Priestess—
Mother—Sacred Sister* (1994) is a challenge to Jewish and Christian feminist theologians attempting to reclaim and reform the ritual practices of
their religious traditions. Sered states that from the perspective of
women-centered religious experiences and needs, it is not self-evident
that women's physiological processes of fecundity and procreation should
be ritually emphasized or even acknowledged.

Due to the rise of women's studies in theology and religion and of
new approaches in ritual studies, rituals concerning the "purification" of
menstruants and parturients are receiving new scholarly attention.[2]

---

1. Susan Starr Sered, *Priestess—Mother—Sacred Sister: Religions Dominated by Women*
(New York: Oxford University Press, 1994), 139.
2. See, e.g., Thomas Buckley, and Alma Gottlieb, eds., *Blood Magic: The Anthropology
of Menstruation* (Berkeley: University of California Press, 1988); Kohlschein, "Die
Vorstellung," 269–88; Shaye Cohen, "Menstruants and the Sacred," 273–99; Jacob
Milgrom, "The Rationale for Biblical Impurity [Lev 12–15]," *JANES* 22 (1993):
107–111; G. L. C. Frank, "Menstruation and Motherhood: Christian Attitudes in
Late Antiquity," *Studiae Historiae Ecclesiasticae* 19 (1993): 185–208; Brakke, "Prob-
lematization of Nocturnal Emissions," 419–60; Sabine Strasser, *Die Unreinheit ist
Fruchtbar: Grenzüberschreidungen in einem türkischen Dorf am Schwarzen Meer*
(Vienna: Wiener Frauenverlag, 1995); Jonathan Magonet, "'But if It Is a Girl, She Is

Purity rituals for women are heavily charged with gendered symbolic meaning, which has motivated Jewish and Christian feminist scholars to investigate, "deconstruct," and in some cases reclaim the purity rituals of their own religious traditions.[3] The existence of these purity rituals for women has also elicited a wide range of reflections on the representation and handling of "female blood" in Western religious thought and practices.[4] Sered's cross-cultural research into "women's religions" departs from very different sources and contexts, including non-Western cultures; moreover, it focuses primarily on women as designers and agents of (their own) rituals. One of Sered's most striking conclusions is that in women's religions, in which ritual is very central, "female blood" rituals are highly exceptional, and sacrificial or bloodletting rituals are almost absent. Therefore, it is very interesting to confront Sered's findings and conclusions with those of the other studies mentioned and to dive into the "ironical difference" Sered points to.

Unclean for Twice Seven Days . . .': The Riddle of Leviticus 12:5," in *Reading Leviticus: A Conversation with Mary Douglas* (ed. J. F. A. Sawyer; JSOTSup 227; Sheffield: Sheffield Academic Press, 1996), 144–52; Jonah Steinberg, "From a 'Pot of Filth' to a 'Hedge of Roses' (and Back): Changing Theorizations of Menstruation in Judaism," *JFSR* 13 (1997): 5–26; Yuko Nakano, "Women and Buddhism—Blood, Impurity, and Motherhood," in *Women and Religion in Japan* (ed. A. Okuda and H. Okano; StOR 420; Wiesbaden: Harrasowitz, 1998), 65–85; Poorthuis and Schwartz, *Purity and Holiness.*

3. See, e.g., Wisse, "De kerkgang van de moeder"; Ilana Be'er, "Blood Discharge: On Female Im/Purity in the Priestly Code and in Biblical Narrative," in *A Feminist Companion to Exodus–Deuteronomy* (ed. A. Brenner; Sheffield: Sheffield Academic Press, 1994), 152–64; Roll, "Churching of Women," 206–29; Joanne M. Pierce, "'Green Women' and Blood Pollution: Some Medieval Rituals for the Churching of Women after Childbirth," *Studia Liturgica* 29 (1995): 191–215; Luise Schottroff and Marie-Theres Wacker, *Von der Wurzel getragen: Christlich-feministische Exegese in Auseinandersetzung mit Antijudaismus* (Leiden: Brill, 1996), 29–80; Fonrobert, "Woman with a Blood-Flow," 121–40; Dresen, *Is dit mijn lichaam?* 41–60; Ulrike Metternich, *"Sie sagte ihm die ganze Wahrheit": Die Erzählung von der "Blutflüssigen"-feministisch gedeutet* (Mainz: Matthias Grünewald, 1999); Anne-Marie Korte, "Reclaiming Ritual: A Gendered Approach to (Im)Purity," in *Purity and Holiness: The Heritage of Leviticus* (ed. M. Poorthuis and J. Schwartz; Jewish and Christian Perspectives 2; Leiden: Brill, 2000), 313–27; Charlotte Elisheva Fonrobert, *Menstrual Purity: Rabbinic and Christian Reconstruction of Biblical Gender* (Stanford, Calif.: Stanford University Press, 2000).

4. See, e.g., Alison Joseph, ed., *Through the Devil's Gateway: Women, Religion, and Taboo* (London: SPCK and Channel Four Television, 1990); Archer, "Bound by Blood," 38–61; Hoffman, *Covenant of Blood*; Richard Whitekettle, "Levitical Thought and the Female Reproductive Cycle: Wombs, Wellsprings, and the Primeval World," *VT* 46 (1996): 376–91; Adriana Destro, "The Witness of Times: An Anthropological Reading of Niddah," in *Reading Leviticus: A Conversation with Mary Douglas* (ed. J. F. A. Sawyer; JSOTSup 227; Sheffield: Sheffield Academic Press, 1996), 124–38.

It is not my intention to examine Sered's concept of "female-dominated religions" or to discuss the anthropological research on which this concept is founded. As a theologian trained in philosophy and women's studies, I have turned to the findings and insights of this anthropological study as incentives for the more theoretical debates on women's rituals and female blood within women's studies in theology and religion. In the first part of this chapter I discuss Sered's conclusions about blood rituals in female-dominated religions, especially the attention paid in these rituals to "female blood" and women's ritual handling of blood. The second part of this chapter deals with the debates on women's rituals in contemporary Jewish and Christian feminist discourse. Do Jewish and Christian feminists indeed construct rituals to celebrate women's physiological passages, as Sered states? And what role does "female blood" play in these rituals? I will argue that the "ironical difference" noticed by Sered can be seen as a "difference in irony," in reference to the different strategies that women develop to distance themselves from androcentric cultural and religious definitions of women's corporeality.

Characteristics of "Women's Religions"

During the past three decades, a weight of evidence and insights has been presented by feminist scholars concerning the marginalization of women in almost all religions worldwide. Sered states having been intrigued by the idea of reversing this approach and delineating the factors that promote the leadership, participation, and influence of women in religions. Examples of religions affirming the voice, autonomy, and authority of women in religious affairs are rare, but do exist, and have been documented to some extent in cultural-anthropological and religious studies. Questions that methodical examination of these studies might answer are: What are the social, historical, and cultural circumstances most likely to allow women to develop autonomy in religious affairs and systems? What are the outstanding features of "women's religions"? Does the fact that women dominate a religious system mean that there is anything "female" about the content or structure of this religion?[5]

To find answers to these questions, Sered has concentrated her research on instances or segments of religion that are "dominated by women," that is to say, in which women are the leaders and the majority of the participants and in which women's concerns are central. According to Sered these women's religions do not stand on their own. Most of

---

5. Sered, *Priestess—Mother—Sacred Sister*, 3–10.

them are part of religions and cultures that are male dominated and phenomenologically not very different from men's religions: in them we find
worship of divine instances, elaborated rituals, privileged mediators,
explanatory worldviews, and practical-ethical guidelines. Nor are these
women's religions very numerous. The twelve examples Sered compares
are almost all the female-dominated religions that have been documented in ethnographic and historical literature. These examples are literally taken from all over the world. Evenly apportioned among Asian,
African, and North American religions, the twelve religions are the
indigenous religion of the Ryukyu Islands (Japan), matrilineal spirit cults
in northern Thailand, shamanism in Korea, and the Nat cults of Burma;
the Sande secret society of West Africa, the Zãr cult of northern Africa,
Afro-Brazilian religions, and Black Carib religion in contemporary
Belize; Shakerism, Christian Science, nineteenth-century spiritualism,
and twentieth-century feminist and womanist spirituality movements in
the United States.[6]

Sered has systematized these examples, looking for common patterns
and characteristics. Analyzing the social contexts that tend to foster
these women's religions, she points to three determining factors. The
first of these is gender dissonance: the occurrence of women's religions
is related to situations in which culturally accepted notions of gender
are highly contradictory or rapidly changing. The second factor is
matrifocality: we find women's religions in social contexts with a cultural
emphasis on the maternal role, often accompanied by either matrilinear-
ity or matrilocality. And the third factor is women's autonomy: women's
religions emerge in social organizations that allow women a relatively
high degree of personal, social, or economic autonomy and that often
have clearly separate male and female spheres or domains.[7]

Women's religions most often occur in societies in which women
control important resources, in which families focus upon mothers, and
in which kinship is matrilineal. According to Sered, family organization, more than any other aspect of social structure, sets the stage for
women's religions. At first sight, this finding seems to confirm the modern Western association of women's activities and interests with "private
life" and relationship as well as the general assumption that interpersonal and familial concerns matter most to women and determine their
lives and choices. Indeed, studies on women's religious participation and
interests demonstrate that women invest considerably in interpersonal

---

6. Ibid., 11–40.
7. Ibid., 43–69.

relationships. Because most religions deny women access to venues of formal power, women tend to be associated with religious modes that stress relationship: "Historical and ethnographical accounts describe women's religious activity as embedded within, complementary to, enriching of, growing out of, and occasionally rebelling against women's familial involvement."[8]

Sered, however, seeks an analysis of this "standing assumption" on a more profound level. Following the cultural anthropologist Melford Spiro, who points to the strong interrelation between family and religion as sociocultural systems and recommends studying religious systems as metaphorical expressions of family relations,[9] Sered shows that there is a strong connection between societies in which kin ties center on mothers (as in matrilineal and/or matrilocal organized societies) and the powerful roles of mothers in religious activity. While a range of identities can describe women's alternating positions within familial relationships (daughter, sister, wife, cowife, mother, grandmother, aunt, cousin, or niece), in female-dominated religions women receive attention primarily as mothers, grandmothers, and sisters. This is in marked contrast to male-dominated religions, which deal with and define women predominantly as wives and daughters, that is to say, in their roles most directly affecting male space and interest. The attention given to women as mothers, grandmothers, and sisters in women's religions corresponds to but also enhances the state of affairs in matrifocal societies that tend toward structural arrangements deemphasizing a definition of women as wives and giving prominence to women as mothers.[10]

Issues and images of motherhood can be prominent in male-dominated as well as in female-dominated religions. Both may address concrete as well as symbolic aspects of motherhood, and almost all religions demonstrate this to a certain degree.[11] But in contrast to male-dominated religions where mothers are perceived from the perspective of children, especially sons, in female-dominated religions motherhood comes to the fore from the perspective of the mothers themselves, that is to say, from an adult and women-centered point of view. Female-dominated religions highlight, not the fears and longings of children for their parents, but the

---

8. Ibid., 6.
9. See, e.g., Benjamin Kilborne and I. I. Langness, *Culture and Human Nature: Theoretical Papers of Melford E. Spiro* (Chicago: University of Chicago Press, 1987).
10. Sered, *Priestess—Mother—Sacred Sister,* 60–66.
11. See, e.g., the Christian veneration of Mary, the mother of Jesus. See also Caroline Walker Bynum, *Jesus as Mother: Studies in the Spirituality of the High Middle Ages* (Berkeley: University of California Press, 1982).

perceptions, insights, and skills of women evoked by their daily and often long-standing care for others who are dependent on them. Motherhood within this frame of reference, according to Sered, forms a fundamental image, a key ritual focus, and a chief theological concern in women's religions. To a large extent, women's religions center on the symbolic and ritual elaboration of this maternal role.[12]

This crucial position of motherhood forms the central thesis and conclusions of Sered's research. To Sered, who follows an established line of critical reflection on motherhood in women's studies that started with Adrienne Rich and Nancy Chodorow, motherhood is a cultural construction in the first place.[13] Physiological and social motherhood are to be seen as two interrelated but distinct aspects of women's identities and activities. Sered counts conception, pregnancy, childbirth, lactation, and maternal mortality among the physiological aspects of motherhood, whereas the social aspects of motherhood include the activities, rights, responsibilities, relationships, and social statuses that construct motherhood in particular cultural contexts. Because these social aspects can differ widely from culture to culture, the symbolic and ritual elaboration of the maternal role takes on very different forms.

The distinction between the biological and social aspects of motherhood guides Sered's interpretation of the "staging" of maternal roles in women's religions. Female-dominated religions, according to Sered, hardly ever offer women conceptions of motherhood that are merely biological. On the contrary, female-dominated rituals often "spiritualize" motherhood and emphasize that motherhood has social meaning and value. Birth is seldom extolled or separately ritualized in women's religions, and women are more honored in their roles as nurturers than as birth givers. In women's religions, mothers are powerful beings whose social bonds with their children give them ritual and spiritual strength. The symbolic and practical aspects of motherhood reflected and dramatized in women's religions are, above all, nurturing and care for the well-being of other persons. In most women's religions food and healing rituals are very important and elaborated: "Ornate fertility rituals, myths of mother goddesses who give birth to the world, and ceremonies that extol the wonders of lactation are almost totally absent from women's

---

12. Sered, *Priestess—Mother—Sacred Sister*, 71–85.
13. Ibid., 284; Adrienne Rich, *Of Woman Born: Motherhood as Experience and Institution* (New York: Bantam, 1977); Nancy Chodorow, *The Reproduction of Mothering: Psychoanalysis and the Sociology of Gender* (Berkeley: University of California Press, 1978).

religions."[14] Sered is reticent about giving comprehensive explanations for this state of affairs and points to several striking exceptions and anomalies in her findings. However, she shows that the recurrence of the pattern in her cross-cultural comparative analysis of women's religions is considerable.

Blood Rituals in Women's Religions

Although women's religions generally have a strong emphasis on ritual, blood rituals ([animal] sacrifice, bloodletting, or wounding) prove to be highly exceptional in their ritual practices. This also applies to rituals concerning the "natural bloodshed" of women in menstruation and childbirth. Sered's research as presented in *Priestess—Mother—Sacred Sister* does not deal systematically with this state of affairs, but she offers several insights that throw light on this very complex matter. I will gather these insights and relate them to the exceptional situations in women's religions where blood rituals and rituals concerning the "natural bloodshed" of women do occur. This will give me the opportunity for an in-depth discussion on the premises and the interpretative model of Sered's research.

According to Sered, the rituals and belief systems in women's religions primarily function to strengthen bonds between people. The fostering of social ties is a main focus of female-dominated religions. These social ties mainly consist of family and kinship relations but are not restricted to blood ties. Kinship relations as such are not ritually or symbolically focused upon in women's religions. The most distinguishing and common theme in the ritual systems of women's religions is not blood, but food and food preparation. Since in most cultures women are responsible for the preparation of meals, food is a resource that women control, and food rituals are par excellence capable of sacralizing women's everyday activities of cooking and serving. In women's religions, food rituals are public, communal, and abundant, and they involve both the supernatural and natural domains. In many cultures, food appears to be an especially sacred symbol because it is ingested, that is to say, incorporated into the body of the believer. Food rituals therefore create bridges between this world and other worlds. Sharing food emphasizes good relationships with the living and the dead, with the ancestors, the spirits, and the gods.[15]

---

14. Sered, *Priestess—Mother—Sacred Sister,* 286.
15. Ibid., 133–38.

Remarkably, in women's religions food rituals rarely include animal sacrifice. No slaughtered or burnt offerings are eaten or sent up to heaven. Instead, cooked and mainly vegetable foods are communally shared. Joining cultural anthropologist Nancy Jay, who has delineated the connection between blood sacrificial religion and patrilineal social organization,[16] Sered suggests that in women's religions bonds between people do not need to be strengthened in, or by, blood. Since blood ties between males are less certain and controllable than matrilineal-defined relationships, the ritual or symbolical affirmation of blood bonds between men is of great importance, as many male-dominated religions demonstrate. As Jay has shown, this also applies to the central rituals of the Jewish and of the Christian religions, in particular to the cultic types of the Anglican, the Roman Catholic, and the Eastern Orthodox churches. Rituals of (animal) sacrifice—sharing the flesh and the blood of the animal or "totem"—serve as confirmation of patrilineal descent and function to constitute and maintain patrilineal descent systems. But in women's religions, Sered declares, the bonds between people are already empirically "in the blood," and no (sacrificial) blood is needed to strengthen, prove, or dramatize that bond. Kinship ties do not need to be symbolically or ritually stressed because they are self-evident.[17]

However, could there be situations in women's religions in which relationships between *women* need to be ritually and symbolically enhanced? Sered tries to show that the very exceptional occurrence of clitoridectomy in women's religions may be related to this purpose. In this context, she refers to the African Sande religion. The central ritual complex in the female-dominated part of this religion involves clitoridectomy of adolescent women. In the Sande initiation rite, older women perform surgery on young women; they cut the clitoris and part of the labia minora away. This procedure, so Sande women believe, makes them clean and helps them bear many children. Enigmatic—at least to us as outsiders—is why Sande women, who belong to a well-established and powerful "secret" organization that gives women self-esteem and teaches them how to control their own fertility, assent to the deliberate dismembering of women's bodies. Sered points to several aspects that may indicate the relevance of this ritual for the establishment of bonds between women and the affirmation of the central position of mothers.

16. Jay, *Throughout Your Generations.* See Dresen and Johnson, this volume.
17. Sered, *Priestess—Mother—Sacred Sister,* 136–37.

Firstly, the shared pain and risk of death from infection helps to bring the women together and form a cohesive group. The fact that older women perform the clitoridectomy displays their power and control over the younger women in the group, but the ritual also brings different generations of women close together, for they all have gone through the same experience. Secondly, since blood rituals serve to establish strong interpersonal bonds in nonmatrilineal societies, perhaps female bonding by blood can be seen as a vigorous response to a patriarchal cultural environment. Sande initiation binds women more closely to one another than to their fathers and husbands, which may have important consequences in the patrilineal and virilocal societies in which Sande is located. And finally, clitoridectomy severs maternal functioning from sexual functioning. Genital mutilation deemphasizes sexuality and sexual pleasure, and so emphasizes childbearing. Considering that Sande women have higher status as mothers than as wives, perhaps the women opt to downplay their identities as wives in order to enhance their identities as mothers, even at the expense of sexual enjoyment: "By splitting off maternity from sexuality, clitoridectomy serves to raise the status of women through accentuating the part of women's identities that is most culturally esteemed."[18] Thus, conceiving of how clitoridectomy establishes bonds between women and affirms the central position of mothers, Sered is able to include this extraordinary violent blood ritual in the common patterns of women's religions.

However, this inclusion seems questionable to me on several grounds. In the first place, in Sered's interpretation no distinction is made between enhancing the position of women as mothers from an androcentric and from a women-centered perspective (acknowledging, of course, that sometimes these perspectives converge and may reinforce each other). In an androcentric context, being defined foremost or exclusively as a mother is primarily related to male control over women's sexuality and fertility,[19] while in a women-centered context this definition refers to women's autonomy, authority, and responsibilities. To relate clitoridectomy to a women-centered understanding of motherhood, as Sered seems to endeavor, requires a more thorough and convincing argumentation than she offers.

In addition, the idea that the clitoridectomy ritual establishes bonds between women is very problematic. The symbolic meaning Sered ascribes to this cliterodectomy ritual is derived by analogy from the symbolic

18. Ibid., 128.
19. Ibid., 71–86

meaning of sacrificial blood rituals in male-dominated religions that function to create "blood ties" between men. Although this analogy is intriguing, substantial elements of the clitoridectomy ritual cannot be related to the "blood-bonding model," and this also applies to the meaning the participants attribute to it. Phenomenologically, the clitoridectomy ritual is more related to initiation rituals like male circumcision than to sacrificial "blood-bond" rituals with shared meals.

Further, the account of the participants that this ritual makes them clean and helps them to bear many children cannot be intrinsically connected to this "women-bonding" interpretation. Sered's disregard of the cleansing explanation especially seems unjustified to me because this element deserves special attention. As Sered states, cleansing or purification rituals are practically absent in women's religions—with the exception of some "housecleaning" customs.[20] The explicit mention of "cleansing" in relation to women's bodies may indicate that an androcentric point of view is dominant here. Moreover, since neither self-sacrifice nor martyrdom are ritually elaborated in women's religions, the inclusion of a violent and dismembering ritual like adolescent clitoridectomy in the pattern of women's religions causes great friction.

We should rather assume that these women, despite having their own "secret society," are in the first place part of a male-dominated culture and religion. As Mary Daly has stated in her critical analysis of worldwide ritual practices of female mutilation, we should not hesitate to acknowledge that clitoridectomy rituals serve as confirmation and endorsement of patriarchal ideology.[21] Instead of trying to accommodate the clitoridectomy ritual to the pattern of women's religions, our research should postulate less clear-cut distinctions between male- and female-dominated religions. The idea of a "double-voiced" performance of women, supposing that the discourses and activities of dominant and marginalized groups differ from each other but also partly overlap,[22] can help us here. This concept acknowledges that women, as in the case of

---

20. Ibid., 151. In some cultures, however, housecleaning is part of the purification rituals that women perform at the end of their menstrual period. In Bangladesh, for example, washing the bed and bedding, cleaning the house, and sweeping and mopping the house are among these rituals. Cf. "Misconceptions about Menstruation," *Women's International Network News* 20 (1994): 2, 45–50.

21. Mary Daly, *Gyn/Ecology: The Metaethics of Radical Feminism* (Boston: Beacon, 1978).

22. Anthropologists Edwin and Shirley Ardener developed a model for studying the cultural expressions of marginalized groups in society. The model assumes that marginalized groups are for the most part included in the dominant culture—while recognizing

the Sande initiation rite, submit to an androcentric purification ritual but also assign their own meaning and value to this ritual. In this frame of reference, it is no longer necessary to reconcile the clitoridectomy ritual with the general pattern of women's religions.

"Female Blood" Rituals in Women's Religions

Sered's study also contains a set of insights concerning the absence of "female-blood" rituals in women's religions. According to Sered, one of the common characteristics of women's religions is that female bodies in processes of fecundity and procreation are not symbolically or ritually focused upon. Although (bodily) suffering and affliction are taken very seriously and rituals of healing have a momentous role in women's religions, rituals related to the specific physiological aspects of women's lives are scarce. "Rites of passage," an important ritual component of many religions worldwide, are relatively rare and unelaborated in women's religions. Birth, for example, is not a focus of ritual in most women's religions, and neither are menarche, marriage, sexuality, conception, or menopause. In women's religions, no initiation or maturation rites concentrate on menstruation.[23]

Sered points to several facts that may explain these findings. In the first place, in women's religions the social aspects of mothering are far more important than the physiological aspects. Moreover, the rituals in women's religions show that social cohesion, communality, and solidarity are more cherished than individual and personal change. Individual bodies are more valued as dwelling places or intermediaries of spirit(s) than as material markers of unique personalities, which may explain why the "normal" physiological processes of individuals do not receive much ritual attention in women's religions, at least not in the form of "rites of passage." In the second place, the absence of specific female "rites of passage" may be perceived as an absence only from the point of view of male-dominated religions, which view female bodies predominantly as "other" and "uncontrollable." These "unique" or "characteristic" physiological processes may not necessarily be considered unique or

---

that they are also excluded from it to some extent. When applied to women, the model indicates that their utterances and actions may be "double voiced"; that is, their expressions may contain irreconcilable tensions between the given women's culture and a dominant androcentric culture. See Edwin Ardener, "Belief and the Problem of Women: The Problem Revisited," in *Perceiving Women* (ed. S. Ardener. New York: Halsted, 1978), 1–27.
23. Sered, *Priestess—Mother—Sacred Sister*, 138–41, 152–55.

paradigmatic from the perspective of women themselves, especially not as experienced in their day-to-day repetitiveness. Moreover, considering that male-dominated religions often emphasize these "unique" or "characteristic" female physiological processes in relation to male control over women's fertility, it becomes conceivable that women tend to deemphasize these aspects. For example, women's religions do not ritualize the transfer of rights to women's bodies from one group of men to another, so wedding ceremonies are marginal."[24]

Sered's research reveals that major differences exist between male-dominated and female-dominated religions with regard to female blood rituals. Examining rituals related to menstruation makes these differences clear. Whereas women's religions do not view female bodies as particularly polluted or polluting and do not require "purifying" rituals in the case of menstruation and childbirth, many male-dominated religions affirm menstrual and childbirth pollution and use it to explain women's "otherness." This affirmation of pollution frequently results in the exclusion of women from religious places and from religious practices like prayer, fasting, studying holy texts, or attending religious services.[25] Further, menstrual and childbirth taboos in male-dominated religions are obviously defined from the husband's perspective. For example, a woman's children or her parents are rarely identified as affected by her menstruation.[26] This does not mean that menstrual and childbirth taboos are totally absent from women's religions. However, in women's religions the social and physical separation that these taboos entail seems to underscore not women's "otherness," but the empowering and spiritual aspects of menstruation and childbirth.[27]

In one of the twelve religions Sered studied, the above-mentioned pattern concerning the absence of ritual attention to women's physiological processes is not as clear and evident as in the other cases. In the feminist spirituality movement of North America and Western Europe, which mainly consists of white, middle-class, well-educated, and feminist women, rituals celebrating all stages of the female life cycle are very prominent. That is to say, in the extensive collection of fiction, art, prayer, and ritual instruction books of this movement, female life-cycle passages are frequently mentioned and celebrated in all kinds of ways.[28]

---

24. Ibid., 140.
25. See above, nn. 2–4.
26. Sered, *Priestess—Mother—Sacred Sister,* 71–72.
27. Ibid., 200–201.
28. See, e.g., Judy Grahn, "From Sacred Blood to the Curse and Beyond," in *The Politics of Women's Spirituality: Essays on the Rise of Spiritual Power within the Feminist*

Actually, to outsiders this movement has become somewhat notorious for its association with "female blood" rituals.

Sered does not expand upon the concrete rituals of this movement. She states that they center on "the celebration of womanhood" and points to the central role of motherhood and women's experiences of giving birth in the spirituality and symbols of the movement. Furthermore, she advances that the social context of this movement can be seen as "matrifocal," for its participants are very often single mothers or lesbian couples, whether or not accompanied by children. Moreover, according to Sered the substantial attention paid to interpersonal relationships and to the spiritual dimensions of daily life in this movement also shows remarkable conformity to the general pattern of women's religions.[29]

But in my opinion, in many respects this movement differs substantially from the other examples of female-dominated religions Sered discusses. This movement is located in a modern, Western, multireligious, and partially secularized context; its members are highly educated and engaged in political and culture-critical organizations for women's and homosexuals' rights, ecology, and antimilitarism; the movement has a far more explicit and elaborated gender ideology than the other female-dominated religions mentioned. Furthermore, it is the only one that venerates a single all-female deity.[30]

Sered does not reflect on this exceptional position and context of the feminist spirituality movement, nor does she investigate the momentous role that rituals celebrating women's physiological processes play in this movement. She also does not consider how these rituals relate to the general pattern of women's religions. But considering the uniqueness of the feminist spirituality movement as stated above, this last question does not seem to be the most fruitful one. It is more productive to study the similarities between this movement and the Jewish and Christian feminists who also try to construct rituals to celebrate women's physiological

---

Movement (ed. C. Spretnak; Garden City, N.Y.: Doubleday/Anchor, 1982), 265–79; Barbara Walker, *Women's Rituals* (San Francisco: Harper & Row, 1990); Lynn V. Andrews, *Woman at the Edge of Two Worlds: The Spiritual Journey through Menopause* (New York: HarperCollins, 1993); Lara Owen, *Her Blood Is Gold: Celebrating the Power of Menstruation* (New York: HarperCollins, 1993).

29. Sered, *Priestess—Mother—Sacred Sister*, 26–27, 56–57, 173–74, 258, 273.

30. In all these aspects, the feminist spirituality movement differs considerably from the Afro-American, or womanist, spirituality movement. In the womanist movement, not the biological, but the social and historical experiences of motherhood are central, and no "(Mother) Goddess" comes to the fore. In general, Sered's concept of a female-dominated religion is more adequate in the case of the womanist spirituality movement than in that of the feminist spirituality movement.

passages, and who also live in the modern Western context. As Sered has
remarked, the Jewish and Christian feminists who are interested in the
creation of these rituals are often involved in or influenced by the feminist spirituality movement.[31] And the opposite is observable in the aversion of some Jewish and Christian feminists to the celebration of
women's physiological passages as often related to their denouncement
of these rituals as performed and discussed in the feminist spirituality
movement.

"Female Blood" Rituals in Contemporary Jewish and Christian Feminist Debates

The celebrating of woman's life cycle is a very controversial subject
among Jewish, as well as among Christian, feminists. Moreover, the
nature of the debate in Jewish feminist circles differs substantially from
that among Christian feminists. Since in the more orthodox parts of
Judaism the purity rituals for menstruants and parturients are still
observed, the issue has more relevance and implications for Jewish feminists than Christian feminists. When we turn to the current discussions
among Jewish feminists concerning the traditional purification rituals
for menstruants and parturients, totally contrary positions appear to be
held. On the one hand, orthodox women hold a feminist plea for the
observance of these purity laws.[32] Some of them point to the deep spiritual meaning that the laws of purity and the rituals surrounding menstruation and childbirth can have to the women observing them. For
example, personal accounts testify to the spiritual renewal gained from
the ritual bath at the end of the "unclean" menstrual period.[33] Apart
from a spiritual meaning, the laws of purity may also have a positive
social significance. Women who were explicitly asked to indicate what
these regulations meant in their own lives associated observance of the
laws with an affirmation of their identity as women and as members of a
religious community.[34] Some Jewish women also mentioned that observing the purity laws allows them to exert some control over their sex lives

---

31. Sered, *Priestess—Mother—Sacred Sister,* 27.

32. E.g., Blu Greenberg, "Female Sexuality," 1–44, esp. 29; Susan Grossman, "Feminism, Midrash, and Mikveh," *Conservative Judaism* 44 (1992): 7–17.

33. E.g., Linda Sireling, "The Jewish Women: Different and Equal," in *Through the
Devil's Gateway: Women, Religion, and Taboo* (ed. A. Joseph; London: SPCK and
Channel Four Television, 1990), 87–96.

34. Rachel Wasserfall, "Menstruation and Identity: The Meaning of Niddah for
Moroccan Immigrants to Israel," in *People of the Body: Jews and Judaism Form an*

and the number of children they bear. Since they can, to some extent, decide when they go to the ritual bath, they can also influence the timing of their sexual relations.[35] Another positive aspect is the ritual bath's function as a social meeting place for women, without (their duties toward) their husbands and children.[36] But many feminist Jewish women cannot ascribe positive meaning to these ancient rituals, nor can they ignore their patriarchal social and political incorporation as it emerges in the theological legitimization of the purity laws as punishment for "the sin of Eve"[37] or in their nationalistic idealization in the "land of Israel" politics.[38]

Christian feminists, on the other hand, have to deal with a far more inarticulate heritage. Although in contemporary Western Christian religious practices the idea of cultic impurity of persons, based upon their physical state or condition, has almost completely faded, women's impurity as menstruants and parturients has been one of the most persistent ritual issues and still marks religious practice and reflection. For example, in the Catholic Church the "churching rite" for mothers after childbirth was practiced until the 1960s. The rite was conducted four to ten weeks after childbirth. The new mother was brought into the church, "from the dark into the light," by a priest, who led her in prayers of gratitude and penance. The Second Vatican Council (1962–65) rescinded this special custom for postpartum mothers. Churching was replaced under the liturgical renewal of Vatican II by a blessing for both parents at the christening of their child, thereby erasing any explicit reference to women's "bodily state" from Catholic ritual.[39] However, the notion of women's cultic impurity still lurks in Catholic discourse on liturgy, theology, and canonical law. The exclusion of women from ecclesiastical offices and liturgical performances in the Catholic Church and particularly the inconsistencies in these regulations cannot adequately be

---

Embodied Perspective (ed. H. Eilberg-Schwartz; Albany: State University of New York Press, 1992), 309–28; Carol Delaney, "Mortal Flow," 75–93.

35. Wasserfall, "Menstruation and Identity," 321–22.

36. Monika Fander, "Reinheit/Unreinheit," in *Wörterbuch der feministischen Theologie* (ed. E. Gössmann et al.; Gütersloh, Germany: Mohn, 1991), 349–51.

37. "Niddah," in *Encyclopaedia Judaica* (ed. C. Roth; Jerusalem: Keter, 1972), 1147; Weissler, "Mizvot Built into the Body," 103–4, 112–13 nn. 7–9. The same argumentation can be found in the Christian interpretation of the churching rite. See Wisse, "De kerkgang van de moeder," esp. 95–102.

38. See, e.g., Niza Yanay and Tamar Rapoport, "Ritual Impurity and Religious Discourse on Women and Nationality," *Women's Studies International Forum* 20 (1997): 651–56.

39. See Roll and Dresen, this volume.

explained without reference to (reminiscences of) the specific cultic impurity of women. Although there is no explicit mention of menstruation or other types of female blood flow in this context, only the notion of cultic impurity can explain why women, regardless of their religious or personal status, must keep their distance from sacred spaces and objects in Catholic churches.[40]

However, these two ancient religious traditions that still ritually assign meaning to the (female) body have definitely inspired women to reflect on the religious meaning of corporeality from their own points of view. For especially in Orthodox Judaism and Roman Catholicism, everyday physical experiences and practicalities are still linked to the quest for personal sanctification and closeness to God. Feminist initiatives to reclaim and re-create rituals that affirm the daily life and bodily experiences of women initially sprang from these two religious contexts.[41] However, the creation of new rituals that focus on women's bodily functions elicits fierce debate among Jewish, as well as among Christian, feminists. These debates are fired by a "paradoxical affection," a mixture of a fascination for and a repugnance to the glorification of the female body. Initially, feminist theologians from the United States and Western Europe have scrutinized concepts and representations of "the female body" in a very critical and analytical way. They have shown to what extent androcentric and misogynist assumptions concerning corporeality and female bodiliness have determined philosophical and theological discourse as well as ritual practice. To them, the affirmation of women's subjectivity and agency in religious affairs demands women no longer be identified with and addressed in terms of their (essentialistic conceived) body or corporeality.

This necessary critical stance toward essentialism, biological determinism, and body/spirit dualism in feminist-theological reflection has burdened the exploration of bodiliness from a woman's perspective. Goddess veneration and life-cycle rituals as performed in the feminist spirituality movement have been looked at with Argus's eyes by a substantial

---

40. *Instructio Fidei Custos* (1969); see Kohlschein, "Die Vorstellung," 269–71.
41. See, e.g., Ellen M. Umansky and Dianne Ashton, eds., *Four Centuries of Jewish Women's Spirituality: A Sourcebook* (Boston: Beacon, 1992); Sue Levi Elwell, "Reclaiming Jewish Women's Oral Tradition? An Analysis of Rosh Hodesh," in *Women at Worship: Interpretations of North American Diversity* (ed. M. Procter-Smith and J. Walton; Louisville: Westminster John Knox, 1993), 111–26; Debra Orenstein, ed., *Lifecycles: Jewish Women on Life Passages and Personal Milestones* (Jerusalem: Jewish Lights, 1995); Susan Berrin, *Celebrating the New Moon: A Rosh Hodesh Anthology* (London: Jason Aronson, 1996).

number of Jewish and Christian feminists. They cannot deny that goddess veneration, life-cycle rituals, and the appeal to a female or motherly "moral stance" express an extraordinarily strong feminist cultural critique because these practices affirm both directly and very positively the "female values" of giving life, caring, nurturing, and protecting that are maligned and repressed in Western culture. But the premises of this affirmation are highly problematic. It is difficult to distinguish the appeal to women's involvement in the creation and sustenance of life as cherished by the feminist spirituality movement from the traditional theological and moral views that define women's status and responsibilities on the basis of the purpose of their "female organs."[42] The fear of feminist theologians to reaffirm essentialism and gender dualism and to confirm the gender stereotypes of their own religious traditions has resulted in restraint in reclaiming or creating rituals that center on the female body. Two examples demonstrate the ambivalent stance of feminist theologians regarding this type of ritual.

The Struggle for Revaluation of Women's Corporeality

An impressive example of an attempt to reinterpret Jewish purity laws for women from a critical, antiessentialist feminist point of view is the noted article "Tumah and Taharah: Ends and Beginnings," which was written about twenty-five years ago by the Jewish feminist theologian Rachel Adler. In this article Adler most carefully reframed Jewish regulations on menstruating women, placing them in the wider context of Jewish purity regulations as a whole, which concern, for example, contact with corpses or leprosy sufferers. In these situations, people are literally handling matters of life and death. The confrontation with death and mortality (*tumah*) is ritually followed by a reaffirmation of life and vitality (*taharah*). Menstruation and birth are directly related to the boundaries between life and death, for the womb is the site of transformation from death to life, and vice versa: "We think of death as a return to the womb because the womb is the place of birth."[43] The *mikveh*, which transforms the bather from *tumah* to *taharah* after menstruation, is a sort of rebirth or a resurrection from death. In Adler's interpretation, *tumah*

---

42. See also Anne-Marie Korte, "Die Erfahrung unseres Leibes: 'Leiblichkeit' als hermeneutische Kategorie in der feministischen Theologie," in *Abschied von Männergott: Schöphungsverantwortung für Frauen und Männer. Catharina Halkes zum 75. Geburtstag.* (ed. J. Jäger-Sommer; Lucerne: Exodus, 1995), 288–314.
43. Rachael Adler, "Tumah and Taharah: Ends and Beginnings," *The Jewish Women* (ed. Elizabeth Koltun; New York: Schocken, 1976), 66. See De Troyer, this volume.

does not denote a state of evil, sin, uncleanliness, or danger but it has a spiritual significance, which means wearing the veil or the shadow of death. Adler's new theological explanation of the purity laws broke with the tradition of speaking about women in terms of (un)touchability and sexual availability. She did not set women's experiences apart but rather saw them as part of a set of situations that have a profound, universally accessible, religious meaning in which people are confronted with the boundaries of physical existence.

Even when she published this view in 1976, Adler immediately had to concede that her reading was hardly supported by historical fact. After all, practically every justification for the purity laws had been rooted in a deep revulsion of the female experience and the association of women with lust, sin, and evil. Despite her universalizing argumentation, Adler also had to admit that observance of the *tumah/taharah* symbolism was, in practice, an exclusively female responsibility. Since the destruction of the Second Temple, the purity laws dealing with the functions of procreation in an individual's body apply to married women only. The purity laws concerning the sexual functions of the male body were never emphasized, developed, and practiced to the same extent.

However, Adler still felt that none of these concessions detracted from the validity of the laws of menstruation. For the sake of women's religious experiences, she argued, it was better to observe the laws but do so with a view to *tumah/taharah*: "Tumah/taharah remains one of the few major Jewish symbolisms in which women had a place. Having so few authentic traditional experiences on which to build, is it worthwhile to reject *niddah*, because later generations of men have projected their repugnance for women upon it?"[44] Adler ended her argument with a plea for the reintroduction of the purity laws for men, for example, those concerning ejaculation. This would give men an opportunity to acknowledge the process of death and rejuvenation in their own bodies.

Two decades later, however, Adler wrote a moving article in which she retracted her theological reinterpretation of the laws of menstruation. She had started to feel increasingly doubtful about precisely those aspects of her interpretation that she had originally considered so positive, namely, her theological justification of the laws of menstruation without reference to the usual "feminine topics" of family purity, sexual relations, menstrual impurity, and the ritual bath. Her *tumah/taharah* interpretation had deliberately neutralized any gender-specific aspects of the laws of menstruation, whether theological, moral, or social. Her universalizing

---

44. Adler, "Tumah and Taharah," 71.

approach disregarded the particular pain and conflict, both internal and external, that women suffer due to the menstruation laws. She had effectively eliminated any way to discuss these aspects.

Over the years, Adler had come to realize that her universalizing explanation of the *tumah/taharah* system and her abstract equation of women and men had left her no room to deal with her own religious queries: "I needed to understand how a body that menstruates, a body that pollutes, could be a holy body. The male writers were concerned about how women were to comport themselves in their impurity. I wanted to know what it might mean to be pure . . . to become holier and closer to God."[45] An answer to these questions could hardly be expected from traditional theological justifications, Adler concluded, because they did not address the issue from a women-centered perspective:

[T]he otherness and the instrumentality of women were foundational presumptions of the men who wrote about these laws. What was significant about menstruation for them was that it made women uniquely capable of causing men to sin by transmitting pollution to them. They never asked themselves how it would feel to be someone to whom such a capacity had been assigned, or whether menstruation might have other meanings to those who menstruated.[46]

Adler turned against the observance of women's purity rituals, considering them "unjust."

In her latest book, *Engendering Judaism: An Inclusive Theology and Ethics* (1998), Adler cites the following story told by Rabbi Laura Geller:

One day when I sat in a class in my Rabbinical seminary . . . we studied the tradition of the *berakoth*—blessings, blessings of enjoyment, blessings related to the performance of *mizvot* (commandments) and blessings of praise and thanksgiving. My teacher explained. . . . "There is no important moment in the lifetime of a Jew for which there is no blessing." Suddenly I realized it was not true. There had been important moments in my life for which there was no blessing. One such moment was when I . . . first got my period.[47]

---

45. Rachel Adler, "In Your Blood, Live: Re-visions of a Theology of Purity," *Tikkun* 8 (1992): 39.
46. Ibid.
47. Rachel Adler, *Engendering Judaism: An Inclusive Theology and Ethics* (Boston: Beacon, 1998), 61.

This story forms the overture to Adler's plea for the incorporation of unacknowledged life-cycle events like first menstruation and menopause in Jewish religious ceremonies and religious language, as Jewish women have started practicing during the past two decades.[48] Adler keeps to her denouncement of the traditional religious justifications of the purity laws for women; however, she holds it possible to reclaim these laws in a contemporary religious and moral setting, as when the laws about "sexual boundaries" are interpreted as "a subset of laws about justice to our neighbor" or as "rules that make trust possible" in all kinds of personal and professional relationships.[49]

In the very extensive oeuvre of the Roman Catholic feminist theologian Rosemary Radford Ruether, we can find a similar itinerary toward the reclaiming and creation of "bodily rituals," as in the works of Adler. In her initial feminist publications Ruether held a strong antiessentialist position. She pointed to the detrimental consequences of women's identification with (their) corporeality and more generally with "lower things" like matter, chaos, and the demonic.[50] In her early works, Ruether critically analyzed this identification in its different appearances in theological and philosophical texts. She was one of the first feminist theologians who openly condemned the symbolic and ritual affirmation of "womanhood" in the feminist spirituality and goddess movements.[51] She opposed its romantic, uncritical embrace of women's "otherness." But, like Adler, Ruether subsequently began to recognize the importance of the reclaiming and creation of rituals that acknowledge and affirm women's bodily existence from a women-centered point of view.

In *Women-Church* (1983), her book on community formation, prayer, and ritual "from the perspective of religious feminists who seek to reclaim aspects of the biblical tradition,"[52] Ruether spends several chap-

---

48. Ibid., 69.
49. Ibid., 132.
50. Rosemary Radford Ruether, "Motherearth and the Megamachine: A Theology of Liberation in a Feminine, Somatic, and Ecological Perspective," *Christianity and Crisis* 31 (1971): 267–73; "Misogynism and Virginal Feminism in the Fathers of the Church," in *Religion and Sexism: Images of Woman in the Jewish and Christian Traditions* (ed. R. Radford Ruether; New York: Simon & Schuster, 1973), 150–84; *New Woman—New Earth: Sexist Ideologies and Human Liberation.*(New York: Seabury, 1975).
51. Rosemary Radford Ruether, "A Religion for Women: Sources and Strategies," *Christianity and Crisis* 39 (1979): 307–11; "Goddesses and Witches: Liberation and Countercultural Feminism, *ChrCent* 94 (1980): 842–47.
52. Rosemary Radford Ruether, *Women-Church: Theology and Practice of Feminist Liturgical Communities* (San Francisco: Harper & Row, 1986), 3.

ters presenting examples of the celebrating of stages of the life cycle and seasonal events. Menstruation, marriage, giving birth, and menopause are all mentioned and receive their own prayers and rituals. The prayers and gestures that are presented here are very similar to those in the handbooks of the feminist spirituality movement, and Ruether herself states that she has composed this book as an alternative to the manuals of feminist spiritualists.

In the four chapters of *Women-Church* presenting examples of women-centered liturgies, rituals related to the cycles of body and nature constitute the greater part. Ruether has designed a "puberty rite for a young woman," to be held after a girl's first menstruation in the presence of women and girls who already have begun to menstruate. The rite symbolically stresses the girl's entrance into the reign of womanhood, sexuality, and fertility. A menopause liturgy and rituals for menstruation and new moon are also elaborated. Ruether admonishes women to reclaim and reevaluate menstruation. Women need to find their own female-defined way of affirming the menstrual cycle: "We should not deny that menstruation is the 'autumn' within the female body, in which capacity for new life is shed and preparation is made for the birth of new potency."[53] However, although the rituals offered by Ruether are very similar in style and gesture to the rituals of the feminist spirituality and goddess movements, the instructions and reflections Ruether adds demonstrate a steady awareness of the contesting and contested meaning of these rituals. To prevent naive assent of these rituals, she has placed the "body and nature" rituals in second position following more critical and political liturgies that focus on (home) violence, incest, rape, abortion, and similar feminist issues. And in her commentaries on the "body and nature" rituals, Ruether hardly refers to ancient "female" religious myths and traditions, as in the feminist spirituality and goddess movements. Ruether prefers to connect the rituals she describes to contemporary (religious) celebrations of political-feminist events and issues, especially those in nonwhite and non-Western contexts. In later publications, Ruether has underlined her critical stance towards the traditional religious justification of women's "otherness" founded in their corporeality and "nature."[54]

---

53. Ibid., 218.
54. Ruether, "Women's Body and Blood," 7–21.

"Female Blood" as a Symbol of Feminist Cultural Critique

Remarkably menarche and menstruation are the events to which feminist theologians from different religious traditions pay substantial attention in their projects to reclaim and to create women-centered rituals. Probably this is related to the fact that in modern Western cultures menstruation is still considered an anomaly: a state to conceal and not to be associated with, as the common representation of menstruation in the media and especially in advertisement demonstrates. After all, menstruation sets women apart, even in modern, Western, and secularized countries. It forms the physical fact that marks persons as *women*.[55] It is hardly surprising that feminist theologians greatly dissent over the question if a ritual for menarche (like a blessing or celebration) should be performed only among women, or rather should be part of a more general ritual with a mixed audience. The fear of affirming gender stereotypes versus the need to break taboos fuels the debate.[56] In addition, this particular attention on (the first) menstruation might also mirror the fact that the Jewish and Christian religions in their texts and rituals have stored, paradoxically as it may sound, an interest for the religious meaning of menstruation and thus of the female body as well.[57] By ritually enhancing (first) menstruation, this religious significance of the female body can be recaptured and explored.

The fact that feminist theologians attempting to reclaim and to create women-centered rituals particularly focus on (the first) menstruation indicates that *revaluation* of women's corporeality from a women-centered point of view constitutes a strong motive. Menstruation preeminently symbolizes this intention because of its obvious associations with taboo, defilement, and secrecy.[58] This revaluation, however, cannot be reduced to a straightforward "celebration of womanhood." As we have seen, feminist theologians like Adler and Ruether who advocate ritual affirmation of life-cycle events also critically scrutinize their own religious heritages and argue for a complete transformation of the discourse on corporeality, sexuality, and relationships within their religious

---

55. See Janet Lee and Jennifer Sasser-Coen, *Blood Stories: Menarche and the Politics of the Female Body in Contemporary Western Societies* (New York: Routledge, 1996).
56. See also Lesley A. Northup, ed., *Women and Religious Ritual* (Washington, D.C.: Pastoral Press, 1993); Leslie Smith Kendrick, "A Woman Bleeding: Integrating Female Embodiment into Pastoral Theology and Practice," *Journal of Pastoral Care* 48 (1994): 145–53.
57. See Fonrobert, "Woman with a Blood-Flow."
58. See O'Grady, this volume.

traditions. Moreover, they keep a (self-)critical pose toward all kinds of feminist attempts to reclaim and create rituals that concentrate on women's bodily experiences.

In my opinion, the bodily rituals of the feminist spirituality movement are more cognate with this contemporary project of feminist cultural critique than with Sered's cultural-anthropological pattern of "women's religions." Placed in their own Western context, these rituals are in the first place cultural-critical statements and might be considered examples of "mimetic strategy" to bring about cultural transformation as proposed by the French feminist philosopher Luce Irigaray.[59] These rituals in their form and content relate to contemporary Western developments in art and literature in which personal statement, artistic expression, and ritual performance increasingly intertangle. These developments are related to the disappearance of rituals with formal status and universal significance in Western culture and the ascension of rituals as context-bound and individually orientated public statements.

At the same time the Jewish and Christian (re-)creation of women-centered rituals differs considerably from the celebration of women's bodily existence in the feminist spirituality movement. In the Jewish and Christian approaches we find complex maneuvers around old and new intellectual and moral taboos concerning the presence and presentation of women's corporeality. These maneuvers lack the iconoclastic force and the revolutionary imagination that characterize the symbols and rituals of the feminist spirituality and the goddess movements. However, the Jewish and Christian approaches facilitate an appropriation of women's corporeality that leaves room for ambivalence, diversity, and historical account. The self-critical stance in the Jewish and Christian approaches is more capable of acknowledging women's often contradictory experiences with their bodies than the romantic and mythic imagination of the feminist spirituality and the goddess movements is able to. The pain and dismay that may accompany the (re)presentation of a "female body" are more reckoned with, as is the historical awareness that sacrificing, starving, and mutilating of their own bodies have been common reactions of women confronted with the normative image of their "uncontrollable" corporeality. The same goes for the "silent history" of shame for menstruation, pregnancy, parturition, miscarriage, abortion, and "women's diseases" that has marked the lives of so many women.

---

59. See, e.g., Luce Irigaray, *An Ethics of Sexual Differences* (Ithaca, N.Y.: Cornell University Press, 1993); *Thinking the Difference: For a Peaceful Revolution* (New York: Routledge, 1994).

The feminist spirituality and the goddess movements offer a joyous, imaginative, and often ecstatic form of revaluation of women's corporeality that renders very positive connotations to "female blood."[60] More earnest and much less ironic are the Jewish and Christian attempts to recapture women-centered rituals. Here the history and experiences of women within the dominant Western religions are kept present and accounted for. "Female blood" is connected to a great diversity of experiences and is not given the unambiguous positive meaning attributed to it by the feminist spirituality and the goddess movements.

To conclude, Jewish and Christian feminists indeed construct rituals to celebrate women's physiological passages, as Sered has observed, but the same holds true for the feminist spirituality and the goddess movements, which are credited by Sered as "women's religions" that generally are not interested in ritually emphasizing women's physiological processes of fecundity and procreation. Moreover, Jewish and Christian feminists create these rituals with great reservation and with a historical and (self-)critical awareness that cannot be found to the same extent within the feminist spirituality and the goddess movements. The "ironical difference" noticed by Sered might rather be seen as a "difference in irony," in reference to the different strategies that contemporary women develop to distance themselves from ancient and ingrained androcentric cultural and religious definitions of women's corporeality.

---

60. See, e.g., Carol P. Christ, *Daughter of Aphrodite: Reflections on a Journey to the Goddess* (San Francisco: Harper & Row, 1987); Genia Pauli Haddon, *Body Metaphors: Releasing the God-Feminine in Us All* (New York: Crossroad Continuum, 1988); Zsuzsanna Emesse Budapest, *The Goddess in the Office: A Personal Energy Guide for the Spiritual Warrior at Work* (San Francisco: Harper, 1993); *The Grandmother of Time: A Women's Book of Celebrations, Spells, and Sacred Objects for Every Month of the Year* (San Francisco: Harper & Row, 1989); Cynthia Eller, *Living in the Lap of the Goddess: New Feminist Spiritual Movements* (New York: Crossroad, 1993); Melissa Raphael, *Theology and Embodiment: The Post-Patriarchal Reconstruction of Female Sacrality* (Sheffield: Sheffield Academic Press, 1996).

10

Shedding Blood
The Sanctifying Rite of Heroes
Judith Ann Johnson

> Bloodshed is a cleansing and sanctifying rite and the nation which
> regards it as a final horror has lost its manhood.
>
> —FROM AN UNNAMED IRISH SOURCE

> God intended for man to become one with God. We are going to
> become one with God. We are going to have almost as much knowl-
> edge and almost as much power as God.
>
> —RICHARD SEED,
> CHICAGO PHYSICIST ENGAGED IN HUMAN CLONING

From the preceding essays in this book, as diverse as they are, one can
draw many parallel conclusions about the flow or shedding of blood and
the assignment of pure or impure status to the person incurring the flow.
In ancient Judaic tradition, the human shedding of blood recalls the flow
of life forces and is, paradoxically, both unclean and sacred at the same
time—as Kathleen O'Grady points out.[1] Both the unclean and the
sacred inspire fear and awe. And both are highly dangerous. The natural
shedding of blood (and other bodily fluids such as semen) conjures up
images of Life. Conversely, the "unnatural" or unexpected shedding of
blood projects images into the mind of fear, terror, and the torments of
convulsing Death.

Blood is the central motif of Life and Death—and whether it is male
or female, more often than not, determines whether it is pure or impure,
clean or unclean, appalling or redemptive, or even a channel to the
Divine. All sacrifice, the ultimate drama of death seeking a divine
rebirth, revolves around this life-sustaining fluid in some way or another.

---

1. The Hebrew term *k-d-sh* (holy) builds principally on the concept of separation.
Both that which is sacred and that which is unclean are kept separate.

As we have seen, in Western religious traditions, the release of blood (or body fluids) from a woman has too often been identified with impurity and shame, with a type of contaminated or desecrated nature; mysteriously, she brings forth new life into a world fraught with evil. A fairly parallel release of blood or fluids from a man is aligned with redemption and honor, the release of a divine flow of life. *She* may produce a monster, but *he* always contributes the perfect form. Her role in history has generally been confined to that lottery called pregnancy; her wager is her blood, her very life. He may have suspected that his fluid, milky donation to the generation of a new human being was needed only once; after that he was expendable, if not repulsed. Indeed, if I may paraphrase Margaret Mead's assessment of a half century ago, men, viewing the birth process like visitors from an alien planet, inevitably sought their own dramas to encounter the mysterious powers that both give and take life. Controlling the regeneration of human life became a primary goal, if not the original passion.

What have men produced to equal the birth of human life? How did they create for themselves a greater role in this drama of life? A close reading of several of the preceding essays allows us to see that an image parallel, yet arguably opposite, to that of the menstruating woman emerges in that of holy man, *nazirite,* or priest. This new, sacred drama invites a communal surge of awe at the release of powers that cannot be contained in one woman; it involves a "rebirth" now in that "perfect" form, which, left to the devices of women, all too often came out at least a little bit mangled—or female. In contrast, in the drama of a communal, religious sacrifice to divine life, when blood flows, it is at the expected time, under the control of the set-apart holy man in communication with a preternatural force. Death and the divine powers that produced human life now come for an awe-filled instance of sacrificial reality in covenant with, if not in control of, the holy men in charge of the ritual.

Still we must ask: Is the priest, the conductor of ritual sacrifice, the *sole masculine* motif that manifests a redemption/rebirth theme through blood in Western traditions or ancient religious myths?

This commentary will seek to move beyond the image of the bloodletting woman and even beyond that of the "holy man" or priest/sacrificer to another side of the holy-man image—to that of another divinely ordained leader of sacrifice, the warrior-priest who does earthly battle, whose killings are real human sacrifices as well as metaphorical ones. Found in both biblical accounts and classic myths, as well as history itself, accounts of the mythic warrior-hero show a different kind of "priest"—the man who risked or shed his own blood in *self*-sacrifice. In

the hero cults of the ancient Greeks, the divine hero whose blood mysteriously saves others brings to them a sacred rebirth in new life beyond
the contaminations of the less controllable evil world. In the savior-hero
the image of holy man and warrior merge. The hero icon is but a mirror
of the priest or *nadir/nazirite*. If one gazes more deeply into that mirror,
one may even see, in the hero-priest's passion to maintain the purity of
his descent line, patriarchy's craving to control death. One can begin to
perceive the warrior-priest and the "hero cult" as fuller, more complex,
and sacralized surrogates for the life-giving woman.

Let me first reflect on some remarks from prior essays in this book.
When I speak of a male need for a "pure" descent line, I am picking up
on strands of Leviticus and warnings in other ancient texts, as my "fore-
mothers" in this volume have also done. As O'Grady reminds us, Aristotle, Augustine, Aquinas, and even John Calvin in our more classic
Christian European traditions allude to the type of deformed creatures
women could produce. Churning up biological "facts" from his own
philosophical stance, Aristotle warned against sex with a menstruating
woman, for it generated baby monsters and other physical abominations.
Citing Leviticus, Augustine exhorts men to shun their wives literally, not
only because of possible abominations but because sex in itself was
shameful. The impure "blood" made it doubly shameful. Aquinas echoes
both Aristotle and Aquinas: "Men ought to keep away from their [men-
struous] wives, because thus is a deformed, blind, lame, leprous offspring
conceived" (*Summa Theologica* 2802 [q. 64, art. 3, suppl.], as quoted in
O'Grady'). Thus, women's defective matter, in a release of their blood,
could turn men's perfect-form offering into a monstrous miscreant.

Alongside this ancient "explanation" for human deformities existed
the corollary longing of the archetypal/collective male mind for a *pure*
male descent line, uncontaminated by female blood, outside the uncontrollable power of women. The priesthood and the warrior-elite provided
those lines.

Among priesthoods, the Levirite and the Catholic/Orthodox
churches reproduce two such purely male descent lines, with priests created through a mystical anointing process.[2] Both take charge of ritual
related to the shedding of blood. As we have seen, both defined laws
related to strictures on both menstruating and parturient women.[3] For

---

2. Also, all other Christian "high" churches and all sacrificial religions would most
likely be on this list.
3. Episcopal celibacy, as early as the fourth century, became necessary in order to keep
inheritance and the right to conduct sacrifice within the pure line of the "anointed,"
that is, to prevent handing it over to the sons of women/wives.

example, up to Vatican II, Catholic penitential books demanded that couples refrain from sex for at least six weeks after childbirth—the time during which women continued to bleed sporadically. Even though confessors in the twentieth century liked to say that this was to "help" the new mother regain her health, one still wonders whether the "ancients" or even the Romans knew this. The umbrage of Augustinian shame and punishment for abominations persisted in hanging over women's bodies that continued to bleed, wallowing in impurities ready to contaminate the male body, morals, and soul-making capacity. Both the baby-matter and the sex partner were at risk.

But I am getting ahead of myself with this summary. Such embedded fears, based on ancient religious customs, are not limited to Judaic and Christian traditions. As one reads Sigmund Freud,[4] two things stand out: The *rituals* of religion are devised to transfer life-giving power to men, as well as control over their own descent line, a new beginning for a perfected (male) human life, with a promise of communal and personal perpetuity. Arthur Schopenhauer, Freud reminds us, said that the damnation of death "stands at the outset of every philosophy"—that we ponder life as we face death, for no sacrificial lamb or family totem can protect us from the ultimate end of physical life.[5] Thus religion took form around issues of birth, death, and rebirth, becoming one generative dynamic leading toward the human dream of perpetuity—a male-defined and controlled perpetuity.[6]

Blood and Sacrifice

Human blood has been the singular motif that brings together issues of life and death. We carry on "bloodlines"; we are red-blooded Americans or English blue bloods. We drink the blood of Christ in liturgical Communion and shed blood in both giving birth and taking life. As the pages of this volume have reiterated, both female and male blood and the (male) body's "other" major fluid-of-power, the fluid called semen, are mysteriously and dangerously potent liquids of life, human and divine—male fluid to create life and female blood to contaminate it. To expose the mythic power of male blood remains largely an issue for this final chapter.

---

4. References here are mostly gleaned from Freud's *Totem and Taboo*.
5. See esp. Freud, *Totem and Taboo*, 109.
6. How girls comprehended this process is, of course, unknown.

If the disparate chapters in this book can be brought together under any one thesis, it would be the meeting ground for two intrinsically related issues: (1) how the different ways blood is shed has operated as a factor in determining the relative "value" or purpose of the two identifiable human sexes; and (2) how in the androcentric view of patriarchal (in this case, Western) society, blood sacrifices were attempts to find a way to control life and death. One might further conclude, arguably, that the moment when "man" identified himself as in control of form/soul production may also have been the moment when he first sought to control all the processes of life, to elevate male blood shedding to a sacred art, as an expression of a divinely sanctioned male sovereignty over life and death. Above stood the first "superman" with his battle plan: to concentrate the forces of life and death under his aegis as king/high priest/hero.

Since there is no historical record of any such original or archaic moment, I will begin outside biblical sources with the anthropological work of Sir James George Frazer, for Frazer provides so many detailed records of nineteenth-century societies, virtually untouched by technology, rich in memories of ancient religious rituals steeped in human blood and alive with metaphoric stories describing the workings of "taboo" to control the uncontrollable mystery of blood shedding.[7]

O'Grady cites Frazer in her essay on "The Semantics of Taboo: Menstrual Prohibition in the Hebrew Bible," when she observes the correspondence between the vows of the *nazir* and the concept of "taboo." Both distinguish someone or something "separated" as well as "consecrated." We detect a nuanced fusion wrought with danger rather than a distinction of meanings. She further emphasizes Frazer's observation that the "uncleanness" of "girls at puberty" *and* the "sanctity of holy men" did not differ "materially" from one another but, instead, were "different manifestations of the same mysterious energy" that "becomes beneficent or maleficent according to its application." Uniting these elements (impurity and sanctity), O'Grady quotes further, is the elemental power of "danger"—danger as an intrusion from *outside,* a danger that must be kept from the community at all costs.[8] Keeping that power at bay in early Israel was the work of kings and priests, especially warrior-priests in contact with the divine.

---

7. Frazer's fatal flaw may also be his prime value to us today: he leaves us with a tapestry of vivid scenes on a threadbare bed of presumptive scholarship. It is up to us to rebuild the frame of that bed.

8. Her theories are, of course, reminiscent of Mary Douglas. See O'Grady, this volume, with quotes from Frazer (*Golden Bough,* 587) as cited in her chapter.

In *The Golden Bough* Frazer gives us cogent examples of the transfer of female-to-male life-giving power; I will use one definitive example, that of the sacrifice of a female stand-in for a goddess. In this scenario Frazer produces a parallel to O'Grady's *niddah-nazir* image, which provides us with clues to the *niddah-nazir* (or menstrual woman and holy priest) relationship.[9]

Frazer describes in elaborate detail an ancient harvest festival in which the Aztecs "sanctified" a pubescent slave girl (of twelve or thirteen years) by investing her with the dress, crown, and accoutrements of the goddess Chicomecohuatl and the symbolic fruits of the harvest. As goddess personified, the girl ritually reigns for three ceremonial days[10] before the priests throw her incensed body on a heap of corn and seeds, cut off her head, and catch "the gushing blood in a tub; they then sprinkle the blood on the wooden image of the goddess, [on] the walls of the chamber, and [over the seed] offerings [on] the floor. After that they flayed the headless trunk, one priest squeezed himself into the bloody skin"; once clad in the "sanctified" robes the girl had worn, he dons the goddess's crown. (Whether the girl was devested or not before she was beheaded is unclear.) What is clear is that the priest usurps the power of the "goddess" by becoming the sacrificed girl.

What is perhaps even less clear but most meaningful is the symbolism of the double rebirth of the goddess and the transfer of her life-giving power to the priest. Even though the girl is crowned and attired as the goddess, "she was specially chosen as a young girl to represent the young maize, . . . not yet fully ripened"—that is, *almost* fertile.[11] She was both the corn and the Corn Goddess. Filled with the polluting power of fertility-about-to-explode, she was like the corn; exuding an aura of danger implicit in her role as an "outsider," she was more than a slave living among free Aztecs. She is the ideal sacrifice, the "perfect kill." Both like the sacrificers, as part of the community, and unlike them (as foreign slave), she was a harbinger of death. And she was more. Representing the "homage and blood offerings of the whole people," she becomes both the ideal sacrifice and the personification of the Corn Goddess. Through her sacrifice, she confers on the priests of the sacrifice—as an extension of

9. Here I go outside of O'Grady's work and directly to Frazer and his "killing the god in Mexico."
10. As Douglas might say, as a "marginal" person at the edge of the community, she personified outside danger and impure infiltration both from external enemies and nonphysical (divine) powers: both exist beyond the margins.
11. And again, as Mary Douglas would in all likelihood remind us, as "almost" fertile she existed on one of the dangerous and polluting margins of life.

her goddess role—the "character of a divinity." Goddess, community, and the fruit of the earth become one through the ritual shedding of a (newly menstruant) girl's blood.

One might loosely identify the slave girl as a type of female savior image, but she is little more than the vessel for transferring that image to the priest.[12] In a very physical ritual of flowing blood, the high priest takes on her crown, vestments, and flayed skin. She is dead, but he— anointed in the continuing flow of her blood—is "god," the divine (now male) power. In the ritual process the very contact of femaleness with divinity has also been flayed.

Curiously, although Frazer presents us with the full ceremony, his explanation stops with the beheading and the spreading of the girl's blood over the crops to infuse them (or pray that they be infused) with the strength and life of the goddess. The rest of the interpretation, in a feminist deconstruction, took nearly another century to reach the point where the symbolism jumps right out of the story. The crops are now, in a sense, reborn in the parturient gush of the young virgin's flowing blood. The least pure (if not impure) human blood becomes the purifying (now holy) blood. Frazer sensed the presence of the deeper symbolism, however, for he seeks to build comparisons with other North American ethnic groups in order to support the above conclusions: "If the Mexican girl, whose blood was sprinkled on the maize, indeed personated the Maize Goddess, it becomes more than ever probable that the girl whose blood the Pawnees similarly sprinkled on the seed corn personated in like manner the female Spirit of the Corn; and so with the other human beings whom other races have slaughtered for . . . crops."[13] Frazer senses the connection within several societies between the pubescent or premenstrual girl and the power of the goddess. Frazer also seems to sense (without comment) that the symbolic but real sacrifice of the girl-goddess also transferred control over human and divine life from sacrificed girl to sacrificer-priest—from women to men.

Doused in the bloody skin of the girl, the priest becomes the transfer point for divine power. For three days she had entered the mysterious and dangerous womb of the earth, to merge with the divine powers resting there and become the communal sacrifice to those powers. But the powers themselves were to be reborn in or transferred to the male priest who had sacrificed her. The blood of the Aztec *niddah* literally

---

12. I am now comparing her to Iphigenia. I will argue against the female-savior theory (as applied to Iphigenia) later in this commentary.
13. Frazer, *Golden Bough*, 591.

became the garment of blessing and divine power for the Aztec version of *nazir*.

The Aztec ritual killing reflects, in the context of a nonbiblical culture, the relation between the menstrual (and sexually alluring) maiden and the priest/*nazir* image. I present it here in order to expand the *niddah-nazir* dynamic to a more universal level. In virtually all sacrificial patriarchal societies, a similar transfer of life-giving power takes place within such rituals. What was contaminated becomes the vehicle for sanctification. Boundaries between the impure and the sacred are transgressed, yet sanctified, by the transfer from female to male. The ultimate purification of the female comes with the release of all her blood in death: the slave girl is, after all, only a slave girl, not a respected member of that society.

Taking a cue from Nancy Jay, however, I must acknowledge that "[n]o sacrificial system can be taken as representative of others." Yet Jay cautiously admits that there is a "logic of sacrifice," despite the variations from society to society. Even though biblical accounts of Israelite sacrifices come from different "strands of tradition" and "different historical periods," one can detect generic links from one to the next.[14] The expiatory sacrifice of the "red heifer" exemplifies an arguable progression in the "logic of sacrifice"—from human sacrifices among Israel's neighbors to animal sacrifices (in Israel). For the ritual slaughter, the priest and his entourage of devotees lead the heifer outside the camp to slaughter it. Here the priest sprinkles the heifer's blood in the direction of the altar. The priest then tosses "cedar, hyssop, and a red cloth" into a fire where the heifer becomes a burnt offering to expiate the sins of the community; that is, to separate them from the "uncleanness" that had angered their deity. Afterwards the priest must bathe and wash his clothes since he remains "unclean" until evening "as if he had touched a menstruating woman."[15]

In many ways the red heifer illustrates an eerie parallel to the Aztec slave girl. Jay remarks: "I suspect that the 'scarlet cloth' which must be burnt with the red heifer (notice that the victim is both female and red) is a euphemism for what the Hebrew Bible calls a 'menstruous rag.' By the intensifications of uncleanness, this sacrifice creates a pole of absolute otherness from cleanness that works like a magnet to draw away uncleanness."[16] The red heifer parallels the slave girl in her value to the

---

14. Jay, *Throughout Your Generations*, 24.
15. Ibid., 26.
16. Ibid., 29.

community but belongs outside that community. Jay also explains that the men who burn the heifer and gather the ashes also become unclean. The heifer's ashes are thus both a pollutant—from the menstruating female—and a sacralized conduit for a type of divine expiatory power. What was indicative of the menstruating maiden, with the potential to produce life, is now both "unclean" and "holy," overcoming the contaminating power of death through a type of metamorphosis (from blood to ashes) of its own life-giving power. The polluting properties of female blood have been transformed from the unclean into the cleansing; the remedy for pollution now rests in the hands of a holy man. All femaleness has been destroyed; the symbolic *niddah* has been sacrificed, her power placed in the hands of the *nazir*. With her ashes he distributes a divine blessing.

O'Grady makes a salient statement, so applicable to both the red-heifer sacrifice and that of the Aztec girl: "To say that 'impurity' underwrites the sacred, not as polar opposites but as part of the same order. . . . is not to say the obvious—that the impure and the holy are *the same thing*—but rather that they are . . . inscribed within one another."[17] Both impurity and the sacred demand separation from normal society, for better or worse. The parallels that O'Grady finds between the *niddah* and the *nazir* are *not* only not incidental but can be found in traditional religious customs, in one form or another, in a myriad of cultures where sacrificial religion holds or has held sway.

Aware of the above scenarios and the scholarly conclusions drawn from them, we must now, before making any further deductions, ask some very basic questions about the relationship between blood and sacrifice, which we have all too briefly set up. Can we argue that *all* ritual sacrifice relates to blood, especially women's blood? When all is said, can we arrive at the "true reasons" for any ancient or so-called "primitive" blood ritual?[18] Since ritual actions and interpretations are not the same, can we legitimately defend the social/cultural inferences we have already made? Do rituals contain universal symbolism or premises? Do they provide any "clues" for detecting and interpreting the "true reasons" for sacrifices we see as alien to our own culture?

Jay, who made some of the most valuable contributions to the cross-cultural study of sacrificial patriarchal societies, cautions us to remember

---

17. See O'Grady, this volume.
18. I use the term "primitive," not as opposed to "civilized," but as Douglas would have used the term, that is, to identify a simpler (nontechnological) culture existing on the tribal or clan level and involved with hunting and possibly rudimentary agriculture, with oral traditions rather than written laws, under some form of patriarchal rule.

before making any deductions that (1) the "nature of an interpretation of action depends as much or more on the interests . . . of the interpreter as it does on those of the actor" and (2) "that an action is not the same as an interpretation of it." Thus, the meaning of an action, she concludes, is "not the same as the interpretations of it"—even when it is the actor or religious believer (rather than the researcher) doing the interpreting—for "meaning is not a simple and direct product of action itself, but of reflection upon it." And *that* reflection is no less than *another* act, "socially situated in its own way."[19] For example, when Hebrew Scriptures give us no explanatory rationale for the origins of its sacrificial rituals—and even the "actors" (in contemporary sacrificial cultures) provide only vague or superficial explanations—from where do we recover a valid interpretive analysis?

Jay points out, "What enables us to interpret ritual *at all* is also what prevents us from interpreting it perfectly": our "bodily situatedness," that is, what the Germans call *Sitz im Leben*—one's own social-historical context. What we must remember (and the chapters in this volume substantiate) is that sacrifice links people together in one community and, "conversely, it separates them from defilement, disease, and other dangers." "Trying to understand ritual" is "a work of relating."[20]

Although social-historical context, with its interplay of "roles" in community and tradition, provides us with the main clues to the meaning of rituals—yet never the "full" meaning, for "there is no perfect meaning"—we must still examine our own premises and "situatedness."[21] As Kathleen Rushton stated in her chapter, historical, anthropological, and exegetical criticism has been up to the last few decades exclusively patriarchal and androcentric. Questions relating to gender division and subordination, for example, have not been deemed relevant. In a feminist reading, this issue is critical. For example, gender divisions in sacrificial religions are/were regarded as socially significant in ways totally unlike the gender distinctions considered the norm in today's egalitarian societies. Even sexual or gender identity was different in ancient times. Today we assume we have basically two gender poles, male and female, on a continuum one to the other; both (and any identified "variants" in between) represent the fullness of human nature. But we still think in positive, yet somewhat polarized, male-female terms; such a

---

19. Jay, *Throughout Your Generations*, 8.
20. Ibid., 12–13.
21. For Jay's full explanation of this process of interpretation, see ibid., 10–13.

"truth" is engrained in the structure of European languages (with two genders and possibly an "it")—or so we think.[22]

Such was not the assumption in sacrificial (ancient) societies—and I am referring here principally to the root traditions of Western culture, especially Greek and Hebrew cultures. As Jay makes clear, the more ancient roles assigned the fullness of human nature to men only. Women had no *positive* identity. Human beings were men and "not men." Men, like pure vacuums, contain no contaminants. Only when women infiltrated their hallowed circle did they become contaminated, impure. Women were thought to have more in common with the beasts of the earth than with men. A philosophical opposition between men and women became a cultural given; man levitated to the "integrated one"; woman, personifying the negative, fell into Chaos. With Aristotelian precision, Jay argues: "What is integrated is One. What is differentiated is logically without limit and can be expressed in a single term only negatively, as not the integrated whole, as opposed to it as disorder is to order, as unclean is to clean, or in formal logical terms, as Not-A is to A."[23] The rules for the A/Not-A distinction, as Jay acknowledges, derive from Aristotle's principles of identity and contradiction, which simply specify that nothing can be both A and Not-A and, conversely, that "anything and everything must be either A or Not-A" (creating the principle of the excluded middle). Thus, "when the sexes are conceived as contradictories, only one sex can have positive reality. (Guess which.)"[24] Today's scholars, however, like modern scientists, tend to see an A/B distinction in which both terms can be seen positively, as continuous one with the other, with flexible boundaries and a possible "middle" between them where the two might mingle to greater or lesser degrees. Without this middle ground, the blending of (or interchange between) the two "opposite" but positive poles is impossible.

Those of us seeing the "continuum" between sexes may hark back to Gen 1 (as well as modern biology) to support our case that "in the beginning God created them male and female," rather than to Hesiod, who said that in the original Golden Age of Greece, all people were male. It is with the Greeks that we find our best examples of the A/Not-A dichotomy. Men, with their perfect souls, could—albeit under rare circumstances—participate in a continuum with the divine. As men

---

22. Language roots may go back further than the wellspring of patriarchy. I find it interesting that in Indo-European languages, the female gender (not the male) is the root/source of the grammatical structure of substantives (nouns and their adjectives).
23. Jay, *Throughout Your Generations*, 19.
24. Ibid.

practiced honorable virtues such as courage and valor, they became heroes for others to emulate; heroes became (in even rarer circumstances) demigods, and eventually they consorted with the gods, became more and more godlike. A "cult of heroes" evolved. But no parallel heaven-bound road lay before women. The best they could hope for was to sleep with a god or demigod or get rescued by a hero—at least until the Christian religion became entangled in the roots of Greek philosophy: now "there is no longer male nor female" (Gal 3:28 NRSV). At the time, even this amalgamation meant a woman could only reach the divine by losing her femaleness and becoming, as the Gospel of Thomas assures us, a "man."[25] Humanness was pure masculinity of the highest order. We see this in the martyrdom of Perpetua, who willingly gave up suckling her baby. Agnes sacrificed her life to her virginity. Neither would allow their bodily fluids to further contaminate men; their blood would no longer perpetuate physical life in all its monstrous forms. Instead they both would shed their blood like men—they would become male. Only then could they enter, *like men,* into the aura of divine life.

Baptism into Christianity, we should not forget, was a release into maleness, a bloodless "virgin birth" in which believers became, like Christ, "specifically male": the "enlightened receive the features and the image of the manliness of Christ."[26] From this more penetrating interpretation of fundamental gender division and roles in the social context of ancient Western cultures, we can form a basic premise upon which to begin a more accurate determination of the meaning of blood-related rituals in sacrificial religions. We understand a little better the world within which "sacrifice is meaningfully performed."[27] It was sacrifice that allowed for a type of *spiritual* social ordering. Both the Greek and Hebrew systems of sacrifice—unique as each is to its own complex social structure—allow us to draw some conclusions about how attitudes toward women and blood, as well as about men and their relation to divine power, have come down to us in Western traditions. I will begin with the clearer examples from the Greek.

---

25. Saying 114, "The Gospel According to Thomas," *The Nag Hammadi Library,* James M. Robinson, ed., 138. (Jesus is said to have said: "I myself shall lead her in order to make her male, so that she too may become a living spirit resembling you males.")

26. From Symposium 8.7, as quoted in Gail Paterson Corrington, *Her Image of Salvation: Female Saviors and Formative Christianity* (Louisville: Westminster John Knox, 1992), 25.

27. Jay, *Throughout Your Generations,* 13.

As Jay demonstrates, the social/sexual distinctions found in human culture rather than in nature were defined through symbols and myths and integrated into the fabric of ancient society through the repetition of religious (especially sacrificial) rituals. Women were, for the ancient Greeks, the "gift" produced by an original sacrifice during the Golden Age. When Prometheus discovered the middle ground between eating raw meat like carnivorous beasts and offering burnt sacrifices to the Olympic gods, he appears to have had a very human ulterior motive: he was cooking meat for human (male) consumption and fooling the gods. (He attempted to fool the gods by only half burning the sacrificial ox and sending the "fragrant smoke" to the gods to inhale while men feasted on the cooked flesh.) When Zeus detected he was being denied his full burnt offering, he took revenge. He sent Pandora as a gift, and with her into this pure-male paradise entered all the evils of hunger, sweaty labor, disease, and death. Now the "pollution of childbirth" and the evil of death became associated in Greek tradition.[28]

And marriage too came into being. Like his own sacrificial food, man himself was now caught halfway between the beasts and the divine, his all-male purity sacrificed to the patriarchal bloodlines. Never again would man spring spontaneously and perfectly formed from the earth, rather, he would be impelled through the birthing canal in a rush of woman's blood. Only in marriage could a man control his filial descent line and only in cleansing sacrifice—in a rebirth by fire—could he expiate his "crime" of consorting with women. Once again he began to climb the ladder to the gods—but no longer from the bottom rung.[29]

In such myths, affirms Jay, is the "fatal flaw of having been born of woman overcome." But the long climb back to original perfection involves heroic acts and blood sacrifice. She cites the mythic story of Herakles (or Hercules), who redeemed himself by dying in a sacrificial fire that burned not only him but also the "poisoned" items his wife and

---

28. Ibid., 29. One can also see this motif in early Christianity. In "On the Origin of the World," as contained in *The Nag Hammadi Library*, we see how "dissolution followed birth," and also how the earth's plants and vegetation sprung from the blood that female spirits shed, 178–79.

29. For a more comprehensive digest of the material in this paragraph, see ibid., 21–22, as well as 30–31. Jay points out that Greek sacrifices to the underworld gods included "those mythic mortals who once had dealings with the gods, the heroes." Defiled persons could sacrifice at the grave of a hero where sacrificial blood could purify blood pollution. Drawing upon the work of Jean-Pierre Vernant, she observes the crucial point that "[w]ithout marriage there can be no paternal filiation, no male line of descent, no family, all of which presuppose a line which is not natural, but religious and social" (p. 30).

his mother had given him—in other words, all the pollution from the women in his life. We now have the strongest of mortal heroes, freed from female contamination, rising in a rebirth with the immortals, as we read in the *Metamorphoses*:

> All that his mother gave him burned away.
> Only the image of his father's likeness
> Rose from the ashes of his funeral pyre . . .
> So Hercules stepped free of mortal being . . .
> And with an air of gravity and power
> Grew tall, magnificent as any god.[30]

As both mortal hero and immortal god, purified of female connectedness, Hercules now could become an example of deified "supermasculinity"—the ultimate hero icon.

In ancient Israel, we find the image of the hero blends even more with that of the priest, so too blood rites appear less easily (and more symbolically) defined. Yet one can still detect how the tribe's own interpretations of sexual distinctions or opposition effect rituals. In partially burnt peace offerings, the "flesh of victims offered for the sins of common people and leaders" was "eaten only by males of priestly families, for its sacredness spreads to anything it touches"—a type of "contagious sanctity," or contamination in reverse.[31] We have already discussed the red heifer, but the paschal lamb provides an opposite symbol: the "perfect male lamb" was slaughtered "according to their fathers' houses, a lamb for each [patriarchal] household."[32] And its redeeming blood is put on the door of the Israelite house where it will be eaten.[33] In memory of a male descent line in covenant with an all-powerful male deity, the perfect communion-expiatory sacrifice was completed (Exod 12).

Thus, sacrificial rituals can be defined in part as an integral element in patriarchal religion as it became rooted in the evolving paradigm of

---

30. From *The Metamorphoses* (p. 248), as quoted in Jay, *Throughout Your Generations*, 31.

31. Jay, *Throughout Your Generations*, 24.

32. Ibid., 26.

33. Corrington explains the difference between redemption and salvation, which is beyond the scope of this chapter (*Her Image of Salvation*, esp. 46–54). In the paradigm of redemption, one "experiences the power of the divine"; in the paradigm of salvation, one's very existence is "transformed from the powerless to the powerful by partaking of the divinity." One can detect the paradigm of redemption at work in the Hebraic texts and the Jewish interpretation of the messiah more readily than in the Greek, where the paradigm of salvation seems more operative.

Western culture. Across traditions, researchers find a convergence of femaleness with evil that must be expiated.[34] Sacrifice also was a means of "male" birthing through a flow of purified and purifying blood, from ancient times to the present.[35] For the patriarchal community, male descent lines were reaffirmed. These "descent lines" can briefly be identified as being produced and safeguarded in and through marriage and sacrificial blood rites, both heroic (concerned with feats of bravery in the "external" world) and symbolic, in communion and expiatory sacrifices. Through patrilineal marriage, a man became the head of a household and, if he was favored by the gods, a clan or nation; he became chief or king. Through heroic sacrifice combined with some communion rites, he might reach the level of masculine purity needed to be a hallowed hero, perhaps even a demigod honored by the myths of future generations; as a priest or even a high priest he could begin or continue the "rebirth" of an all-male descent line. Combining all three, he became king-hero-priest, the perfect trinitarian reflection of perfect masculinity, of supermasculinity itself. If he could combine the mythic power of a demigod with the mystique of the holy-of-holiest high priests, he could become the soteriological hero who could save other men through his own sacrificial blood.[36]

In speaking of soteriological heroes, or savior figures, I am making no attempt to deconstruct the Christian figure of Jesus the Savior; rather, I merely attempt to show how elements from the ritual-sexual context of a society at least prepare a body of knowledge, paradigmatic myths, and ritual language that make the understanding of such a religious figure possible or even probable. Like the father figure itself, the hero icon has its roots in the patriarchal family, with its social (rather than purely biological) relationships.[37] "Fatherhood" can be legally decided by the fact that one's wife has a child, regardless of who fathered it. On the other hand, "illegitimate" children often have little, if any, rights of inheritance: they exist outside the social unit called "family." Thus fatherhood has evolved traditionally as more of a social and legal relationship than a recognition of filial bloodlines. Motherhood is another matter. Leaving

---

34. Jay summarizes this (*Throughout Your Generations*, 28–29).
35. As both Susan Roll and Kathleen Rushton describe in their chapters, the "churching of women" in twentieth-century (pre-Vatican II) Catholicism demonstrates this process.
36. For a fuller description of the types of sacrifices that benefited men, see Jay, *Throughout Your Generations*, 22–28.
37. A sequel to this book might well include Freud's primal father and René Girard's analysis of violence and the sacred—both of which ignore women.

aside adoptions, motherhood is established pretty much by blood alone. In a family, woman's role is like that of her children. She belongs to the man who provides her social station.[38] In monogamous unions we have one wife, and in polygamy many—but (in these two common forms) that "union" remains one "marriage" based on the presence of one husband, the *pater*, who as paterfamilias functions as lord, magistrate, and priest within his own socially defined family.[39]

Like the institution of the paterfamilias, patterns of priesthood have come down to us only externally modified or restricted. The male descent line remains, for example, inured in the "apostolic succession" of the Christian churches that retain an anointed priesthood and sacrificial tradition. As Nancy Jay observes, "Even in settings where various kinds of descent through women are valued, and also in social organizations with no actual family base (such as the clerical hierarchy of the Roman Church), sacrificing produces and reproduces forms of intergenerational continuity through women."[40] As Marcel Detienne had pointed out, the Greek word for butcher-sacrificer-cook had no female form. While some women in some societies (even in the ancient West) may have wielded the sacrificial knife on occasion, they are virtually always found to be postmenopausal or possibly a "virgin" priestess or rich surrogate "male" under the control of men. Never, it appears, does she conduct the sacrifice for her own lineage, Jay tells us.[41]

Thus blood sacrifices strongly relate to male-descent lineages as in opposition to female lineages founded on parturient blood. For the ritual, the active leadership or participation of a woman of childbearing age, a menstruating woman, was forbidden. O'Grady summarizes in closing that "menstrual blood, more clearly than any other taboo substance or

---

38. Even in matrilineal families, a woman is subject to men; usually two—her brother and her husband.

39. Jay fully discusses this subject in *Throughout Your Generations*. Particularly illuminating for this chapter are her examples on pp. 45 and 54: "In Rome as in Greece, birth did not give family membership. Should the paterfamilias withhold his ritual recognition, legally the child did not exist. A name and paternal recognition were given on the "day of purification," when the proper "sacrifice removed the pollution of childbirth." Also, an illegitimate son had no right to sacrifice in the cult of his birth father, or genitor. On the other hand, legal descent from a pater could be created ritually: "Only those families organized around a pater . . . were maintained sacrificially" (Jay, *Throughout Your Generations*, 45).

40. Ibid., 153. Jacob here refers to Marcel Detienne's discussion of "The Violence of Well Born Ladies: Women in the Thesmophoria" in *The Cuisine of Sacrifice Among the Greeks*.

41. Ibid.

state," brings together "the "blood of life itself, the most sacred of substances, with the shedding of blood, in a 'sacrificial' gesture." As symbol
of evil and death, menstrual blood was identified with the blood of the
sacrifice, never of the priest. (In sacrifice alone, metamorphosis was possible. As Jay observed, communion rituals also evolve out of blood rituals: the communion of a divine-energy-giving "food" arises from the
blood and ashes of sacrifice.) Thus, the relationship between the *niddah*
and the *nazir* is, indeed, not incidental but integral to an understanding
of sacrificial religions. When that relationship merges, we see a one-way
transfer of the "mysterious energy," flowing from the most submissive
female to the most dominant male.

For the second part of this chapter, I would like to take the theories of
this book one step further, to examine the relationship between the
nazir, or holy man, and the priest-sacrificer-warrior-hero in Western tradition—the fully masculine complement to the image of the birthing,
bleeding woman. Certainly the warrior-hero, even Hercules, relates to
the shedding of blood. This leaves many questions begging. What does
the warrior-hero have to do with women, especially menstruating
women? or with birth? purity? shame? In taking the sources of Western
"religion" back to their roots, the authors in this book have found the
inseparable relationship between symbolic and real sacrifice of life.

But the most significant question remains to be asked: Why does
"sacrifice" have such appeal that it, cross-culturally, is used as a tool to
replace the natural birth process and elevate the "masculine" to the role
of life generator? From the time of Abraham, "sacrifice" has taken the
place of Isaac's birth in identifying him as a member of his father's
household, as heir apparent. He might be called the first "Born Again" in
the Judeo-Christian tradition. The "sacrifice remedies having been born
of woman, establishing bonds of intergenerational continuity between
males."[42] Mom is out; Pop is in. Equally important, a second androcentric unit is also created: the fraternal circle—the defenders of the fathers'
line, the collective out of which the ultimate hero, the savior figure,
arises—in a new configuration of sacrifice.

Divine Sacrifice Reserved for Males Only

To many religious thinkers even today, menstrual blood remains a contaminating fluid that identified a person as ineligible for ordination/eleva-
tion to priestly status. In early Christianity, the Council of Laodicea (ca.

---

42. Ibid., 149.

360) banned women from the sacred area of the official Eucharistic "sacrifice" for fear of "the *pollutio* of the divine sacraments," were they to be
"distributed by women." Virginity came to offset this female impurity
somewhat, but never enough to allow women to be priests officially. (For
Augustine and later Aquinas, woman's only ordained purpose was to give
birth.) Many contemporary scholars see the fear/awe of female "blood"
as a more nuanced situation, however.

Kristin De Troyer, in "Blood: A Threat to Holiness or toward (Aan-
other) Holiness?" sees the concept of blood-purification needs for
woman, coupled with her banishment from the arena of cultic sacrifice,
as "traces of a perceived threat from other religions and other gods."
Thus, women's marginal position of bringing forth not only monsters
but divine-like male babies put her in mysterious commune with dangerous divine energies beyond natural forces, as well as human enemies
beyond clan/community life. In De Troyer's view: the Hebrews feared
(according to Leviticus) that in as much as a woman is capable of giving
life, she is on the border of life and nonlife, and she should, therefore, be
kept away from the sacred.[43] De Troyer infers—then abruptly ends her
argument—that it was the female deities they served (and represented),
not her fertility, that brought on the fear of woman's oracular energy.[44]
This leads one to suspect that women-led rituals may have focused more
on communication and celebration than on obsequious blood sacrifice—
but that, again, lies beyond the scope of this volume.

More to the point, De Troyer is leading us in a crucial direction: "fertility," as a central motif of "life," as the source of all human life, did in
fact identify woman as not only capable of bringing forth human life but
of existing on the border between life and nonlife, between physical
nature and divine mystery, between the sweetness of life and the terror of
death, as our Aztec slave girl did. Between A and Not-A. Set upon this
border, under certain controlled circumstances, woman could still be a
mediator for incoming life and nonlife, or death. Fear of her powers as
well as her pollution led to banning her from priesthood. Indeed, were
she handed this power too, what would be left for men? Thus, the "male"
longing for power over the forces of life and death, from the prehistoric

---

43. De Troyer might have stayed more grounded in history than I have. She argues
that researchers have, indeed, demonstrated that "this 'rule' presupposes the existence
of pagan fertility religions" in which women priests controlled the rites—including
fertility rites.

44. As Mary Daly noted in her later works, men most feared not woman's polluting
body, but her wisdom and her prophetic mind, which appeared so easily to communicate with the divine. See also Douglas, *Purity and Danger*, 67–68.

beginnings of Western civilization (as we know it) to the present, has not only created patriarchal cultures but has aspired to relocate generative powers—the life force itself—away from women and solely in men; if women indeed brought physical life into this world, it was men who had the power to expel it from this world. Men reserved for themselves sole power over killing and rebirthing, over shedding blood and extending bloodlines on the divine level—as "new Adams."

Such forces were not only priests but warrior-priests in ancient Israel; the early Israelites were a war-plagued people ruled by a caste of warrior-priests identified as the Levite tribe of Moses, Aaron, and Joshua. In this generic society, power and dominant authority—often carrying out the will of a fierce and angry god of war—rested in warrior-priests; it was a matter of survival in a chaotic and cruel world. The priest was not a magic worker but a guardian of the community against evil forces. As Mary Douglas says: rituals are designed to "control situations and to *modify* experience," especially the experience of death.[45] Let us take a simple example outside of Israel. Among the Dinka herdsmen of Africa, as Douglas points out, "certain men, closely in contact with Divinity, should not be seen to enter upon physical death." That was for women. These elders were not necessarily priests but hunters, and their deaths were to appear deliberate, neither a killing nor a suicide but an occasion for public celebration—a combination of ritual and reality. (One might think of it as the original "virtual reality"!) Douglas explains: "The Master of the Fishing Spear does not kill himself. He requests a special form of death which is given by his people, for their own sake, not for his. If he were to die an ordinary death, the life of his people, goes with him. Everyone should rejoice, because on this occasion there is a social triumph over death."[46] In this instance, the triune king-priest-warrior appears as the performer/celebrant of his own death ritual for the community: he is priest. Man goes from controlling birth (through a social rebirth) to trumping natural death—a "social triumph." The Dinka are aware, Douglas stresses, that this act has no magical efficacy to change death processes or to preempt them. But much of the fear is removed; in the action itself control transfers from uncontrollable forces to deliberate ones in the hands of the power-leader, at least on the symbolic level. It is, like all Dinka rituals, a religious act. And for them (as for us in all our religious rituals), "that is enough."[47]

---

45. Douglas, *Purity and Danger,* 67
46. Ibid., 67–68.
47. Ibid., 68.

In the earliest biblical times, as recorded in the Book of Numbers, the warrior-priest buffeted and absorbed the most dangerous risks of the people, from risks of approaching the altar of God to approaching the human enemy of God. Bearing all the "iniquities" of their people: they would "walk through the valley of death and fear no evil," so to speak. Little did they differentiate between enemies beyond their camps and beyond nature. In fact, "redemption" was more of a physical than spiritual act, like being "brought up out of the land of Egypt"— more the rescue by a warrior-god than a spiritual soteriological act. The warrior-priest ruled as both a channel to God and a shield from his wrath.[48]

The hero icon is one of three faces of the warrior-priest-king (a soteriological figure) in ancient (eastern Mediterranean) *historical* as well as prehistoric, or mythic, times. As we see in ancient warrior-heroes, such as Alexander the Great, the "king" displayed his divine power over human life in all three roles. As high priest and as hero/warrior chief, he controlled divine life through the shedding of blood, through killing:. "With Alexander. . . . His day began with his plunging of a blade into the living body of an animal and his uttering of prayer as the blood flowed. Before Gaugamela [his final battle with Darius], uniquely in his whole kingship, he performed sacrifice in honour of Fear."[49] Within the sanctuary of his "sacred" inner circle of delegated heroes, Alexander's sacerdotal role incited awe and fear, suggesting a metaphysical presence that was both worshiped and defiled. As he plunges the blade, uttering the prayer, Alexander fuses with the very meaning of the ritual itself, a symbol of death as a prelude to new life, a symbol of a heroic surrender of life, respecting or "honoring fear" rather than running in shame.

As I write, I am mindful of Grietje Dresen's words in her chapter on the sacrifice and churching of women:

> The only action that is as serious as giving birth . . . is killing. This is one way to interpret the common sacrificial metaphors of birth and rebirth, or birth done better. . . . Unlike childbirth, sacrificial killing is deliberate, purposeful, "rational" action, under perfect control. Both birth and killing are acts of power, but . . . [unlike sacrificial killing,

---

48. I am making a distinction here (and below) between salvation and redemption based on Corrington's work (*Her Image of Salvation,* 46). (See also pp. 47–55 for her definitive description of "redemption" in Hebrew biblical times.)

49. John Keegan, *The Mask of Command* (New York: Penguin. 1988), 47.

society tends to see] childbirth as the quintessence of vulnerability, pas-
sivity, and powerless suffering.[50]

Although Dresen points out as obvious the conclusions that the "only
action that is as serious as giving birth . . . is killing" and that sacrificial
killing is an act of "power" parallel to childbirth, she does not expand
upon the image of the male killer-sacrificer—indeed, it was beyond the
scope of her chapter.

I, for one, cannot help but speculate on how the salvific warrior-hero,
like the priest-sacrificer, not only represents the ritually pure (sexually
uncontaminated) man but also, as Alexander did, symbolizes the *pater*—
the essence of sexually uncontaminated fatherhood. He endows his sons,
not with the power to give mortals birth, but with power and permission
to kill and, especially, to seek the glory of self-sacrifice, not as the Master
of the Fishing Spear did, in order to cheat death, but rather in order to
overcome death. Such a hero, shedding his own male blood, is "reborn" as
a demigod continuing to energize the "warrior spirit" in his brother warriors. Through killing he comes in control of killing, a power never really
controlled by women.[51] Through self-sacrifice on the battlefield, the
body and blood of "man" passes through death to rebirth.

Until he delegated his sacrificial power and his right to be a communal hero, Alexander embodied the whole mystique of hero-savior in his
person. Only by delegating that mystique to his highest level of subordinates—the circle of elite warriors/potential heroes surrounding him, his
"senior officers"—did he extend the powers of hero-savior to his family
of warriors and their descent line. Beginning at least with Alexander, we
see the origin of a military "chain of command" engendering a form of
"pure" male descent line. The hero collective, banded in warriors' blood,
now shares in the sacred mandate and awesome power to kill enemies.

As part of Alexander's legacy, we know that a heroic surrender of
life—whether on the battlefield or on the altar—was a type of uncontaminated, female-free birth that "both glorified the victim and best legit-
imized his blood-heir's succession to his title" as trinitarian king, warlord,
and high priest.[52] His fraternal circle of potential heroes knew, without
conscious reflection, that the sacrificial hero-warrior/war-chief/demigod

---

50. See Dresen, this volume.
51. While woman may have been the active vehicle for the entrance of life and evil in
the world, she was no more than the vehicle or passive vessel for uncontrollable death.
Killing is another matter, reserved for hunters, communally or divinely delegated exe-
cutioners, and warriors.
52. Keegan, *Mask of Command,* 312.

must be a male leader (*Führer*) who literally survives death as he suc-
cumbs in the heat of battle; that is, his bloodline continues, is born in his
own spilled blood.[53] His mission is to kill enemy powers, not himself, to
risk and survive, or resurrect from death to demigod—not to die. His
image was no different than that of the classic mythic hero.

What Alexander did in history, ancient Greek "heroes" did before
him, recorded in mythic poetry and drama, where we get the full story of
how woman's blood was spilled in sacrifice for the inspiration and divine
blessing of the warrior-heroes. In the story of Iphigenia, while Agamemnon's army stood waiting to sail to Troy, his warriors grew restless; his
heroes were losing physical and emotional strength. Worse yet, they
insisted that Athena, the goddess of war—born from the limb of Zeus,
not from a woman—demanded the sacrifice of Agamemnon's daughter,
Iphigenia. Agamemnon summoned his daughter to the camp, telling her
mother to bedeck her as a bride. Iphigenia thought she was to marry
Achilles, a hero of her father's army, but instead her bridal garments were
to be her sacrificial robes—her death shroud. With her sacrifice, Athena
was appeased and the elite circle of waiting heroes regained their courage
and drive. But there is far more to the story.

Like so many Greek legends, Iphigenia's powerful drama has been
psychoanalyzed and symbolically interpreted. Like the drama of *Oedipus
Rex*, it conveys intense psychosociological content conveyed on the level
of high metaphor. But even feminist scholars, in an effort to strengthen
Iphigenia's positive symbolic value, miss the point. For example, Gail
Paterson Corrington identifies Iphigenia as a "female savior," a woman
in active control of her own sacrifice—which she was not. Corrington
says, "The model of heroic, self-sacrifice in Greek mythology is Iphigenia," the virgin daughter of Agamemnon, who "allows herself to be
killed" to ensure a Greek victory against the Trojans. As Corrington
argues, Euripides presents her in *Iphigenia at Aulis* as a willing victim,
conscious of her role in the unfolding "salvific history" of Hellas.[54] But
what is that role? Like Mary of Nazareth's *Magnificat*, Iphigenia's lyrical
tribute to Greece points to her own divine destiny, but not necessarily to
her "willingness":

All Greece turns
Her eyes to me, to me only, great Greece
In her might—for through me is the sailing

---

53. Ibid., 312 f.
54. Corrington, *Her Image of Salvation*, 72.

Of the fleet, through me the sack and overthrow
Of Troy.[55]

Even if she is the delegated victim who will prevent rape and pillage, does her death not have a more symbolic interpretation? Her sacrificial story retains all the attributes and significant details needed to alert us to a much deeper or universal meaning.

The story line tells us: Agamemnon hoodwinks his wife and daughter into coming to the campsite in expectation of a festive wedding between Iphigenia and Achilles. Such duplicity is necessary because Agamemnon knows his wife would never have brought her daughter to her doom. Despite his deep love for his daughter, Agamemnon never wavers; he seems to understand the cosmic meaning of her pending sacrifice. Iphigenia herself is kept oblivious to the truth until the very last minutes. Involved as she is in the nuptial preparations, she becomes part of the flow of the ritual mood building around her. When she learns of her pending death, she knows she cannot change it; it will happen no matter what she does. As psychologists undoubtedly would agree, a numbness sets in.[56] Passive acceptance and the ease of merely slipping into step with the ritual movements, without thought or will—like the victims of recent genocidal atrocities—take over. The ritual itself dominates.

Finally, the symbolism, on a more abstract level, lifts the story into the realm of metaphor: it becomes the drama of a cataclysmic cultural evolution. The "eyes" and future of Greece—and all Western patriarchal culture—are indeed bearing down of her: "Through me" Greece will overthrow Troy. "For . . . all these things . . . my death will achieve. . . . I, savior (*eleutherosa*) of Greece will be honored and my name shall be blessed."[57]

Why, I ask, "*through* Iphigenia"? Why is no other sacrifice possible? (Indeed, if it were possible, her father would have done it.) The answer, I believe, is more than merely the whim of Athena. If Agamemnon appeared unmoved by the pending slaughter of his beloved child, the reasons become clearer as the symbolism reveals itself. Iphigenia represented the female presence within Agamemnon's descent line—a female child beget by her father through her mother's blood, who now has to be replaced by a male-only descent line. To the collective mind of Agamemnon's heroes, Iphigenia existed beyond the boundaries of the

---

55. Ibid., 72–73.
56. I am arguing on the basis of studies of victims of atrocities.
57. From *Iphigenia at Aulis*, quoted by Corrington, *Her Image of Salvation*, 73.

evolving fraternal collective attempting to assert itself in its all-male purity. The vertical descent line father-son-(grand)son was widening laterally with each new generation, into son-son-son, a brotherhood magnetically bonded together by past heroic feats and dreams of superheroic deeds of glory in the future.

The cult of heroes was being birthed.[58]

Indeed, no one (or thing) *except* Iphigenia could have been sacrificed, for it was her very blood that needed to be shed. A young and fertile virgin at the point of becoming a bride (and of contaminating men and bearing children in blood) is dressed in the whiteness of an innocent bride, then led to her sacrificial bed. By a stroke of the knife, Agamemnon, as high priest of the sacrifice, severed his tie to the regeneration of the female presence.[59] That presence, consumed on a pyre of fire, became smoke for Athena. Like the Aztec slave girl, Iphigenia became the channel for the transfer of a type of mystical power to men. In her sacrificial death, the unclean became purified, changed into the "mysterious energy" that would generate a superwarrior "spirit." Athena—born of her father—was appeased in the process.[60] The royal daughter's blood had been shed—cleansed—and, in the cleansing, purified and spiritually transformed into that of the new heroic descent line. Like Athena, the heroes could now claim their heritage from their warrior-leader. Troy could now be conquered and the heroes engraved in the Book of Gods.

Iphigenia is the story of the transformation of the filial line of descent from the societal unit under the paterfamilias—in this case, the warrior-leader Agamemnon—to that leader's circle of elite heroes. Ajax, Achilles, and Odysseus could now aspire to become demigods.

In many ways the blood of women, like that of Iphigenia as archetypal personification, imbues the story of the rise of patriarchy in many cultures. From the Hebrews we have the images of the daughter of Zion.

---

58. Jay argues that the Greeks have no true ancestral cult because "heroes" had replaced siblings (*Throughout Your Generations*, 41). She, however, made this statement without comment. The statement does nonetheless support the hypothesis I have developed: the hero cult represents the sacralizing of a purely male descent line; heroes replaced siblings (who included sisters and were born from women).

59. The Agamemnon-Iphigenia (father-daughter) sacrificial rite mirrors the Abraham-Isaac scenario. Unlike Isaac's sacrifice, however, no divinity stops her father's hand: Iphigenia must be killed in order to initiate the all-male descent line.

60. As a combatant male, the Christian martyr Perpetua can be seen within the motif of Iphigenia: she became male in death, symbolized in her dream of herself as a male warrior-hero engaged in an unearthly combat. In her dream rather than her actual death she becomes a savior-hero figure.

(See Rushton's article.) In Christianity we have Mary of Nazareth.[61] If the early Christian community observed that God triumphs through the "agency of the normally powerless," as Corrington reminds us, is this triumph not God's alone? Iphigenia may have been an *eleutherosa*, but she was no *sotera*. From the earliest stages of human civilization as we know it in Western culture, the sacrifice of female (that is, *not male*) impurities by the high priest was, in turn, closely allied with the very real blood sacrifice of warriors. Iphigenia is perhaps the best example of the symbolism of a woman's blood sacrificed to bring about the glorification of heroes. In her myth, ritual and reality mingle as gods and men did. Yet, ignored through succeeding aeons, women faced the threat of death on the sacrificial birthing bed, as did men on the sacrificial battlefield.

As in the Oedipus story, strong archetypal characters fill out the drama of Ipighenia's story, revealing the depth of the patriarchal soul in a legend rife with symbols of earth-shattering cultural change. Instead of the Oedipal father-son struggle, Iphighenia's story is a sibling struggle between male and female blood rights in the family. Which will "inherit the earth"? so to speak. From the upheaval arises a clear image of a basic paradigm of patriarchy: through the cleansing of male-controlled sacrificial rituals, a collective of fraternal heroes arises to share in the awesome powers of supermasculinity—maybe even to become demigods and savior figures. This is the natural religion of patriarchy itself, expressed through the warrior-hero cult for close to three millennia, not to be decimated until a "new" Alexander appeared in the twentieth-century's own version of Gaugamela, controlling life and death through the power of ritual killing.[62]

A Strange Thing Happened on the Way to Kuwait

Not far from where Alexander battled the Persians at Gaugamela, in the desert sands of the Middle East, United States Army General Norman Schwartzkopf gathered his militia to do battle against the modern Mesopotamians. In the last decade of the second millennia of this era,

---

61. A devotee of Mary might well argue that she could have said no; therefore, she was a willing savior figure.
62. In the writings of not only Durkheim but also all the classic religion theorists—from Frazer and Freud through Weber and on to Girard and Burkert today, through several generations of theorists of psychology, sociology, and religion—we see extensive military allusions related to the "origins" or archetypes of rituals of religion. In light of this, we might ask what are the implicit (or even archetypal) "ritual prescriptions" at the root of military ideological theory today?

Schwartzkopf became a type of sanitized/cybernetic Alexander, as far from a "religious" leader as one can get. Or was he?

Unlike Alexander, Schwartzkopf held a heretofore unknown titanic power: he could prevent the shedding of all heroes' blood! Yet, like Alexander, he became the sole hero, the godlike icon himself. Standing before a television screen, for all the world to see, Schwartzkopf appeared to control the direction of his thunderbolts as if from above. He became not an antihero, but a transformed resurrection of his Alexandrine ancestor, displaying a new type of omnipotence and mystery without the need for the immolation of a hero's death.[63]

If nothing else, this reversed the "rules" of the game. Once the hero-leader controlled the strike of death, he rose above the need to challenge death further; his major responsibility evolved into seeing that none of his subordinates sacrificed their lives or spilled their blood. In the new Gaugamela, for the first time in the history of warfare, an entire consortium of nations sent their commanding general out to conduct a war with the explicit and oft repeated dictum to do all in his power to see that no soldier or aviator died in battle—that no heroes be produced except for the hero-leader himself.

With the Gulf War, two millennia of heroic "progress," of warfare itself, was turned on its head: public opinion and politics as well as cybernetics had infiltrated the purity of command. With the entry of computer expertise as a key ingredient in the "strategy for victory," the very future of the "chain of command" was at stake. After more than two millennia, the Alexandrine terms had reversed. A network of technicians had taken the officers' place, and a new Alexander, half cyber, half cyberus, was controlling its moves. The virtues of ritual segued into virtual reality. The electronic override of heroic sacrifice may have sounded the death knell on militarism as the "savior" religion of Western civilization.

At the same time as the shedding of heroes' blood becomes anathema rather than a divine command—as fate would have it—women are entering the ranks of combat officers in record numbers. With their integration, we may finally have been given the opportunity to see militarism for what it is: the natural "religion" of traditional patriarchy. As we see in Alexander the Great's military-religious ritual, a sacred sacrifice

---

63. The heroic image evolving from Alexander to today is more fully explained in my doctoral dissertation: "Military Aristocrat or Warrior-Monk? The Religious and Ethical Formation of the American Military Officer" (Claremont Graduate University, May 2002).

(to that nemesis of the warrior, "fear") is an intrinsic element in the core of the societal paradigm of military culture.

Could it be that warfare itself—like blood-shedding heroes—no longer fulfills a purpose in our society? Could we be that lucky?

Contemporary Western society, particularly as it veers on into the heady cyberspace of twenty-first century aerotechnology, consciously rejects all recognition of the sacrosanct side of our military icons; we cast such ideology aside as Neanderthal remnants of prehistory. Yet, to do so is only to bury our heads in sand—or cosmic dust; fundamental religious motifs endure; vestiges of a patriarchal past still inspire our fervor for heroes, for a regeneration of an undefined "warrior spirit." Even as we come to assume that our nominal or normative religion, be it Judaism or Christianity or Islam or any other, is our "one" religion, a deeper but vaguely indefinable "natural" religious identity continues to impress itself on our Western/patriarchal psyche, to set its mark on religious imagination, if not on the totality of our religious identification.

Tailhook as a Sacrificial Ritual

If Alexander the Great embodied all heroic virtues in himself as the "Father" of all heroes, the hero icon and sole sacrificer—and Norman Schwartzkopf usurped that title over two millennia later—who do we have as the descendants of the original, filial hero cult? Who now represents Alexander's and Agamemnon's subordinates and the aspiring superheroes seeking to become the new Achilles?

In the U.S. Navy the most elite circle of air warriors are the precision aviators who take off—become "air-born[e]"—as they blast off the deck of their aircraft-carrying motherships. They carry the name of Tailhookers.[64] Their landing is no less perilous:

> In the split second the plane hits the deck, the pilot pushes the throttle to full power in case he needs to lift off for another pass. If the hook grabs one of the cables, the tension yanks the speeding, straining plane to a halt in a hail of metal-on-metal sparks amid the deafening roar of supersonic engines . . . roughly equivalent to stomping on the gas pedal and jamming on the brakes at the same time at a speed of up to 150 mph [to stop within four hundred feet].[65]

---

64. The sexual double entendre in the dual term tail/hookers is preserved, if not intended.

65. Tony Perry, "Dangers in the Night," *Los Angeles Times,* 6 February 1995. A-19.

Among the aviation officers of the U.S. Navy and its Marine Corps, the aircraft-carrier pilots are officially the *crème de la crème*[66] of the military elite, the "top guns," the risk-taking heroes, ready to make the "ultimate sacrifice"[67] in service to their country or, perhaps more accurately, to set their mark as inspiring heroes on the legends of their elite fraternal circle. As bearers of the military myth, they personify the "masculine mystique": blood bonded, they are heroes before the deed; dead, they are deified.[68] Since the end of World War I, common sailors and their ships' commanders have had to deal with these new titans—the gods *descending* among them "like angels, floating down from the skies above the ships to accomplish their impossible landings."[69] Aviators have assumed a place at the top of virtually every Western naval hierarchy, with far-reaching "rights," which are more ancient and tribal than legal. Like heroes at any time and place, naval aviators—as a brotherhood, in control of their own sacrifices—assume they can do no wrong, will "live forever," and have the right to go crazy on occasion. In giving an account of the "Tailhook" scandal of 1991, which radically changed the gender awareness of the military in America, one Tailhook pilot said: "We were always taught in flight school to be . . . the wildest, most adventurous, both in the cockpit and out of it. It sounds like hogwash, but if you're in naval aviation, you know that that's how it is. And you become leader of the squadron by being leader on liberty. . . . Naval aviation rewards those that are the wildest."[70] Seeing himself as immune "from orthodox control,"[71] the fighter pilot "on leave" (or off duty) assumes that the right to "go crazy" comes "with the territory," according to one chronicler.[72] Military

---

66. This phrase is used frequently. One reference is in Roger A. Beaumont, *Military Ethics: Special Fighting Units in the Modern World* (New York: Bobbs-Merrill, 1974), 179.
67. Francke reminds us that "high-risk" specialty groups define the "masculine edge" as putting military elitists, such as aviators, "high on the masculine role-model scale" (Linda Bird Francke, *Ground Zero: The Gender Wars in the Military* [New York: Simon & Schuster, 1997], 153). She cites "the ultimate sacrifice" as the "term the military uses to ennoble death" (p. 35).
68. Jeanne Holm, *Women in the Military: An Unfinished Revolution* (rev. ed.; Novato, Calif.: Presidio, 1992), 16; see Beaumont for his explanation of this type of elite warrior as a "hero before the fact," merely because his specific heroes' circle upheld a tradition of heroism: such men are said to descend from heroes (*Military Ethics*, esp. 71 and 78).
69. Jean Zimmerman, *Tailspin: Women in War at the Wake of Tailhook* (New York: Doubleday, 1995), 28.
70. Ibid., 52–54.
71. See ibid., 51; and Beaumont, *Military Ethics*, 3.
72. Jean Zimmerman, *Tailspin*, 51.

researcher Roger Beaumont cites the military airborne elite as "all children of a dream, an old dream of armies moving on the air, and the myth is more powerful than reality."[73] The symbolic image and its myth touch on a reality far more significant to the aviator (who identifies with it) than does his functional role as pilot. Part aristocratic war leader, part bonded aviator, and part mythic hero, this archetypal image appears less as an individual than as an icon, an *individuation* of a cultural ideal: the ultimate lone warrior, elevated from his fraternal collective to an illusory demigod; he becomes the heroic icon embodied in naval aviation mythology.[74]

The Tailhook collective is the same group of close to two hundred elite officers who, in 1991, created the "Tailhook" scandal—the symbolic pinnacle on a heap of Navy scandals ignited around that time, when the aviation "heroes" first faced the threat of women being integrated into their elite combat-ready ranks, and they literally went "crazy." At night they performed a bizarre ritual called the "gauntlet,"[75] complete with chants and yells—a ritual ceremony designed to entrap, terrorize, and "sacrifice" women up and down a long and narrow hotel corridor jammed with close to two hundred men. One victim described her immolation thus: one man put his head under her legs and lifted her into the air; like the bodies of dozens of other women, her body was passed hand to hand over the heads of the men, then dumped at the end of the hallway. Another victim recalled how men "grabbed her on the breast, buttocks, and crotch," hit her in the mouth, and "put their hands under her skirt, while she feverishly tried to protect herself with her arms. . . . Totally in shock," she "squeezed her eyes shut" as she finally was passed man to man through the long and well-packed crowd.[76] No one seemed to care; not one man was ever court-martialed.

Tailhook '91 was a complex phenomenon within the culture of militarism. More than a scandalous incident of "spontaneous" sexual violence

---

73. Beaumont, *Military Ethics,* 78.
74. Noddings makes the distinction between individual and individuation. See Nel Noddings, *Women and Evil* (Berkeley: University of California Press, 1989).
75. These issues are more extensively covered in my dissertation, "The Military Aristocrat or Warrior-Monk?" In the Department of Defense, the inspector general's report did draw the blunt conclusion that the "gauntlet" was a lineup of "drunk" and "'obnoxious' junior officers" who vomited, pushed, shoved, groped, and hurled insults at passersby, mostly women, in a quasi-organized fashion, along the narrow sixty-to-eighty-foot-long third-floor hallway of the Hilton—principally in front of three or four squadron hospitality suites—on Saturday, September 7, 1991.
76. Derek Vander Schaaf, *The Tailhook Report (The Official Inquiry into the Events of Tailhook '91)* (New York: St. Martin's, 1993), app. F, 29.

arising in a context of "consensual" group sex play, the hostile, misogynist actions at Tailhook '91 provide "symbolic evidence" of a fierce melding of the identification of a combat pilot's maleness and his blood-brother-hood with a fear of women so strong that the collective itself developed rituals to exorcize her from the purity of their heroes' circle. Like Iphige-nia, she needed to be sacrificed to maintain the purity of the heroes' cult. In *Women in the Military,* retired Air Force General Jeanne Holm detects a (masculine-idealizing) gender "undercode" in the pervasive presence of what she calls the "masculine mystique" among elitist military men who see the military as "a man's world," a type of mysterious, woman-free self-worshiping society with cultic overtones—a veritable "cult of mas-culinity." [77]

Holm's "cult of masculinity" produces its own value-laden symbols, ethos, and mystique, not unlike that of a priestly institution. The sym-bols and rituals of this "cult of masculinity," which was so clearly revealed at Tailhook '91, have yet to be examined critically as a cultic expression. [78] Like their military forebears through history (and in myths such as *Iphi-genia*), carrier-squadron aviators have formed a pure-male familial social structure more cohesive than any biological family, rooted in a sense of their own mortality, compensated for by the (totem) brotherhood's (and nation or clan's) immortality. Since each "hero" lives at the edge of real death, life is sustained as a tension between two inveterate beliefs: (1) that the officer must put his life on the line every time he flies and (2) that he will never die. Thus he commits himself to fulfill the obligatory ritual, ready to sacrifice with his brother-aviators, and always remains the priest in control of the sacrifice, never the helpless victim. The issue of self-sacrifice now operates on a taboo level; repressed in thought, it will resurrect in sacrificial rituals and seek out surrogate victims, such as those handed down the gauntlet at Tailhook '91.

---

77. Holm quotes John Fowles's narrator's reference [in *The Magus*]: to "what the Americans call 'a man's world'"—"a world governed by brute force, humorless arro-gance, illusory prestige, and primeval stupidity . . . Men love war because it allows them to look serious" (*Women in the Military*, 16–17).

Bal refers to gender codes as among the most basic or primary of human commu-nication codes used to interpret experiences and relationships in social groups—as "underlying" methods of interpretation that operate on a more fundamental level than specific academic codes. See Mieke Bal, *Murder and Difference: Gender, Genre, and Scholarship of Sisera's Death* (trans. M. Gumpert; Bloomington: Indiana University Press, 1988), 10. These "undercodes" determine the paradigmatic premises of our cul-tures.

78. I have attempted to begin that process with "Military Aristocrat or Warrior-Monk." See Johnson, 2002.

Such sacrificial rites—like all "blood" sacrifices through the ages—are both empirical and ethereal, both essential and contiguous, governed by the dream of attaining and sustaining a purely masculine descent line. Women's blood is unwelcome, except as it flows from a victim.

A New Cult of Heroes

My third example of the "hero cult" today—if I may include Schwartzkopf as a new "prototype" in that group—may surprise my readers. As noted at the beginning of this article, David Noble has hypothesized that science and "the present enchantment with things technological"—the very measure of modern enlightenment—is rooted in religious myths and ancient imaginings. The army project for the world's first manned spaceflight was called Project Adam.[79] The new technologists of space travel, cybertechnology, and genetic research assume the title of the New Adam, creating new worlds and even new human beings. Astronaut John Glenn became, literally, the first New Adam. Why were men sent into space? Noble quotes Wernher von Braun, the man who named and headed the "Adam" project. "It was God's purpose," von Braun wrote, "to send his Son to other worlds to bring the gospel to them." (Who, exactly, was included in the soteriological image of "son," he does not say.) But if the Adam analogy has meaning, it is not the proclamation of the gospel that space technology seeks, but a new creation of life, as well as redemption. Noble explains:

> Von Braun had come to view spaceflight as a millennial "new beginning" for mankind, the second and final phase of his divinely ordained destiny. The astronaut . . . was another Adam, conceived to extend the promise of redemption across the celestial sea. . . . [Von Braun said:] "If man is Alpha and Omega . . . it may be Man's destiny *to assure immortality*, not only of his race but even of the life spark itself."[80]

Could it be that twenty-first century technology is attempting to do what sacrificial cults did in nontechnological (patriarchal) societies: to put men in control of life and death by usurping, for men, the power of women's blood? As Rushton demonstrates in her chapter earlier in this

---

79. This military agency became the Mercury Project of the National Aeronautics and Space Administration (NASA). President Dwight Eisenhower created NASA in order to put space research in the hands of civilians. Nonetheless, just about all the astronauts were military (mostly Navy) aviators.
80. Noble, *Religion of Technology*, 126–27, emphasis added.

volume, the first Adam was the original *genitor* of the human race—not Eve. In technology, modern man seeks to extend that (male) generative power into immortality.

Noble also predicates a "powerful affinity" between technology and masculinity and speaks of a "masculinized" "religion of technology" that derives from medieval celibate monks and identifies with "elite males" (such as aviators and astronauts)—men carrying on military operations transformed by giant "advances" in technology.[81] Noble relates such significant advances in technology and warfare to the "core monotheistic Judeo-Christian male creation myth"; inspired by both androcentric myths and scientific aspirations, men consciously seek "to imitate their male god." He reminds us that "the recovery of mankind's image-likeness to God was understood by orthodox Christians from the outset to be restricted to males"—Augustine's "sons of promise." And he reminds us of the medieval image that stands as a root metaphor for technological advance: "In medieval [artistic] representations, however, God has become a mere midwife, removing the fully formed Eve from the side of Adam, who has, in effect, given birth to her—a procreation reversal common to male creation myths. Here only Adam, the male, was created in the image of God."[82]

This "first birth" or "spermist" view of creation was as bloodless as it was pure, creating a patrilineal line of descent without the instrumentality of women's blood or birthing powers.[83] Even less than "marginal," Eve was now excluded entirely from a share in the original divine likeness and in all future divine creation. Only man, as priest, as king, as warrior-hero, as astronaut, and even as a second Creator God (the geneticist), shares in the bloodless divine likeness and performs *bloodless* acts of divine creation: the "restoration of perfection was a male-only pursuit . . . Eden without Eve."[84]

Western patriarchal religion and the spiritually significant technology spawned in its medieval monasteries became intertwined in the exaltation of a bloodless, pure, and female-free masculine cosmos and divine

---

81. I refer my reader again to the work of Bal (*Murder and Difference*) on gender undercodes.
82. Noble, *Religion of Technology*, 213. (As Rushton defined earlier in this volume: God may have been the midwife, but Adam was the physical source—the birthing genitor.)
83. Noble here speaks in anthropological terms (*Religion of Technology*, 214).
84. Ibid. (Also, as Noble observes, medieval cleric Joachim of Fiore "understood that millenarian redemption was restricted to males—and only those not 'defiled by women.'")

destiny. The ultimate example of the sacrificial priest—slaughtering the female element in order to give birth bloodlessly—may well be geneticists (such as Richard Seed, quoted at the beginning of this chapter) seeking to control the creation of life itself. As Noble observes: "Religious preoccupations pervade the space program. . . . Genetic engineers imagine themselves divinely inspired participants in a new creation . . . the recovery of mankind's lost divinity."[85] In the "myth of a masculine millennium," such a birth-giving/redemptive process is not only bloodless but also far loftier than the monstrous deformities that occasionally occur in woman's life-giving labors.

Perhaps some good can come of it. Perhaps the reversal of female-controlled birthing to male-controlled killing can now be replaced with a bloodless creation of life instead. But before any good can come of it, we must begin to comprehend it as the creative/redemptive sacrificial rite that it is.

Conclusions

In both the mysterious role of high priest and in the courageous role of warrior-hero, man sought to create his own descent line, his own bloodline purified of all female blood. Thus, the two roles, priest and warrior or combat-hero—and now geneticist—have been handed down generations as male-only roles. Over physical life, born of woman, men had taken control at the familial/social or tribal level, as paterfamilias or chief, for example, and ultimately as king. Society was now male determined. Only in the role of high priest and warrior-hero could the "king" (or any leader/chief) gain full control of Life and Death, with full right to sacrifice it, to shed human blood, to kill. Just as woman (nonmale) could produce human (male) life, men now can turn human life into nonlife.

Thus, the priesthood and the military officer corps are parallel all-male descent lines, purifying the patriarchy of female influence and control as it reaches for the unknown power of Supermasculinity. But such an egocentric illusion of collective might can become an outrageously abusive force.

Lastly, in the shadow of technology we must approach the issue of blood as a global symbol for life and (for those of us who are Americans) begin to question the ideological overtones of one country's identifying itself as the one "superpower" in control of life, death, and killing on that

---

85. Ibid., 5.

globe. Certainly, the need to create a "superpower" that "saves" the world or civilization is a soteriological fantasy. It not only represents a dangerous religious goal but also seeks to usurp all sacrificial power on the grandest scale imaginable. Just as the genecist becomes humankind's new Creator God, astronauts, by "conquering" military and super/astro/cybertechnological space, become the West's ultimate hero, ready to replant (and save) human life in outer space.

What knights of old have called their covenant-in-blood has been "purified" into a covenant of steel and cyberbytes and genomes.

BIBLIOGRAPHY

Adler, Rachel. *Engendering Judaism: An Inclusive Theology and Ethics.* Boston: Beacon, 1998.

———."In Your Blood, Live: Re-visions of a Theology of Purity." *Tikkun* 8 (1992): 38–41.

———. "A Mother in Israel: Aspects of the Mother Role in Jewish Myth." Pages 237–55 in *Beyond Androcentrism: Essays on Women and Religion.* Edited by R. M. Gross. Missoula: Scholars Press, 1977.

———. "Tumah and Taharah: Ends and Beginnings." Pages 63–71 in *The Jewish Woman: New Perspectives.* Edited by E. Koltun. New York: Schocken, 1976.

———. "Tumah and Taharah—Mikveh." Pages 167–71 in *The Jewish Catalogue.* Edited by M. Strassfeld et al. New York: Jewish Publication Society, 1972.

Alfes, Georg. *Die kirchliche Weihe des Familienlebens.* Cologne: Bachen, 1998.

Allison, Dale C. *The End of the Ages Has Come.* Philadelphia: Fortress, 1985.

American Heritage Dictionary. New York: Delta, 1992.

Anderson, Gary. "Celibacy or Consummation in the Garden? Reflections on Early Jewish and Christian Interpretations of the Garden of Eden." *Harvard Theological Review* 82 (1989): 121–48.

Andrews, Lynn V. *Woman at the Edge of Two Worlds: The Spiritual Journey through Menopause.* New York: HarperCollins, 1993.

Annas, Julia. *The Hellenistic Philosophy of Mind.* Berkeley: University of California Press, 1992.

Antonelli, Judith S. *In the Image of God: A Feminist Commentary on the Torah.* London: Jason Aronson, 1995.

The Apostolic Constitutions: Translations of the Writings of the Fathers. Edited by A. Roberts and J. Donaldson. Ante-Nicene Library 17. Edinburgh: T&T Clark, 1870.

Archer, Leonie J. "Bound by Blood: Circumcision and Menstrual Taboo in Post-Exilic Judaism." Pages 38–61 in *After Eve: Women, Theology, and the Christian Traditions.* Edited by J. M. Soskice. London: Marshall Pickering, 1990.

———. *Her Price Is beyond Rubies.* Sheffield: Sheffield Academic Press, 1990.

———. "'In Thy Blood Live': Gender and Ritual in the Judaeo-Christian Tradition." Pages 22–49 in *Through the Devil's Gateway: Women, Religion, and Taboo.* Edited by A. Joseph. London: SPCK and Channel Four Television, 1990.

———. "The Role of Jewish Women in the Religion, Ritual, and Cult of Graeco-Roman Palestine." Pages 273–87 in *Images of Women in Antiquity.* Edited by A. Cameron and A. Kuhrt. Detroit: Wayne State University Press, 1983.

Ardener, Edwin. "Belief and the Problem of Women: The Problem Revisited." Pages 1–27 in *Perceiving Women.* Edited by S. Ardener. New York: Halsted, 1978.

Aristotle. *The Generation of Animals.* Translated by A. L. Peck. London: William Heinemann, 1942.

Arndt, William F., and F. Wilbur Grinrich. *Greek-English Lexicon of the New Testament and Other Early Christian Literature.* Chicago: University of Chicago Press, 1979.

Arx, Walter von. "The Churching of Women after Childbirth: History and Significance." *Concilium* 112 (1978): 63–73.

Ashley, Timothy R. *The Book of Numbers.* Grand Rapids: Eerdmans, 1993.

Augustine. "Forgiveness 21, XII, The Precept about Touching the Menstruous Woman Not to Be Figuratively Understood." Online: http://ccel.org/s/schaff/npn/105/htm/x.iii.21.htm.

Baker, Adrienne, ed. *The Jewish Woman in Contemporary Society.* New York: New York University Press, 1993.

Bal, Mieke. *Murder and Difference: Gender, Genre, and Scholarship of Sisera's Death.* Translated by M. Gumpert. Bloomington: Indiana University Press, 1988.

Bamberger, Bernard J. Leviticus, *The Torah: A Modern Commentary.* New York: Union of American Hebrew Congregations, 1981.

Barkley, Gary Wayne. *Origen: Homilies on Leviticus 1–16.* Fathers of the Church. Washington, D.C.: Catholic University of America Press, 1990.

Barnes, Jonathan, ed. *Aristotle: The Complete Works.* Princeton: Princeton University Press, 1982.

Baskin, Judith R. "Rabbinic Reflections on the Barren Wife." *Harvard Theological Review* 82 (1989): 101–14.

———. "Woman as Other in Rabbinic Literature." Pages 177–96 in vol. 2 of *Where We Stand: Issues and Debates in Ancient Judaism.* Part 3 of *Judaism in Late Antiquity.* Edited by J. Neusner and A. J. Avery-Peck. Leiden: Brill, 1999.

Baumgarten, Joseph. "Purification after Childbirth and the Sacred Garden in 4Q265 and Jubilees." Pages 3–10 in *New Qumran Texts and Studies: Proceedings of the First Meeting of the International Organization for Qumran Studies, Paris 1992.* Edited by G. J. Brooke and F. García Martínez. Leiden: Brill, 1994.

Beaumont, Roger A. *Military Ethics: Special Fighting Units in the Modern World.* New York: Bobbs-Merrill, 1974.

Be'er, Ilana. "Blood Discharge: On Female Im/Purity in the Priestly Code and in Biblical Narrative." Pages 152–64 in *A Feminist Companion to Exodus–Deuteronomy.* Edited by A. Brenner. Sheffield: Sheffield Academic Press, 1994.

Beers, William. *Women and Sacrifice: Male Narcissism and the Psychology of Religion.* Detroit: Wayne State University Press, 1992.

Berger, Teresa. "Liturgie und Frauenseele: Die Liturgische Bewegung aus der Sicht der Frauenforschung." *Praktische Theologie heute* 10 (1993).

Berrin, Susan. *Celebrating the New Moon: A Rosh Hodesh Anthology.* London: Jason Aronson, 1996.

Bieler, Ludwig, ed. *The Irish Penitentials.* Dublin: Dublin Institute for Advanced Studies, 1975.

Bingen, Hildegard von. "Voice of the Blood." Sequentia: Deutshe harmonia mundi; BMG Blassics, 1995.

Binns, Leonard Elliot. *Numbers.* Westminster Commentaries. London: Methuen, 1927.

Blenkinsopp, Joseph. "Sacrifice and Social Maintenance: What's at Stake in the (Non-)Ordination of Roman Catholic Women." *Cross Currents* 45 (fall 1995): 359–67.

Bonar, Andrew. *A Commentary on Leviticus.* London: Banner of Truth Trust, 1846.

Børresen, Kari Elisabeth. *Subordination and Equivalence: The Nature and Role of Women in Augustine and Thomas Aquinas.* Repr., Kampen, Netherlands: Kok Pharos, 1993.

———. ed. *The Image of God: Gender Models in Judaeo-Christian Tradition.* Minneapolis: Fortress, 1995.

Boyarin, Daniel. *Carnal Israel: Reading Sex in Talmudic Culture.* Berkeley: University of California Press, 1993.

Bradshaw, Paul, ed. *The Canons of Hippolytus.* Translated by C. Bebawi. Alcuin/Grow Liturgical Study 2; Grove Liturgical Study 50. Bramcote, England: Grove Books, 1987.

Brakke, David. "The Problematization of Nocturnal Emissions in Early Christian Syria, Egypt, and Gaul." *Journal of Early Christian Studies* 3 (1995): 419–60.

Brenton, Lancelot Charles Lee. *The Septuagint Version of the Old Testament and Apocrypha.* London: Bagster, 1851. Repr., Grand Rapids: Zondervan, 1978.

Brewer, David. "Nomological Exegesis in Qumran Divorce Texts." Römische *Quartalschrift für christliche Altertumskunde und Kirchengeschichte* 18 (1998): 561–79.

Brinkhoff, Lucas, et al., eds. *Liturgisch Woordenboek.* Roermond, Netherlands: Romen, 1965.

Bronner, Leah. "Gynomorphic Imagery in Exilic Isaiah (40–66)." *Dor le Dor* 2 (1983–1984): 77.

Broshi, Magen. "The Gigantic Dimensions of the Visionary Temple in the Temple Scroll." *Biblical Archaeology Review* 13, no. 6 (1987): 36–37.

Browe, Peter. *Beiträge zur Sexualethik des Mittelalters.* Breslau [now Wroclaw, Poland]: n.p., 1932.

Brown, Francis, ed. *The New Brown, Driver, and Briggs Hebrew and English Lexicon of the Old Testament, Based on the Lexicon of William Gesenius as Translated by*

Edward Robinson. Edited by Francis Brown with the cooperation of S. R. Driver and Charles A. Briggs. Grand Rapids: Baker, 1981.

———. *The New Brown-Driver-Briggs-Gesenius Hebrew and English Lexicon.* United States: Christian Copyrights, 1983.

Brown, Peter. *The Body and Society: Men, Women, and Sexual Renunciation in Early Christianity.* New York: Columbia University Press, 1988.

Brown, Raymond E. *The Death of the Messiah: From Gethsemane to the Grave.* Vol 1. Anchor Bible Reference Library. Garden City, N.Y.: Doubleday, 1996.

Brown, Raymond E., et al., eds. *Jerome Bible Commentary.* Englewood Cliffs, N.J.: Prentice-Hall, 1968.

Buckley, Thomas, and Alma Gottlieb, eds. *Blood Magic: The Anthropology of Menstruation.* Berkeley: University of California Press, 1988.

Budapest, Zsuzsanna Emesse. *The Goddess in the Office: A Personal Energy Guide for the Spiritual Warrior at Work.* San Francisco: Harper, 1993.

———. *The Grandmother of Time: A Women's Book of Celebrations, Spells, and Sacred Objects for Every Month of the Year.* San Francisco: Harper & Row, 1989.

Budd, Philip J. *Numbers.* Word Biblical Commentary. Waco, Tex.: Word, 1984.

Bujo, Bénézet. "Feminist Theology in Africa." *Theology Digest* 36, no. 1 (1989): 25–30.

Burrus, Virginia. "Word and Flesh: The Bodies and Sexuality of Ascetic Women in Christian Antiquity." *Journal of Feminist Studies in Religion* 10, no. 1 (1994): 27–51.

Buttrick, George Arthur, et al., eds. *The Interpreter's Bible.* Vol 2. New York: Abingdon, 1953.

Bynum, Caroline Walker. *Jesus as Mother: Studies in the Spirituality of the High Middle Ages.* Berkeley: University of California Press, 1982.

Callaway, Mary. *Sing, O Barren One: A Study in Comparative Midrash.* Society of Biblical Literature Dissertation Series 91. Atlanta: Scholars Press, 1986.

Calvin, John. *Commentaries on the Four Last Books of Moses.* Translated by C. W. Bingham. Grand Rapids: Eerdmans, 1950.

Caron, Charlotte. *To Make and Make Again: Feminist Ritual Theology.* New York: Crossroad, 1993.

Carson, Ann. "Dirt and Desire: The Phenomenology of Feminist Pollution in Antiquity." Pages 77–100 in *Constructions of the Classical Body.* Edited by J. I. Porter. Ann Arbor: University of Michigan Press, 1999.

Celsus. *On Medicine.* Translated by W. G. Spencer. 3 vols. Loeb Classical Library. Cambridge: Harvard University Press, 1948.

Chia, Mantak. *Taoist Secrets of Love: Cultivating Male Sexual Energy.* Santa Fe, N.M.: Aurora Press, 1884.

Chodorow, Nancy. *The Reproduction of Mothering: Psychoanalysis and the Sociology of Gender.* Berkeley: University of California Press, 1978.

Christ, Carol P. *Daughter of Aphrodite: Reflections on a Journey to the Goddess.* San Francisco: Harper & Row, 1987.

Clement. *Opera*. Edited by A. Roberts and J. Donaldson. Ante-Nicean Fathers. Grand Rapids: Eerdmans, 1884.

Cleven, Wilhelm. *Fragen um Sakrament und Sakramentalien*. Bonn: Borromäus-Vereins, 1949.

Cicero. *On the Nature of the Gods*. Translated by H. Rackham. Loeb Classical Library. Cambridge: Harvard University Press, 1961.

Cohen, Menahem, ed. *Mikra'ot Gedolot 'Haketer': Ezekiel*. Ramat Gan, Israel: Bar-Ilan University Press, 2000.

Cohen, Shaye J. D. *From the Maccabees to the Mishnah*. Library of Early Christianity. Philadephia: Westminster, 1987.

———. "Menstruants and the Sacred in Judaism and Christianity." Pages 273–99 in *Women's History and Ancient History*. Edited by S. B. Pomeroy. Chapel Hill: University of North Carolina Press, 1991.

Collins New English Dictionary. New York: HarperCollins, 1997.

Connolly, R. Hugh, ed. *Didascalia Apostolorum*. Oxford: Clarendon, 1929.

Corrington, Gail Paterson. *Her Image of Salvation: Female Saviors and Formative Christianity*. Louisville: Westminster John Knox, 1992.

Cuming, Geoffrey J. *Hippolytus: A Text for Students With Introduction, Translation, Commentary and Notes*. 2nd ed. Bramcote, England: Grove Books, 1987.

Daly, Mary. *Gyn/Ecology: The Metaethics of Radical Feminism*. Boston: Beacon, 1978.

Danby, Herbert. *The Mishnah*. Oxford: Oxford University Press, 1933.

Darr, Katheryn Pfisterer. *Isaiah's Vision of the Family of God: Literary Currents in Biblical Interpretation*. Louisville: Westminster John Knox, 1994.

———. "Like Warrior, like Woman: Destruction and Deliverance in Isaiah 42:117." *Catholic Biblical Quarterly* 49 (1987): 564–71.

Dausend, Hugo. "Der Mutter erster Gang zur Kirche." *Bibel und Liturgie* 9 (1934–35): 448–50.

Davies, Philip. "The Dead Sea Writings, the Judaism(s) of." Pages 182–96 in vol. 1 of *The Encyclopaedia of Judaism*. Edited by J. Neusner, A. J. Avery-Peck, and W. S. Green. Leiden: Brill, 2000.

Dean-Jones, Lesley. "Menstrual Bleeding according to the Hippocratics and Aristotle." *Transactions of the American Philological Association* 119 (1989): 177–92.

———. *Women's Bodies in Classical Greek Science*. Oxford: Clarendon, 1994.

Delaney, Carol. "Mortal Flow: Menstruation in Turkish Village Society." Pages 75–93 in *Blood Magic: The Anthropology of Menstruation*. Edited by Th. Buckley and A. Gottlieb. Berkeley: University of California Press, 1988.

Delaney, Janice. *The Curse: A Cultural History of Menstruation*. Chicago: University of Illinois Press, 1988.

Destro, Adriana. "The Witness of Times: An Anthropological Reading of Niddah." Pages 124–38 in *Reading Leviticus: A Conversation with Mary Douglas*. Edited by J. F. A. Sawyer. Journal for the Study of the Old Testament: Supplement Series 227. Sheffield: Sheffield Academic Press, 1996.

De Troyer, Kristin. *The End of the Alpha Text of Esther: Translation and Narrative Technique in MT* 8:1–17, LXX 8:1–17, and AT 7, 14–41. Septuagint and Cognate Studies 48. Atlanta: SBL, 2000.

Didascalia Apostolorum in Syriac. Vol. 2, chs. 11–26. Edited by A. Vööbus. Corpus Scriptorum Christianorum Orientalium, 407–408. Louvain: Catholic University of Louvain, 1979.

Dionysius. *Extant Fragments.* Edited by A. Roberts and J. Donaldson. Ante-Nicean Fathers. Grand Rapids: Eerdmans, 1884.

Dionysus of Alexandria. *Canon II: Response to Letter from Basilidea the Bishop.* Online: http://ccel.wheaton.edu/fathers/NPNF2–14/7 appndx/dionysiu.htm.

Dioscordies. *Greek Herbal.* Translated by J. Good. Edited by R.T. Gunther. New York: Hafner, 1959.

Dix, Gregory, ed. *The Treatise on the Apostolic Tradition of St. Hippolytus of Rome.* 2d ed. London: SPCK, 1969.

Douglas, Mary. *Purity and Danger: An Analysis of the Concepts of Pollution and Taboo.* London: Routledge, 1966, 1992.

Dresen, Grietje. "Einde van de inquisitie, geboorte van een ander. Verhalen van de liefde in een voorstel tot ethiek." *Te Elfder Ure* 29, no. 2 (1986): 178–212.

———. "Het betere bloed." *Mara* 6 (1992–93): 28–40.

———. *Is dit mijn lichaam? Visioenen van het volmaakte lichaam in katholieke moraal en mystiek.* Nijmegen, Netherlands: Valkhof Pers, 1998.

———. *Onschuldfantasieën: Offerzin en heilsverlangen in feminisme en mystiek.* Nijmegen, Netherlands: SUN, 1990.

Driver, Samuel R. *Exodus.* Cambridge Bible. Cambridge: Cambridge University Press, 1911.

Edwards, Robert G. *Conception in the Human Female.* London: Academic Press, 1980.

Eilberg-Schwartz, Howard. *The Savage in Judaism.* Bloomington: Indiana University Press, 1990.

Ellens, Deborah. "A Comparison of the Conceptualization of Women in the Sex Laws of Leviticus and in the Sex Laws of Deuteronomy." Ph.D. diss., Claremont Graduate University, 1998.

———. "Leviticus 15: Contrasting Conceptual Associations regarding Women." Pages 124–51 in vol. 2 of *Reading the Hebrew Bible for a New Millennium.* Edited by W. Kim et al. Harrisburg: Trinity Press International, 2000.

Eller, Cynthia. *Living in the Lap of the Goddess: New Feminist Spiritual Movements.* New York: Crossroad, 1993.

Ellis, Richard S. *Foundation Deposits in Ancient Mesopotamia.* New Haven: Yale University Press, 1968.

Elwell, Sue Levi. "Reclaiming Jewish Women's Oral Tradition? An Analysis of Rosh Hodesh." Pages 111–26 in *Women at Worship: Interpretations of North American Diversity.* Edited by M. Procter-Smith and J. Walton. Louisville: Westminster John Knox, 1993.

Empedocles. *The Extant Fragments.* Translated and edited by M. R. Wright. New Haven: Yale University Press, 1982.

Erich, A., and R. Beitel, eds. *Wörterbuch der deutschen Volkskunde.* Stuttgart: Kröner, 1955.

Etienne, Anne. "Birth." *The Ecumenical Review* 34 (1982): 228–37.

Eusebius. *Ecclesiastical History.* Translated by R. J. Deferrari. New York: Fathers of the Church, 1953.

Exum, J. Cheryl. *Fragmented Women: Feminist (Subversions) of Biblical Narratives.* Journal for the Study of the Old Testament: Supplement Series 163. Sheffield: Sheffield Academic Press, 1993.

Fander, Monika. "Reinheit/Unreinheit." Pages 349–51 in *Wörterbuch der feministischen Theologie.* Edited by E. Gössmann et al. Gütersloh, Germany: Mohn, 1991.

Fischer, Balthasar. "Das Rituale Romanum (1614–1964): Die Schicksal eines liturgisches Buches." *Trierer Theologische Zeitschrift* 73 (1964): 257–71.

Fletcher, John, and Andrew Benjamin, eds. *Abjection, Melancholia, and Love: The Work of Julia Kristeva.* London: Routledge, 1990.

Fonrobert, Charlotte. "The Woman with a Blood-Flow (Mark 5.24–34) Revisited: Menstrual Laws and Jewish Culture in Christian Feminist Hermeneutics." Pages 121–40 in *Early Christian Interpretation of the Scriptures of Israel.* Edited by C. A. Evans and J. A. Sanders. Sheffield: Sheffield Academic Press, 1997.

Fortenbaugh, William W., et al., eds. *Theophrastus of Eresus: Sources for His Life, Writings, Thought, and Influence.* Vol. 2. Leiden: Brill, 1992.

Francke, Linda Bird. *Ground Zero: The Gender Wars in the Military.* New York: Simon & Schuster, 1997.

Frank, G. L. C. "Menstruation and Motherhood: Christian Attitudes in Late Antiquity." *Studiae Historiae Ecclesiasticae* 19 (1993): 185–208.

Franz, Adolph. *Die Kirchlichen Benediktionen im Mittelalter.* Freiburg i.B., Germany: Herder, 1909.

Frazer, James. "Taboo." Page 15 in vol. 23 of *The Encyclopedia Britannica.* Edinburgh: Adam and Charles Black, 1898.

———. *The Golden Bough.* Edited by Th. H. Gaster. Criterion Books 490. New York: Criterion Books, 1959.

Frede, Michael, and Gisela Striker, eds. *Rationality in Greek Thought.* Oxford: Clarendon, 1996.

Fredrickson, Paula. "Hysteria and the Gnostic Myths of Creation." *Vigilae christianae* 33 (1979): 287–90.

Freedman, H., and Maurice Simon, eds. *Midrash Rabbah.* Translated by J. J. Slotki. London: Soncino, 1939.

Freud, Sigmund. *New Introductory Lectures on Psychoanalysis.* New York: W. W. Norton, 1965.

———. *Totem and Taboo.* Translated and edited by James Strachey. New York: W. W. Norton, 1989. (Repr. from London: Routledge & Kegan Paul. LTO, 1950).

Freyne, Sean. "Vilifying the Other and Defining the Self: Matthew's and John's Anti-Jewish Polemic in Focus." Pages 117–43 in *"To See Ourselves as Others See Us": Christian, Jews, Other in Late Antiquity.* Edited by J. Neusner and E. S. Frerichs. Chico, Calif.: Scholars Press, 1985.

Friedman, Susan Standford. "Creativity and the Childbirth Metaphor: Gender Difference and Literary Discourse." *Feminist Studies* 13 (1987): 50–51.

Frymer-Kensky, Tikva. "Pollution, Purification, and Purgation in Biblical Israel." Pages 399–414 in *The Word of the Lord Shall Go Forth: Essays in Honor of David Noel Freedman in Celebration of His Sixtieth Birthday.* Edited by C. L. Meyers and M. O'Connor. Winona Lake, Ind.: Eisenbrauns, 1983.

Fuchs, Esther. "The Literary Characterization of Mothers and Sexual Politics in the Hebrew Bible." Pages 117–136 in *Feminist Perspectives on Biblical Scholarship.* Edited by A. Yarbro Collins. Atlanta: Scholars Press, 1985.

Fuller, Reginald C., et al., eds. *A New Catholic Commentary on Holy Scripture.* Don Mills, Ontario: Nelson, 1969.

Funk, F. X., ed. *Didascalia et Constitutiones Apostolorum.* Vol. 1. Paderborn, Germany: Schoeningh, 1905.

Galen. *On the Affected Parts of the Body.* Translated by R.E. Siegel. Basel: Karger, 1976.

Gemf, Conrad. "The Imagery of Birth Pangs in the New Testament." *Tyndale Bulletin* 45 (1994): 120.

Gerstenberger, Erhard S. *Leviticus: A Commentary.* Old Testament Library. Louisville: Westminster John Knox, 1996. Originally published as *Das dritte Buch Moses: Leviticus.* Das Alte Testament Deutsch 6. Göttingen: Vandenhoeck & Ruprecht, 1993.

Gerzon, Mark. *A Choice of Heroes: The Changing Face of American Manhood.* Boston: Houghton Mifflin, 1982.

Ginsberg, Harold Louis. "Studies in Hosea 1–4." Pages 50–69 in *Yehezkel Kaufmann Jubilee Volume.* Edited by M. Haran. Jerusalem: Magnes, 1960.

Grabbe, Lester L. *Leviticus.* Sheffield: Sheffield Academic Press, 1993.

Grahn, Judy. "From Sacred Blood to the Curse and Beyond." Pages 265–79 in *The Politics of Women's Spirituality: Essays on the Rise of Spiritual Power within the Feminist Movement.* Edited by C. Spretnak. Garden City, N.Y.: Doubleday/Anchor, 1982.

Green, Jay P., et al., eds. *A Concise Lexicon to the Biblical Languages.* Peabody, Mass.: Hendrickson, 1987.

Greenberg, Blu. "Female Sexuality and Bodily Functions in the Jewish Tradition." Pages 1–44 in *Women, Religion, and Sexuality: Studies on the Impact of Religious Teaching on Women.* Edited by J. Beecher. Geneva: WCC, 1990.

Greenberg, Moshe. "The Etymology of Niddah '(Menstrual) Impurity.'" Pages 69–77 in *Solving Riddles and Untying Knots: Biblical, Epigraphic, and Semitic Studies in Honor of Jonas C. Greenfield.* Edited by Z. Zevit, S. Gitin, and M. Sokoloff. Winona Lake, Ind.: Eisenbrauns, 1995.

Greenstone, Julius H. *The Holy Scriptures: Numbers, with Commentary.* Philadelphia: Jewish Publication Society, 1939.

Griggs, C. Wilfrid. *Early Egyptian Christianity: From Its Origins to 450 C.E.* Leiden: Brill, 1990.

Grossfeld, B. *The Targum Onkelos to Leviticus and the Targum Onkelos to Numbers.* Aramaic Bible 8. Edinburgh: T&T Clark, 1987.

Grossman, Susan. "Feminism, Midrash, and Mikveh." *Conservative Judaism* 44 (1992): 7–17.

Gruber, Mayer I. *Aspects of Nonverbal Communication in the Ancient Near East.* 2 vols. Rome: Biblical Institute Press, 1980.

———."Breast-Feeding Practices in Biblical Israel and in Old Babylonian Mesopotamia." *Journal of the Ancient Near Eastern Society* 19 (1987): 61–83.

———. *The Motherhood of God and Other Studies.* University of South Florida Studies in the History of Judaism 57. Atlanta: Scholars, 1992.

———. "The Sources of Rashi's Cartography." Pages 61–67 in *Letters and Texts of Jewish History.* Edited by N. Simms. Hamilton, New Zealand: Outrigger, 1999.

———. "The Status of Women in Ancient Judaism." Pages 164–67 in vol. 2 of *Where We Stand: Issues and Debates in Ancient Judaism.* P 3 of *Judaism in Late Antiquity.* Edited by J. Neusner and A. J. Avery-Peck. Leiden: Brill, 1999.

———. "Women in the Cult according to the Priestly Code." Pages 35–48 in *Judaic Perspectives on Ancient Israel.* Edited by J. Neusner, B. A. Levine, and E. S. Frerichs. Philadelphia: Fortress, 1987.

Gundry, Robert H. *Mark: A Commentary on His Apology for the Cross.* Grand Rapids: Eerdmans, 1993.

Gunther, Robert T. *Dioscordies: Greek Herbal.* Translated by J. Goodyer. New York: Hafner, 1959.

Haddon, Genia Pauli. *Body Metaphors: Releasing the God-Feminine in Us All.* New York: Crossroad Continuum, 1988.

Halivni, David. *Sources and Traditions: Tractate Shabbat.* New York: Jewish Theological Seminary, 1982.

Hanson, Ann Ellis. "Hippocrates: Diseases of Women I: Archives." *Signs* 1 (1975): 567–84.

———. "The Medical Writer's Woman." Pages 309–38 in *Before Sexuality: The Construction of the Erotic Experience in the Ancient Greek World.* Edited by D. M. Halperin, J. J. Winkler, and F. I. Zeitlin. Princeton: Princeton University Press, 1990.

Harrington, Hannah K. *The Impurity Systems of Qumran and the Rabbis: Biblical Foundations.* Society of Biblical Literature Dissertation Series 143. Atlanta: Scholars Press, 1993.

Harrison, Roland Kenneth. *Leviticus: An Introduction and Commentary.* Downers Grove, Ill.: InterVarsity Press, 1980.

Hatchett, Marion. *Sanctifying Life, Time, and Space.* New York: Crossroad, 1976.

Hauke, Manfred. *Women in the Priesthood? A Systematic Analysis in the Light of Creation and Redemption.* San Francisco: Ignatius Press, 1988. Originally published as *Die Problematik um das Frauenpriestertum vor dem Hintergrund der Schöphungs- und Erlösungsordnung.* Paderborn, Germany: Bonifatius, 1986.

Haupt, Paul. *The Sacred Books of the Old and New Testament.* New York: Dodd, Mead, 1898.

Hauptman, Judith. *Rereading the Rabbis: A Woman's Voice.* Boulder, Colo.: Westview, 1975.

Hein, Kenneth. *Eucharist and Excommunication: A Study in Early Christian Doctrine and Discipline.* Frankfurt: Peter Lang, 1975.

Hepding, Hugo. "Das Begräbnis der Wöchnerin." Pages 151–65 in *Volkskundliche Beiträge: Festschrift R. Wossidlo.* Neumünster, Germany: n.p., 1939.

Himmelfarb, Martha. "Sexual Relations and Purity in the Temple Scroll." *Dead Sea Discoveries* 6 (1999): 11–36.

Hippocrates. *Genuine Works.* Vol. 1. Translated by F. Adams. London: Sydenham Society, 1849.

———. *The Hippocratic Treatise "On Generation," "On the Nature of the Child," "Diseases IV."* Edited by Ian M. Lonie. New York: de Gruyter, 1981.

———. *Opera.* Translated by W. H. S. Jones and E. T. Withington. Vol. 4. Loeb Classical Library. Cambridge: Harvard University Press, 1939.

Hippolytus. *Refutation of All Heresies and Fragments.* Edited by A. Roberts and J. Donaldson. Ante-Nicean Fathers 5. Grand Rapids: Eerdmans, 1884.

———. *The Treatise on the Apostolic Tradition of St. Hippolytus of Rome.* Edited by G. Dix. 2d ed. London: SPCK, 1969.

Hoffman, Lawrence A. *Covenant of Blood: Circumcision and Gender in Rabbinic Judaism.* Studies in the History of Judaism. Chicago: University of Chicago Press, 1996.

Holm, Jeanne. *Women in the Military: An Unfinished Revolution.* Rev. ed. Novato, Calif.: Presidio, 1992.

The Holy Bible: New Revised Standard Version. New York: Oxford University Press, 1989.

Horowitz, Maryanne Cline. "Aristotle and Woman." *Journal of the History of Biology* 9 (1976): 183–213.

Horsley, G. H. R., ed. *New Documents Illustrating Early Christianity: A Review of the Greek Inscriptions and Papyri Published in 1978.* North Ryde, Australia: Macquarie University, 1983.

———. *New Documents Illustrating Early Christianity: A Review of the Greek Inscriptions and Papyri Published in 1979.* North Ryde, Australia: Macquarie University, 1987.

Ilan, Tal. "Biblical Women's Names in the Apocryphal Traditions." *Journal for the Study of the Pseudepigrapha* 11 (1993): 3–67.

———. *Jewish Women in Greco-Roman Palestine: An Inquiry into Image and Status.* Texte und Studien zum antiken Judentum 44. Tübingen: Mohr-Siebeck, 1995.

Irenaeus. *Against Heresies.* Edited by A. Roberts and J. Donaldson. Ante-Nicean Fathers. Grand Rapids: Eerdmans, 1884.

Irigaray, Luce. *An Ethics of Sexual Differences.* Ithaca, N.Y.: Cornell University Press, 1993.

———. *Thinking the Difference: For a Peaceful Revolution.* New York: Routledge, 1994.

Jacobs, Louis, ed. *The Jewish Religion: A Companion.* Oxford: Oxford University Press, 1995.

Janowski, Bernd. *Sühne als Heilsgesehen.* Neukirchen-Vluyn: Neukirchener Verlag, 1982.

Japhet, Sara. "The Prohibition of the Habitation of Women: The Temple Scroll's Attitude toward Sexual Impurity and Its Biblical Precedents." *Journal of the Ancient Near Eastern Society* 22 (1993): 69–87.

Jay, Nancy. "Sacrifice as Remedy for Having Been Born of a Woman." Pages 283–309 in *Immaculate and Powerful: The Female in Sacred Image and Social Reality.* Edited by C. W. Atkinson. Boston: Beacon, 1985.

———. *Throughout Your Generations Forever: Sacrifice, Religion, and Paternity.* Chicago: University of Chicago Press, 1992.

Jensen, Anne. *God's Self-Confident Daughters: Early Christianity and the Liberation of Women.* Louisville: Westminster John Knox, 1996. Originally published in 1992 as *Gottes selbstbewusste Töchter: Frauenemanzipation im frühen Christentum.* Freiburg i.B., Germany: Herder.

Jerome. *Commentarii in Propheta Zachariam, S. Hieronymi presbyteri opera.* Corpus Christianorum: Series latina. Turnhout, Belgium: Typographi Brepols Editores Pontifici, 1970.

Johnson, Judith Ann. "Military Aristocrat or Warrior-Monk: The Religious and Ethical Formation of the American Military Officer." Ph.D. diss., Claremont Graduate University, May 2002.

Joseph, Alison, ed. *Through the Devil's Gateway: Women, Religion, and Taboo.* London: SPCK and Channel Four Television, 1990.

Josephus, Flavius. *Against Apion.* Translated by W. Whiston. Grand Rapids: Baker, 1974.

———. *Antiquities of the Jews.* Translated by W. Whiston. Grand Rapids: Baker, 1974.

Justin Martyr. *Opera.* Edited by A. Roberts and J. Donaldson. Ante-Nicean Fathers. Grand Rapid: Eerdmans, 1884.

Kee, Howard Clark. *Medicine, Miracle, and Magic in New Testament Times.* Cambridge: Cambridge University Press, 1986.

Keegan, John. *The Mask of Command.* New York: Penguin, 1988.

Keil, Carl Friedrich, and Franz Delitzsch. *Biblical Commentary on the Old Testament.* Grand Rapids: Eerdmans, 1949.

Kelly, Henry Ansgar. *The Devil at Baptism: Ritual, Theology, and Drama.* Ithaca, N.Y.: Cornell University Press, 1985.

Kendrick, Leslie Smith. "A Woman Bleeding: Integrating Female Embodiment into Pastoral Theology and Practice." *Journal of Pastoral Care* 48 (1994): 145–53.

Kikawada, Isaac M. "The Shape of Genesis 11:1–9." Pages 18–32 in *Rhetorical Criticism.* Edited by J. J. Jackson and M. Kessler. Pittsburgh: Pickwick, 1974.

Kilborne, Benjamin, and I. I. Langness. *Culture and Human Nature: Theoretical Papers of Melford E. Spiro.* Chicago: University of Chicago Press, 1987.

King, Helen. "Bound to Bleed: Artemis and Greek Women." Pages 109–28 in *Images of Women in Antiquity*. Edited by A. Cameron and A. Kuhrt. London: Croom Helm, 1983.

———. *Hippocrates' Woman: Reading the Female Body in Ancient Greece*. New York: Routledge, 1998.

Kiuchi, Nobuyoshi. *The Purification Offering in the Priestly Literature: Its Meaning and Function*. Journal for the Study of the Old Testament: Supplement Series 56. Sheffield: Sheffield Academic Press, 1987.

Kleinheyer, Bruno, Emmanuel von Severus, and Reiner Kaczinski. *Sakramentliche Feiern II, Gottesdienst der Kirche*. Handbuch der Liturgiewissenschaft 8. Regensburg, Germany: Pustet, 1984.

Knab, Sophie Hodorowicz. *Polish Customs, Traditions, and Folklore*. New York: Hippocrene, 1993.

Knierim, Rolf P. *Text and Concept in Leviticus 1:1–9: A Case in Exegetical Method*. Tübingen: Mohr, 1992.

Knierim, Rolf P., and Gene M. Tucker, eds. *The Forms of the Old Testament Literature*. Grand Rapids: Eerdmans, 1981.

Knight, George A. F. *Leviticus*. Daily Study Bible Series. Edinburgh: Saint Andrews Press, 1981.

Knödel, Natalie. "Reconsidering an Obsolete Rite: The Churching of Women and Feminist Liturgical Theology." *Feminist Theology* 14 (1997): 106–25.

Koehler, Ludwig, and Walter Baumgartner. *Lexicon in Veteris Testamenti Libros*. Grand Rapids: Eerdmans, 1951.

———. "Het betere bloed." *Mara* 6 (1992–93): 28–40.

Kohlschein, Franz. "Die Vorstellung von der kultischen Unreinheit der Frau. Das weiterwirkende Motiv für eine zweispältige Situation?" Pages 269–88 in *Liturgie und Frauenfrage: Ein Beitrag zur Frauenforschung aud liturgiewissenschaftlicher Sicht*. Edited by T. Berger and A. Gerhards. Pietas Liturgica 7. St. Ottilien: EOS, 1990.

Kornfeld, Walter. Levitikus. *Neue Echter Bibel*. Würzburg, Germany: Echter, 1983.

Korte, Anne-Marie. "Die Erfahrung unseres Leibes: 'Leiblichkeit' als hermeneutische Kategorie in der feministischen Theologie." Pages 288–314 in *Abschied von Männergott: Schöpfungsverantwortung für Frauen und Männer*. Catharina Halkes zum 75. Geburtstag. Edited by J. Jäger-Sommer. Lucerne: Exodus, 1995.

———. "Reclaiming Ritual: A Gendered Approach to (Im)Purity." Pages 313–27 in *Purity and Holiness: The Heritage of Leviticus*. Edited by M. Poorthuis and J. Schwartz. Jewish and Christian Perspectives 2. Leiden: Brill, 2000.

Kottje, Raymund. *Studien zum Einfluss des Alten Testaments auf Recht und Liturgie des frühen Mittelalters (6–8 Jh)*. Bonner Historische Forschungen 23. Bonn: n.p., 1970.

Kraemer, Ross Shepard. *Her Share of the Blessings: Women's Religions among Pagans, Jews, and Christians in the Greco-Roman World*. New York: Oxford University Press, 1992.

————. "Monastic Jewish Women in Greco-Roman Egypt: Philo on the Therapeutrides." *Signs* 14 (1989): 342–47.

Kristeva, Julia. *Des chinoises.* Paris: Des Femmes, 1974.

————. *Pouvoirs de l'horreur: Essai sur l'abjection.* Paris: Du Seuil, 1980.

Lacks, Roslyn. *Woman and Judaism: Myth, History, and Struggle.* Garden City, N.Y.: Doubleday, 1980.

Lane, D. J., et al. *Leviticus-Numbers-Deuteronomy-Joshua. Old Testament in Syriac according to the Peshitta Version.* 1.2. II/1b. Leiden: Brill, 1991.

Lange, John Peter. *Commentary on the Holy Scriptures: Leviticus.* Grand Rapids: Zondervan, 1876.

————. *A Commentary on the Holy Scriptures: Numbers and Deuteronomy.* Translated and edited by P. Schaff. New York: Charles Scribner's Sons, 1879.

Lee, Janet, and Jennifer Sasser-Coen. *Blood Stories: Menarche and the Politics of the Female Body in Contemporary Western Societies.* New York: Routledge, 1996.

Lefkovitz, Lori Hope. "Sacred Screaming: Childbirth in Judaism." Pages 5–15 in vol. 6 of *Lifecycles: Jewish Women on Life Passages and Personal Milestones.* Edited by D. Orenstein. Woodstock, Vt.: Jewish Lights, 1994.

Levine, Baruch A. *Leviticus.* JPS Torah Commentary. Philadelphia: Jewish Publication Society, 1989.

————. Numbers 1–20. *Anchor Bible.* New York: Doubleday, 1993.

————. "The Temple Scroll: Aspects of Its Historical Provenance and Character." *Bulletin of the American Schools of Oriental Research* 232 (1978): 5–23.

Lewis, Jack P. "Baptismal Practice of the Second and Third Century Church." *Restoration Quarterly* 26 (1983): 1–17.

Lieu, Judith. "Scripture and the Feminine in John." Pages 225–40 in *A Feminist Companion to the Hebrew Bible in the New Testament.* Edited by A. Brenner. Sheffield: Sheffield Academic Press, 1996.

Longrigg, James. *Greek Rational Medicine: Philosophy and Medicine from Almaeon to the Alexandrians.* New York: Routledge, 1993.

Lütterbach, Hubertus. "Holy Mass and Holy Communion in the Medieval Penitentials (600–1200): Liturgical and Religio-Historical Perspectives." Pages 61–82 in *Bread of Heaven: Customs and Practices Surrounding Holy Communion.* Essays in the History of Liturgy and Culture. Edited by C. Caspers, G. Lukken, and G. Rouwhorst. Liturgia Condenda 3. Kampen, Netherlands: Kok Pharos, 1995.

Magonet, Jonathan. "'But if It Is a Girl, She Is Unclean for Twice Seven Days . . .': The Riddle of Leviticus 12:5." Pages 144–52 in *Reading Leviticus: A Conversation with Mary Douglas.* Edited by J. F. A. Sawyer. Journal for the Study of the Old Testament: Supplement Series 227. Sheffield: Sheffield Academic Press, 1996.

Maher, Michael. *Targum Pseudo-Jonathan: Leviticus.* Aramaic Bible 3. Edinburgh: T&T Clark, 1994.

Mahoney, E. J. "Moral Cases: Churching a Bad Catholic." *Clergy Review* 5 (1933): 73.

Maimonides, Moses. *Moses Maimonides' Commentary on the Mishnah: Introduction to Seder Zeraim and Commentary on Tractate Berachoth.* Translated by F. Rosner. New York: Feldheim, 1975.

Martin, Dale. *The Corinthian Body.* New Haven: Yale University Press, 1995.

Martin, Emily. *The Woman in the Body.* Boston: Beacon, 1987.

May, Margaret Tallmadge, ed. *Galen on the Usefulness of the Parts of the Body.* Cornell Publications in the History of Science. Ithaca, N.Y.: Cornell University Press, 1968.

McNamara, Martin, and Robert Hayward. *Targum Neofiti 1: Leviticus.* Aramaic Bible 3. Edinburgh: T&T Clark, 1994.

McNeile, Alan Hugh. *The Book of Numbers.* Cambridge: Cambridge University Press, 1931.

Meeks, Wayne A. "Breaking Away: Three New Testament Pictures of Christianity's Separation from the Jewish Communities." Pages 93–115 in *"To See Ourselves as Others See Us": Christian, Jews, Other in Late Antiquity.* Edited by J . Neusner and E. S. Frerichs. Chico, Calif.: Scholars Press, 1985.

Metternich, Ulrike. *"Sie sagte ihm die ganze Wahrheit": Die Erzählung von der "Blutflüssigen" -feministisch gedeutet.* Mainz: Matthias Grünewald, 1999.

Milgrom, Jacob. "The City of the Temple." *Jewish Quarterly Review* 85 (1994): 125–28.

———. *Leviticus 1–16. Anchor Bible.* New York: Doubleday, 1991.

———. "The Rationale for Biblical Impurity [Lev 12–15]." *Journal of the Ancient Near Eastern Society* 22 (1993): 107–111.

———. "The Scriptural Foundations and Deviations in the Laws of Purity of the Temple Scroll." Pages 83–99 in *Archaeology and History in the Dead Sea Scrolls: The New York University Conference in Memory of Yigael Yadin.* Edited by L. H. Schiffman. Journal for the Study of the Pseudepigrapha: Supplement Series 8; Journal for the Study of the Old Testament/American Schools of Oriental Research Monographs 2. Sheffield: Sheffield Academic Press, 1990.

"Misconceptions about Menstruation." *Women's International Network News* 20 (1994): 45–50.

Mitchell, Leonel L. "Development of Catechesis in the Third and Fourth Century: From Hippolytus to Augustine." Pages 49–78 in *The Faithful Church: Issues in the History of Catechesis.* Edited by J. H. Westerhoff .Wilton, Conn.: Morehouse-Barlow, 1981.

Modrak, Deborah K. W. "Aristotle: Women, Deliberation, and Nature." Pages 207–22 in *Engendering Origins: Critical Feminist Readings of Plato and Aristotle.* Edited by Bat-Ami Bar On. Albany: State University of New York Press, 1994.

Moss, Patricia. "Unraveling the Threads: The Origins of Women's Asceticism in the Earliest Christian Communities." *Pacifica* 10 (1997): 137–55.

Müller, Michael. *Die Lehre des Hl. Augustinus von der Paradieselehre und ihre Auswirkung in der Sexualethik des 12. und 13. Jahrhunderts bis Thomas von Aquin.* Regensburg, Germany: Pustet, 1954.

Nakano, Yuko. "Women and Buddhism—Blood, Impurity, and Motherhood." Pages 65–85 in *Women and Religion in Japan.* Edited by A. Okuda and H. Okano. Studies in Oriental Religions 420. Wiesbaden: Harrasowitz, 1998.

Neusner, Jacob. *From Scripture to 70: The Pre-Rabbinic Beginnings of the Halakah.* University of South Florida Studies in the History of Judaism 192. Atlanta: Scholars Press, 1998.

"Niddah." Pages 1141–48 in *Encyclopaedia Judaica.* Edited by C. Roth. Jerusalem: Keter, 1972.

———. *Midrash, Genesis Rabbah: The Judaic Commentary to the Book of Genesis.* Atlanta: Scholars Press, 1985.

———. *The Tosefta Translated from the Hebrew: Third Division: Nashim (The Order of Women).* New York: Ktav, 1979.

Noble, David F. *The Religion of Technology: The Divinity of Man and the Spirit of Invention.* New York: Knopf, 1997; New York: Penguin Putnam, 1999.

Noddings, Nel. *Women and Evil.* Berkeley: University of California Press, 1989.

Noonan, John T. *Contraception: A History of Its Treatment by the Catholic Theologians and Canonists.* Cambridge: Belknap, 1965.

Northup, Lesley A., ed. *Women and Religious Ritual.* Washington, D.C.: Pastoral Press, 1993.

Noth, Martin. *Leviticus: A Commentary.* Translated by J. E. Andersen. London: SCM Press, 1962 .

———. *Leviticus: A Commentary.* Translated by J. E. Andersen. Old Testament Library. Philadelphia: Westminster, 1965.

———. *Numbers: A Commentary.* Translated by J. E. Andersen. Old Testament Library. Philadelphia: Westminster, 1968.

O'Kane, James. *Notes on the Rubrics of the Roman Ritual.* 2d ed. Dublin: Duffy, 1868.

Oliver, Kelly, ed. *Ethics, Politics, and Difference in Julia Kristeva's Writing.* New York: Routledge, 1993.

———. Reading Kristeva: *Unraveling the Double-Blind.* Bloomington: Indiana University Press, 1993.

Olson, Dennis T. *Numbers: Interpretation.* Bible Commentary for Teaching and Preaching. Louisville: John Knox, 1996.

Orenstein, Debra, ed. *Lifecycles: Jewish Women on Life Passages and Personal Milestones.* Jerusalem: Jewish Lights, 1995.

Origen. *Commentaries.* Edited by A. Roberts and J. Donaldson. Ante-Nicean Fathers. Grand Rapids, Eerdmans, 1889.

———. *Homélies sur la Lévitique.* Edited by Marcel Borret. Sources chrétiennes 287. Paris: Cerf, 1981.

———. *Homilies.* Translated by F. Crombie. Fathers of the Church. Edinburgh: T&T Clark, 1869.

———. *Homilies on Leviticus 1–16.* Translated by G.W. Barkley. Fathers of the Church. Washington, D.C.: Catholic University of America Press, 1990.

Owen, Lara. *Her Blood Is Gold: Celebrating the Power of Menstruation.* New York: HarperCollins, 1993.

Parker, Robert. *Miasma: Pollution and Purification in Early Greek Religion.* Oxford: Oxford University Press, 1983.

Parunak, H. Van Dyke. "Transitional Techniques in the Bible." *JBL* 102, no. 4 (1983): 525–48.

Patai, Raphael. *Gates to the Old City.* New York: Avon, 1980.

Patrologia latina. Edited by J.-P. Migne. 217 vols. Paris: 1844–1864.

Payer, Pierre J. *Sex and the Penitentials: The Development of a Sexual Code 550–1150.* Toronto: University of Toronto Press, 1984.

Peisker, Armor D., ed. *The Wesleyan Bible Commentary.* Grand Rapids: Eerdmans, 1967.

Perry, Tony. "Dangers in the Night." *Los Angeles Times,* 6 February 1995. A19.

Phipps, William. "The Menstrual Taboo in Judeo-Christian Tradition." *Journal of Religion and Health* 19 (1980): 298–303.

Pierce, Joanne M. "'Green Women' and Blood Pollution: Some Medieval Rituals for the Churching of Women after Childbirth." *Studia Liturgica* 29 (1995): 191–215.

Plaskow, Judith. *Standing Again at Sinai: Judaism from a Feminist Perspective.* San Francisco: Harper & Row, 1991.

Plato. *The Republic.* Translated by F. M Conford. Oxford: Oxford University Press, 1963.

———. *The Sophist and Statesman.* Translated by A. E. Taylor. Edited by R. Kubansky and E. Anscombe. London: Nelson, 1961.

———. *Timaeus.* Translated by D. Lee. New York: Penguin, 1965.

Plaut, W. Gunther. *The Torah: A Modern Commentary.* New York: Union of American Hebrew Congregations, 1981.

Pliny. *Natural History.* Translated by H. Rackham. Loeb Classical Library. Cambridge: Harvard University Press, 1942.

Poorthuis, Marcel J. H. M., and Joshua Schwartz. *Purity and Holiness: The Heritage of Leviticus.* Jewish and Christian Perspectives 2. Leiden: Brill, 2000.

Porter, Joshua Roy. *Leviticus.* Cambridge: Cambridge University Press, 1976.

Porter, Stanley E. "What Does It Mean to Be 'Saved by Childbirth' (1 Timothy 2:15)." *Journal for the Study of the New Testament* 49 (1993): 87–102.

Qimron, Elisha. "The Biblical Lexicon in the Light of the Dead Sea Scrolls." *Dead Sea Discoveries* 2 (1995): 295–329.

———. "Celibacy in the Dead Sea Scrolls and the Two Kinds of Sectarians." Pages 287–94 in vol. 1 of *The Madrid Qumran Congress: Proceedings of the International Congress of the Dead Sea Scrolls, Madrid 18–21* March, 1991. Edited by J. Trebolle Barrera and L. Vegas Montaner. Studies on the Texts of the Desert of Judah 11:1. Leiden: Brill, 1992.

Qimron, Elisha, and Florentino García Martínez. *The Temple Scroll: A Critical Edition with Extensive Reconstructions and Bibliography.* Beersheba: Ben-Gurion University of the Negev Press, 1996.

Raab, Kelley Ann. "Nancy Jay and a Feminist Psychology of Sacrifice." *Journal of Feminist Studies in Religion* 13 (1997): 75–89.

Ranke-Heinemann, Uta. *Eunuchen voor het hemelrijk: De rooms-katholieke kerk en seksualiteit.* Baarn, Netherlands: Ambo, 1990

Ranke-Heinemann, Uta. *Eunuchs for the Kingdom of Heaven.* New York: Doubleday, 1990.

Raphael, Melissa. *Theology and Embodiment: The Post-Patriarchal Reconstruction of Female Sacrality.* Sheffield: Sheffield Academic Press, 1996.

Rashkow, Ilona N. "Daughters and Fathers in Genesis . . . Or, What Is Wrong with This Picture?" Pages 250–65 in *The New Literary Criticism and the Hebrew Bible.* Edited by J. Cheryl Exum and D. J. A. Clines. Journal for the Study of the Old Testament: Supplement Series 143. Sheffield: Sheffield Academic Press, 1993.

Ravanat, F. "Della Benedictio mulieris post partum." *Perfice munus* 4 (1929): 738–42.

Reider, Joseph. *An Index to Aquila.* Vetus Testamentum Supplements 12. Leiden: Brill, 1966.

Rich, Adrienne. *Of Woman Born: Motherhood as Experience and Institution.* New York: Bantam, 1977.

Riggans, Walter. *Numbers.* Philadelphia: Westminster, 1983.

Rituale Romanum De Benedictionibus: Editio typica. Vatican City: Typis polyglottis Vaticanis, 1984.

The Roman Ritual: Book of Blessings. Collegeville, Minn.: Liturgical Press, 1989.

Roll, Susan K. "The Churching of Women after Childbirth: An Old Rite Raising New Issues." *Questions Liturgiques/Studies in Liturgy* 76 (1995): 206–29.

Roth, Cecil, ed. *Encyclopaedia Judaica.* Jerusalem: Keter, 1972.

Ruddick, Sara. *Maternal Thinking: Towards a Politics of Peace.* London: Women's Press, 1990.

Ruether, Rosemary Radford. "Goddesses and Witches: Liberation and Countercultural Feminism." *Christian Century* 94 (1980): 842–47.

———. "Male Clericalism and the Dread of Women." Pages 1–14 in *Women and Orders.* Edited by R. J. Heyer. New York: Paulist, 1974.

———. "Misogynism and Virginal Feminism in the Fathers of the Church." Pages 150–84 in *Religion and Sexism: Images of Woman in the Jewish and Christian Traditions.* Edited by R. Radford Ruether. New York: Simon & Schuster, 1973.

———. "Motherearth and the Megamachine: A Theology of Liberation in a Feminine, Somatic, and Ecological Perspective." *Christianity and Crisis* 31 (1971): 267–73.

———. *New Woman—New Earth: Sexist Ideologies and Human Liberation.* New York: Seabury, 1975.

————. "A Religion for Women: Sources and Strategies." *Christianity and Crisis* 39 (1979): 307–11.

————. *Women-Church: Theology and Practice of Feminist Liturgical Communities.* San Francisco: Harper & Row, 1986.

————. "Women's Body and Blood: The Sacred and the Impure." Pages 7–21 in *Through the Devil's Gateway: Women, Religion, and Taboo.* Edited by A. Joseph. London: SPCK and Channel Four Television, 1990.

Rushton, Kathleen P. "The Parable of Jn 16:21: A Feminist Socio-Rhetorical Reading of a (Pro)creative Metaphor for the Death-Glory of Jesus." Ph.D. diss., Griffith University, Brisbane, Australia, 2000.

————. "The (Pro)creative Parables of Labour and Childbirth (John 3:1–10 and 16:21–22)." In *The Lost Coin: Parables of Women, Work and Wisdom.* Edited by M. A. Beavis. Journal for the Study of the Old Testament: Supplement Series. Sheffield: Sheffield Academic Press, forthcoming.

Sabatier, Petrus. *Bibliorum Sacrorum Latinae versions antiqua seu vetus italica et caeterae quaecunque in Codicibus Mss. & antiquorum libris reperiri potuerunt.* Reims, France: apud Reginaldus Florentain, 1743. Repr., Turnhout, Belgium: Brepols, 1987.

Satlow, Michael L. *Tasting the Dish: Rabbinic Rhetorics of Sexuality.* Brown Judaic Studies 303. Atlanta: Scholars Press, 1995.

Sawyer, John F. "Daughter of Zion and Servant of the Lord in Isaiah." *Journal for the Study of the Old Testament* 44 (1989): 89–107.

Schiffman, Lawrence H. *The Eschatological Community of the Dead Sea Scrolls.* Society of Biblical Literature Monograph 38. Atlanta: Scholars Press, 1989.

————. "Exclusion from the Sanctuary and the City of the Sanctuary in the Temple Scroll." *Hebrew Annual Review* 9 (1985): 301–20.

————. "Laws Pertaining to Women in the Temple Scroll." Pages 210–28 in *The Dead Sea Scrolls: Forty Years of Research.* Edited by D. Dimant and U. Rappaport. Leiden: Brill, 1992.

Schottroff, Luise. *Lydia's Impatient Sisters: A Feminist Social History of Early Christianity.* Translated by B. and M. Rumscheidt. Louisville: Westminster John Knox, 1995.

Schottroff, Luise, and Marie-Theres Wacker. *Von der Wurzel getragen: Christlich-feministische Exegese in Auseinandersetzung mit Antijudaismus.* Leiden: Brill, 1996.

Schubert, F. "Liturgie und Volksgebrauche." *Theologie und Glaube* 22 (1930): 137–49.

Schuck, Johannes. *Der Segen Gottes: Ein christliches Hausbuch von dem kirchlichen Segnungen und Weihen.* Würzburg, Germany: Fränkische Gesellschaftsdruckerei Würzburg Echter, 1939.

Schwarzenberger, Rudolf. "Der Muttersegen nach der Geburt." Pages 279–84 in *Heute segnen: Werkbuch zum Benediktionale.* Edited by A. Heinz and H. Rennings. Freiburg im B., Germany: Herder, 1987.

Selvidge, Marla J. *Women, Cult, and Miracle Recital: A Redactional Critical Investigation of Mark 5:24–34.* Lewisburg, Pa.: Bucknell University Press, 1990.

Sered, Susan Starr. *Priestess—Mother—acred Sister: Religions Dominated by Women.* New York: Oxford University Press, 1994.

Setel, Drorah O'Donnell. "Exodus." Pages in 26–35 *The Women's Bible Commentary*. Edited by C. A. Newsom and S. H. Ringe. London: Westminster John Knox, 1992.

Siegel, R. E. Galen: *On the Affected Parts*. Basel: Karger, 1976.

Sinclair, Daniel. "Miqveh." Pages 469–70 in *The Oxford Dictionary of the Jewish Religion*. Edited by J. Zwi Werblowsky and G. Wigoder. New York: Oxford University Press, 1997.

Sireling, Linda. "The Jewish Women: Different and Equal." Pages 87–96 in *Through the Devil's Gateway: Women, Religion, and Taboo*. Edited by A. Joseph. London: SPCK and Channel Four Television, 1990.

Smith, W. Robertson. *Lectures on the Religion of the Semites: The Fundamental Institutions*. New York: Ktav, 1969.

Snaith, Norman Henry, ed. *The Century Bible: Leviticus and Numbers*. London: Nelson, 1967.

Soranus. *Gynecology*. Translated by O. Temkin. Baltimore: Johns Hopkins University Press, 1956.

Staden, Heinrich von. Herophilus: *The Art of Medicine in Early Alexandria*. Cambridge: Cambridge University Press, 1989.

———. "Women and Dirt." *Helios* 19 (1992): 7–30.

Steinberg, Jonah. "From a 'Pot of Filth' to a 'Hedge of Roses' (and Back): Changing Theorizations of Menstruation in Judaism." *Journal of Feminist Studies in Religion* 13 (1997): 5–26.

Steiner, Franz. *Taboo*. London: Penguin, 1956.

Stenta, Norbert. "Segnung der Mutter nach der Geburt." *Bibel und Liturgie* 7, no. 1 (1932–33): 193–96.

Stern, Ephraim. "Measures and Weights." Pages 376–88 in vol. 16 of *Encyclopedia Judaica*. Jerusalem: Keter, 1972.

Strasser, Sabine. *Die Unreinheit ist Fruchtbar: Grenzüberschreidungen in einem türkischen Dorf am Schwarzen Meer*. Vienna: Wiener Frauenverlag, 1995.

Stratton, George Malcolm. *Theophrastus and the Greek Physiological Psychology before Aristotle: De Sensu*. London: George Allen & Unwin, 1917.

Sturdy, John. *Numbers*. Cambridge Bible Commentary. Cambridge: Cambridge University Press, 1976.

Te Reile, G. J. M. J. "Une Nouvelle Loi Sacreé en Arcadie." *Bulletin of correspondance hellénique* 102 (1978): 325–31.

Tertullian. *Opera*. Edited by A. Roberts and J. Donaldson. Ante-Nicean Fathers. Grand Rapids: Eerdmans, 1926.

Thalhofer, Valentin. "Aussegnung." In *Weber und Welte, Kirchenlexikon*. Edited by J. Bergenröther. 2d ed. Freiburg i.B., Germany: Herder, 1882.

Thistlethwaite, Susan Brooks. "You May Enjoy the Spoil of Your Enemies: Rape as a Biblical Metaphor for War." *Semeia* 61 (1993): 59–75.

Thomas Aquinas, Summa Theologica. Vol. 2. Translated by Fathers of the Dominican Province. London: Burns & Oates, 1947.

Torjesen, Karen Jo. *When Women Were Priests: Women's Leadership in the Early Church and the Scandal of Their Subordination.* San Francisco: Harper, 1993.

Touito, Eleazar. "The Historical Background of Rashi's Commentary on Gen. 1–5." Pages 97–104 (in Hebrew) in *Rashi Studies.* Edited by Z. A. Steinfeld. Ramat Gan, Israel: Bar-Ilan University Press, 1993.

Tregelles, Samuel Prideaux. *Gesenius's Hebrew and Chaldee Lexicon to the Old Testament Scriptures.* New York: Wiley, 1883.

Trible, Phyllis. *God and the Rhetoric of Sexuality.* London: SCM Press, 1992.

Umansky, Ellen M., and Dianne Ashton, eds. *Four Centuries of Jewish Women's Spirituality: A Sourcebook.* Boston: Beacon, 1992.

Van der Meer, Haye. *Women Priests in the Catholic Church? A Theological-Historical Investigation.* Philadelphia: Temple University Press, 1973. Originally published as *Priestertum der Frau.* Freiburg: Herder, 1969.

Vander Schaaf, Derek. *The Tailhook Report (The Official Inquiry into the Events of Tailhook '91).* New York: St. Martin's, 1993.

Van der Toorn, Karel. *From Her Cradle to Her Grave: The Role of Religion in the Life of the Israelite and the Babylonian Woman.* Translated by S. J. Denning-Bolle. Sheffield: Sheffield Academic Press, 1994.

Walker, Barbara. *Women's Rituals.* San Francisco: Harper & Row, 1990.

Wallis, A. F. *The Latin Version of Hippolytus' Apostolic Tradition.* Edited by F. L. Cross. Studia patristica 1.1. Berlin: Akademie Verlag, 1957.

Waltke, Bruce K., and Michael Patrick O'Conner. *Biblical Hebrew Syntax.* Winona Lake, Ind.: Eisenbrauns, 1990.

Wasserfall, Rachel. "Menstruation and Identity: The Meaning of Niddah for Moroccan Immigrants to Israel." Pages 309–28 in *People of the Body: Jews and Judaism Form an Embodied Perspective.* Edited by H. Eilberg-Schwartz. Albany: State University of New York Press, 1992.

Webster's II New Riverside University Dictionary. Boston: Houghton Mifflin, 1984.

Wegner, Judith Romney. *Chattel or Person: The Status of Women in the Mishnah.* New York: Oxford University Press, 1988.

———. "Leviticus." Pages 36–44 in *The Woman's Bible Commentary.* Edited by C. A. Newson and S. R. Ringe. London: SPCK, 1992.

Weissler, Chava. "Mizvot Built into the Body: Tkhines for Niddah, Pregnancy, and Childbirth." Pages 101–15 in *People of the Body: Jews and Judaism from an Embodied Perspective.* Edited by Howard Eilberg-Schwartz. New York: State University of New York Press, 1992.

Weller, Philip T. *The Roman Ritual.* Milwaukee: Bruce, 1964.

Wendebourg, Dorothea. "Die alttestamentlichen Reinheitsgesetze in der frühen Kirche." *Zeitschrift für Kirchengeschichte* 95 (1984): 149–70.

Wenham, Gordon J. *The Book of Leviticus.* Grand Rapids: Eerdmans, 1979.

———. "Why Does Sexual Intercourse Defile (Lev.15:18)?" *Zeitschrift für die alttestamentliche Wissenschaft* 95 (1983): 432–35.

Werblosky, R. J. Zwi. *On the Baptismal Rite according to St. Hippolytus.* Edited by K. Aland. Studia patristica 2.2. Berlin: Akademie Verlag, 1958.

Wevers, John W. *Notes on the Greek Text of Leviticus.* Septuagint and Cognate Studies 44. Altanta: Scholars Press, 1997.

Whitekettle, Richard. "Levitical Thought and the Female Reproductive Cycle: Wombs, Wellsprings, and the Primeval World." *Vetus Testamentum* 46 (1996): 376–91.

———. "Leviticus 15.18 Reconsidered: Chiasm, Spatial Structure, and the Body." *Journal for the Study of the Old Testament* 49 (1991): 31–45.

Wigoder, Geoffrey, ed. *The Encyclopedia of Judaism.* New York: Macmillan, 1989.

Wintermute, O. S. "Jubilees." Pages 35–142 in vol. 2 of *The Old Testament Pseudepigrapha.* Edited by J. H. Charlesworth. London: Dartmann, Longman & Todd, 1985.

Wisse, Marian. "De kerkgang van de moeder na de geboorte van een kind." Unpublished doctoral qualifying paper. Utrecht, 1984.

Wohlmann, Paul. *Buch der Segnungen.* Lucerne: Rex, 1974.

Wright, Martin R. *Empedocles: The Extant Fragments.* New Haven: Yale University Press, 1981.

Yadin, Yigael, ed. *The Temple Scroll.* 3 vol. Jerusalem: Israel Exploration Society, Institute of Archaeology of the Hebrew University of Jerusalem, and Shrine of the Book, 1983.

Yanay, Niza, and Tamar Rapoport. "Ritual Impurity and Religious Discourse on Women and Nationality." *Women's Studies International Forum* 20 (1997): 651–56.

Zimmerman, Frank. "Origin and Significance of the Jewish Rite of Circumcision." *Psychoanalytic Review* 38 (1951): 103–12.

———. "The Penitential of Theodore." In *Readings in Medieval History.* Edited by P. J. Geary. Peterborough, Ontario: Broadview, 1991.

Zimmerman, Jean. *Tailspin: Women in War at the Wake of Tailhook.* New York: Doubleday, 1995.

INDEX